TWENTIETH CENTURY VIEWS

The aim of this series is to present the best in
contemporary critical opinion on major authors,
providing a twentieth century perspective on
their changing status in an era of profound
revaluation.

Maynard Mack, *Series Editor*
Yale University

T. S. ELIOT

T. S. ELIOT

A COLLECTION OF CRITICAL ESSAYS

Edited by

Hugh Kenner

A SPECTRUM BOOK

Prentice-Hall, Inc., *Englewood Cliffs, N. J.*

Current printing (last digit):

15   14

© 1962

BY PRENTICE-HALL, INC.

ENGLEWOOD CLIFFS, N. J.

LIBRARY OF CONGRESS CATALOG CARD NO.: 62-9290

Printed in the United States of America

27433-C

Table of Contents

vii

11268

T. S. ELIOT

Introduction

by Hugh Kenner

The facts are simple. Thomas Stearns Eliot, M.A., arrived in London, aged twenty-six, late in August 1914, the war with the Central Powers having disrupted his plans for graduate study in philosophy at Marburg. The following year he commenced publishing poems in avant-garde periodicals, and reviewing books in respectable ones. Before long he figured among the "drunken helots" of an enraged reviewer's assault on literary Bolshevism; the Spartans, it seems, used to promote orgies among their serfs, to serve as a horrible example to the well-bred, and this was the only kind of purpose the reviewer in question could imagine such poetry fulfilling. Eliot went on reviewing for *The New Statesman, The Athenaeum,* even *The Times Literary Supplement,* and working in Lloyd's Bank. In 1922 his poetic and critical careers publicly converged, when *The Waste land* appeared (without notes) in the first issue of *The Criterion,* a literary periodical established under his editorship. The *Times* reviewer, with surprising restraint, contented himself with noting that this poem was sometimes "very near the limits of coherency"; it was widely felt to be a scandalous affair. This feeling has never quite died; Sir Arthur Quiller-Couch continued to the end to wonder whether T. S. Eliot had ever composed three consecutive lines of *poetry* in his life[1]; another elder was especially offended by what he took to be the poet's desire to become a crab. Yet by 1932 Eliot was delivering the Charles Eliot Norton lectures at the University where he had failed to complete the work for his doctoral degree; and by 1948 he was the Nobel Prizewinner for Literature, and had been for a decade or more the undisputed literary dictator of London.

This translation from obloquy to eminence came about without any taking of barricades by storm. It was the unforeseen and somewhat irrelevant resultant of a process which derives from the nature of Eliot's writing: from the odd withdrawal of any affirmative per-

---

[1] See the 1943 letter to Lord Alfred Douglas ("Q" then aged 80), quoted in F. Brittain's *Arthur Quiller-Couch* (New York: The Macmillan Company, 1948), p. 151. It would be amusing to compile a sampling of the abuse this generation directed at Eliot, about 1925-1945.

sonality, which has allowed his work to be discussed as though it
were the legacy of a deceased poet, and from that quality in both
his verse and his prose which invades the reader's mind and there
undergoes an assimilation which soon persuades us that we have
always possessed it. "I do not know for certain," writes Mr.
William Empson, "how much of my own mind he invented, let alone how
much of it is a reaction against him or indeed a consequence of
misreading him. He is a very penetrating influence, perhaps not
unlike an east wind." He is also the first major poet of the first age
devoted to serious and systematic, indeed curricular, scrutiny of its
own literature. This fact gives a special status to essays like the ones
collected in the present volume. The various public discussions of
Eliot's work are not so much serial opinions as they are part of the
work's own way of working; part of a complex process of assimilation
from which the work itself can only partly be separated.

Even the poet, and in his own lifetime, has tended to disappear
into this process. It is odd how his impact resists summary. Mr.
Empson's essay was written for a *Festschrift* commemorating the
poet's sixtieth birthday, the only readable contributions to which
came from people who, like Empson, Clive Bell, Conrad Aiken,
John Betjeman, Neville Coghill and Felix Morley, declined "to judge
or define the achievement of Eliot," and instead told anecdotes. The
rest of the book is divided between tributes either faintly grandiose
or faintly facetious, and pieces of autobiography[2]; whoever attempts
to "judge or define the achievement" soon finds himself assessing
how much of his own mind Mr. Eliot invented: "an east wind,"
indeed. Ten years later a second *Festschrift* manifested similar difficulties[3]; its editor even had recourse to a series of statements by
British schoolchildren, presumably as possessing minds new enough
not to have been wholly invented just yet. By 1959 it was relevant
to offer the generalization that "opinion concerning the most influential man of letters of the twentieth century has not freed itself from
a cloud of unknowing. He is the Invisible Poet in an age of system-
atized literary scrutiny, much of it directed at him." [4]

Much of it, furthermore, was instigated by him; for he has been
the most gifted and most influential literary critic in English in the

[2] *T. S. Eliot,* a symposium . . . compiled by Richard March and Tambimuttu
(Chicago: Henry Regnery Company, 1949).

[3] *T. S. Eliot: a Symposium for His 70th Birthday* edited by Neville Braybrooke
(New York: Farrar Straus & Cudahy, Inc., 1958).

[4] Hugh Kenner, *The Invisible Poet: T. S. Eliot* (New York: McDowell, Obolensky Inc., 1959), p. ix.

twentieth century—very likely the best since Coleridge. And the lesson of his criticism has been this: that it is most profitable to examine specific bodies of work. "Analysis and Comparison," he wrote in 1917,

> Analysis and comparison, methodically, with sensitiveness, intelligence, curiosity, intensity of passion and infinite knowledge: all these are necessary to the great critic. Comparison the periodical public does not want much of; it does not like to be made to feel that it ought to have read much more than it has read before it can follow the critic's thought; analysis it is afraid of.[5]

He was writing, on that occasion, in a periodical, reviewing a collection of negligible essays that had been written for the periodical public. The reflexiveness is characteristic: these are words of the kind one would expect to find in a coterie journal, *Partisan Review,* for instance, which the periodical public can be trusted not to hear about, and we find them instead in a weekly paper. Eliot has always sought readers whom his words would oblige to think about their own health, inviting, thus, the complex resistance and assimilation his words have characteristically undergone.

For "comparison and analysis" is only part of the critical process. It is, as Eliot makes clear in his essay on "The Function of Criticism," a metaphor drawn from anatomy. Blandly confronting Wordsworth's complaint that we murder to dissect, Eliot reminds us that we have after all not the poet before us but the poem, and that the poem is in certain respects dead. ("Deadness," wrote Wyndham Lewis in 1914 in a book Eliot admired, "is the first condition of art. . . . Instead of being something impelled like a machine by a little egoistic fire inside, it lives soullessly and deadly by its frontal lines and masses." [6]) But the anatomist's metaphor has always, in Eliot's practice, been crossed with another, that of the dialogue, a process coming to life between two persons. Even pontificating he is playing a role, inciting to self-appraisal readers accustomed to less informed pontification. When he is being a poet, however, he does not *talk,* and the dialogue becomes more elusive, since the reader must supply so much of it. The Eliot poem implies a Voice, but it is not the voice of the poet speaking, nor does it agitate a desert silence; it is audible only in the reader's mind. To an unusual degree, then, the reader takes

[5] From a review of Robert Lynd's *Old and New Masters,* in *The Athenaeum,* No. 4650 (June 13, 1919), pp. 456-7.
[6] Wyndham Lewis, *Tarr* (London: The Egoist Ltd., 1918), p. 295.

possession of an Eliot poem, or suffers it to take possession of him. That is why thinking or discoursing about it comes so much to resemble the processes of self-scrutiny; that is also why so many of the essays and articles which mean to be accounts of Eliot's poetry are actually drafts for the essayist's autobiography, and why hostile accounts pulsate with such vehemence, recording as they do the struggle of newly mobilized antibodies to repel an invader which has lodged itself in the very capillaries of the sensibility.[7] It has been given to very few critics to write about Eliot's work with even a provisional detachment.

The present collection avoids essays which annotate, essays which repudiate, and essays which merely employ Eliot's work for a datum in some discussion of politics, religion, or culture. It confines itself to pieces which either exemplify or tangentially illustrate the process by which the twentieth-century mind puts Eliot's writings to use, in its long attempt to establish its own identity. Putting the work to use has been partly an effort to *see* the work, and the man doing it, partly an effort to define the implications the work has for us, once we have appropriated it. He has never resembled that week-end reviewer's fiction, a poet for a casual hour; what he has written has entered intimately our attempts to become ourselves. If this principle of selection has excluded some excellent essays, even perhaps a few better than some it admitted, it seems nevertheless the most illuminating focus to which the vast Eliot bibliography can be brought.

We commence with Mr. Arthur Mizener's essay, the theme of which is precisely the obsolescence of so many other essays, written as they were out of and on behalf of a time on which Eliot's work impinged with the fascination of contemporary novelty. Or better, out of a succession of such times; for Eliot was in succession the vivid contemporary of the London Vortex (1914-19), of the 1920's (*The Waste Land*), of the 1930's (*Ash-Wednesday* and *Murder in the Cathedral*), and of the war years (*Four Quartets*). To find him at last, as Mr. Mizener puts it, "looked upon with uncomprehending respect as a man no longer expected to contribute anything the spectators care enough about to quarrel with," is yet another novelty, so long has that insouciant magisterial presence haunted the century's intellectual terrain. Even now he continues to haunt discussions of the poetic drama, a topic which would be pursued with greater

---

[7] See for example Karl Shapiro's onslaught in *In Defence of Ignorance* (New York: Random House, 1960).

passion if there were more poetic drama to discuss. Mr. Mizener's survey of the nondramatic poetry, from a plateau guaranteed for the first time in forty years by the virtual certainty that there is not going to be any more of it, supplies a useful minimum account of what the work seems to look like, as tradition at length commences to claim it whole for tomorrow's anthologists.

Each of the four periods enumerated above has contributed testimony worth salvaging. In the days of Vorticism Ezra Pound was Eliot's most prescient spokesman. His 1917 review of *Prufrock and Other Observations* is a small compendium of the things that could relevantly be said when Eliot was an unknown poet with one tiny volume to his credit, though it took, in those days, a Pound's perspicacity to say them:

> After much contemporary work that is merely factitious, much that is good in intention but impotently finished and incomplete; much whose flaws are due to sheer ignorance which a year's study or thought might have remedied, it is a comfort to come upon complete art, naïve despite its intellectual subtlety, lacking all pretence.[8]

Pound drew attention to things we have learned to take for granted:

> Mr. Eliot's two sorts of metaphor: his wholly unrealizable, always apt, half ironic suggestion, and his precise realizable picture, his method of conveying a whole situation and half a character by three words of a quoted phrase, his constant aliveness, his mingling of a very subtle observation with the unexpectedness of a backhanded cliché.

Eliot in the same year compiled and published anonymously a little pamphlet, *Ezra Pound, his Metric and Poetry*. The anonymity was and remains characteristic. "You let *me* throw the bricks through the front window," Pound once admonished his supple ally in those years. "You go in at the back door and take out the swag." Four decades later Wyndham Lewis recalled that time of association; his "Early London Environment," reprinted here, is the most authoritative image we have of the context in which our minds were beginning to be invented. Not its least engaging feature is the role Lewis himself elects to play: "On this most solemn occasion, I shall do my best." As good as his word, he provides with affectionate detachment a context in which live personalities move, reminding us how much

---

[8] This review is reprinted in *The Literary Essays of Ezra Pound* (New York: New Directions, 1954), pp. 418-422.

of the prodigious operation of genius we must remember to refer to a frail, faintly disproportionate human vessel; for the ventriloquial powers of "Gerontion" or *XXX Cantos* emanated—it is not always easy to remember—from men having at one time no special prominence, who paid visits, held conversation, sat in chairs. Around Eliot at least legend very rapidly closed; Mr. Empson's testament to "The Style of the Master" presents very well the gravity of the role he soon learned to play.

Our next three essays take some stock of the revolution's scope. Eliot was equipped for his decisive achievement by fortune as well as by talent and temperament; and an important ingredient in his fortune was the close academic confrontation with the British philosopher Francis Herbert Bradley. It was not that Bradley told him things he needed to know, as Fenollosa's papers told Pound, nor supplied him with doctrines to versify, as Bolingbroke's treatise was once thought to have supplied Pope; rather, the experience of coming to terms with Bradley's account of "immediate experience" liberated him to pursue with confidence the implications of a kind of verse he had already commenced to write. For he had begun by writing resonant monologues; and had it not been for Bradley he might easily have been persuaded that the way to develop that gift was Browning's way, reaching out from the central Voice into its enclosing circumstance, the details of time and place, the four-walled box of particulars that enclose Andrea del Sarto or the Bishop Ordering his Tomb: mediating, so, between the deliverances of the Voice and the curiosities of a reader who demands to know who is speaking and when. But the conviction, borne upon him by Bradley's metaphysic, that such demands were essentially meaningless; that the mere Voice, without accessories, itself imitated with unsettling accuracy our experience of being, knowing, speaking, experiencing—so that the reader comes to accept it as his own—this conviction doubtless helped save him from the fate of a minor poet stranded by epistemological orthodoxies. And Mr. R. P. Blackmur indicates how modern poetry, however liberated (for though Eliot was liberated by Bradley no one else need feel obligated by that particular prescription), itself engages in "Irregular Metaphysics," supplying in turn new analogies for a time of "new knowledges." The poet makes analogies, not statements.

The reason why "Prufrock" is *now* a popular poem (though it was a very difficult poem for most people during its first twenty years of life) is that the analogies with which it is composed have had time to sink in. This too is how poems change and grow and even sometimes disappear: in relation to our apprehension of what is in analogy, where the elements go on working. The obscurity is like that of the womb.

Mr. Blackmur is right in noting that the parts of *The Waste Land* which have received the greatest share of exegetical attention are in fact its structural members, not its planes of discourse. Taking his cue perhaps from the final lines of "Gerontion," he compares the poem to a house which we have learned to inhabit, and which we therefore allow (this is its real function) to shape our experience in nondiscursive ways: an environment, not a body of propositions. Miss Elizabeth Sewell next suggests that it is just such a structuring of our intellectual environment that the English have chosen, misleadingly, to denominate as Nonsense. Saluting Lewis Carroll as the Mallarmé of England, she prolongs what is in effect Mr. Blackmur's proposition, that the poet's service is to make us a liberating structure. "The genre or game of Nonsense has strict rules. The aim is to construct with words a logical universe of discourse meticulously selected and controlled; within this playground the mind can then manipulate its material, consisting largely of names of things and numbers." If this sounds like a whimsical formulation (and Miss Sewell's essay, composed in the homeland of the British grin, disconcerts here and there with unstable recourses to whimsy), we have only to check its aptness to a body of work whose impact on the 1960's will not be denied: the fiction of Samuel Beckett. Mr. Eliot's little jokes, as when he converts the lift and the spiral staircase at the Gloucester Road Station of the London Underground into the Two Ways by one of which we must "descend lower" and leave the "strained time-ridden faces," tend to disconcert his votaries when someone points them out, and confirm the worst suspicions of the disaffected. They are nevertheless intimate features of his way of working—which Miss Sewell suggests is the only way for modern poetry to work.

For Eliot's method again and again is to deprive of its context some perfectly natural statement, or else some quotation, and leave the words to echo by themselves, often in a new context, where the echoes multiply. "I had not thought death had undone so many"— this stirs in *The Waste Land* a rustle of suggestions of which it was innocent when it lay embedded in *The Inferno*. Or lines not quoted sound as though they ought to be quotations ("Come in under the shadow of this red rock"—can all that sinister power lurk in nine words?). Or perfectly straightforward statements, stripped of their occasions, vibrate portentously, the poet perhaps steadied in the back of his mind by his knowledge of what the original contexts were:

> Footfalls echo in the memory
> Down the passage which we did not take
> Towards the door we never opened
> Into the rose-garden.

It is easy to infer that these lines were composed in full awareness of a specific experience, that of a child reading *Alice in Wonderland,* in the first chapter of which the White Rabbit's footfalls scamper away down a passage at the end of which is a far too tiny door. But having composed them so as to describe exactly a recollection of reading Carroll's pages, Eliot simply breaks the mold away. There is no reason, when we encounter them in the first movement of "Burnt Norton," for being reminded of *Alice in Wonderland;* in fact the chances are good that hardly any reader will be so reminded. They have an echoing gravity of their own, as the poet candidly goes on to acknowledge:

>   My words echo
> Thus, in your mind.

What he is telling us, at this instant, is exactly how his poetic method works. But even the formula by which he utters the exact truth proceeds itself to echo in the mind—until the poem, as Mr. D. W. Harding notes, becomes "an achievement in the creation of concepts," shaping our own experience of reading it with a freedom that depends on our *not* being sharply aware of some particular subject that is being talked about.

One way in which the poems alter with time is this: that as commentary proliferates it becomes harder and harder to undergo an innocent experience of the verse working as it first worked. Several exegetes, for instance, have identified *Alice in Wonderland* as a "source" for "Burnt Norton," so that today's reader is put to the trouble of ingesting such information and then learning how to disregard it. What commentary provides can be very distracting. Commentary took its cue however from Mr. Eliot himself, who supplied

Notes to *The Waste Land*,[9] and commentary then bedeviled itself further with what deserves to be called the Genetic Fallacy. The Genetic Fallacy supposes that what the poem "means" is what the poet experienced when he wrote it. Let us recover, then, the books he was reading, the places he was visiting, the authors he was quoting; let us assemble and combine this material, let us write it into the margins of the pages, and let us then suppose that we have recovered the poetic experience, of which the written text is merely a trace, as the trace in a cloud-chamber shows where a proton has been.

Eliot himself at one time devoted considerable attention to the implications of hypotheses of this kind, which involve, in their various forms, an attempt to *become* the poet, on the supposition that Art works by a transfusion of personality. And just here is Eliot's point of dissent from them. For as no one will argue (he uses this figure in writing on Bradley) that the "real" geranium is the geranium's experience of itself, just so it is meaningless to argue that the "real" poem is the poet's experience of it. Hence in ascertaining sources we are learning something about the process of composition, perhaps something about the poet, but not about the poem. Nevertheless, such knowledge, as we acquire it, cannot but color our sense of what the poem is, its way of existing in our minds. But this is not to elucidate the poem so much as to alter it into something less intransigent.

These points are neatly illustrated by the two essays on Eliot's dealings with "sources," S. Musgrove's on the Tennysonian imprint and George L. K. Morris's on the origin of *The Waste Land*'s "Marie." Eliot dealt with the autobiography of the Countess Marie Larisch as he dealt with the numerous other books on which *The Waste Land* drew, extracting details and suppressing their original context so that they vibrate with inexplicable mysteriousness:

> In the mountains, there you feel free.
> I read, much of the night, and go south in the winter.

He merely neglected to register it in the notes; so until Mr. Morris turned it up by chance in 1954, it lay quietly, distracting no one.

[9] Not, however, to inform the reader, so much as "with a view to spiking the guns of critics of my earlier poems who had accused me of plagiarism." The notes were later expanded because the publisher needed a few more pages filled, and Eliot came to regret "having sent so many enquirers off on a wild goose chase after Tarot cards and the Holy Grail." (See his lecture "The Frontiers of Criticism" in *On Poetry and Poets*.)

It seems, now that we know about it, a slight thing to have been turned into something so wonderful.

The Musgrove pages deal with a different order of indebtedness entirely, a system of echoes, no doubt largely unconscious, of recent poetic ancestors. The book from which these pages are excerpted concerns itself with Eliot and Whitman, and concludes that Eliot's vocabulary of "physical image and emotional evocation"—not his speculative passages but details like

> When evening quickens faintly in the street

or

> Now that lilacs are in bloom

or

> Where the hermit-thrush sings in the pine-trees

—depends on a web of attachments and repulsions formed in childhood and in his native country, not on such a process of deliberate fabrication as transformed the Countess into "Marie, Marie." Eliot himself has said as much:

> Why for all of us, out of all that we have heard, seen, felt, in a lifetime, do certain images recur, charged with emotion, rather than others? The song of one bird, the leap of one fish, at a particular place and time, the scent of one flower, an old woman on a German mountain path, six ruffians seen through an open window playing cards at night at a small French railway junction where there was a watermill: such memories may have symbolic value, but of what we cannot tell, for they come to represent the depths of feeling into which we cannot peer.

These sentences from *The Use of Poetry and the Use of Criticism* (1933) have often been quoted, and several lines of "Journey of the Magi" as often glossed in their light. Mr. Musgrove, however, has carried the general principle a good deal further, for he has shown that the poet's early pattern of feeling associated itself not only with remembered images of this kind, about which we can never learn unless the poet chooses to identify them for us, but also with half explicit reminiscences of poets, like Tennyson, in whom he steeped himself while still young.[10] Hence the elusively familiar overtones

---

[10] Though Eliot by his own account did not steep himself in Whitman, the argument of Mr. Musgrove's book is that he identified Whitman with qualities of American experience in which he did steep himself.

behind some of his most individual effects; hence, too, perhaps, the noted capacity of his verse for "communicating before it is understood."

Discussions of this kind throw light on the kind of verse it is and the way it came into being. There remains—has remained from the first—the obligation to relate the poems as explicitly as possible to our own capacity for response: indeed, to read them. To construe the lines, to analyse the prosody, to assign the images their place in some prior tradition—this is not to read. "We can have the poem," wrote F. R. Leavis in 1940, "only by an inner kind of possession," for an approach to works of literature "is personal or it is nothing: you cannot take over the appreciation of a poem, and unappreciated, the poem isn't 'there.'" [11] It is the principal lesson of much Eliot commentary, that for a great many readers and writers the poems are only provisionally "there." Between the communication which *precedes* any disciplined understanding, and which public discussion takes for granted, and the pursuit of rationale for the poems' surface novelties, with which much public discussion concerns itself, lies a gulf seldom explored, a region in which the reader owes it to the poem to take detailed possession of what it is doing, what it does for him. To conduct a discussion in this region is not to explain but to clarify,

> to bring into sharp focus, in turn, this, that and the other detail, juncture or relation in our total response; or (since "sharp focus" may be a misleading account of the kind of attention sometimes required), what we are doing is to dwell with a deliberate, considering responsiveness on this, that or the other node or focal point in the complete organization that the poem is, in so far as we have it.

And this focussing and dwelling, Dr. Leavis continues, is "a more deliberate following-through of that process of creation in response to the poet's words which reading is. It is a recreation in which, by a considering attentiveness, we ensure a more than ordinary faithfulness and completeness."

Such discussion is not flashy and is seldom anthologized; it does not issue in debatable conclusions, since it seeks instead to involve the reader in a process of disciplined apprehension which he completes by assent, dissent, even resistance. Of this difficult, self-effacing critical genre Dr. Leavis's discussion of *The Waste Land* and *Coriolan*,

---

[11] In "Literary Studies," *Scrutiny* IX (March, 1941). Reprinted in F. R. Leavis, *Education and the University* (New York: George W. Stewart, Inc., 1948), pp. 66-86.

and the mutually supplementary articles on the *Quartets* contributed
by him and D. W. Harding to *Scrutiny,* are among the most distinguished contemporary examples. They do not provide information,
but guide our response to the poems' organization of gesture. Indeed
they were written before most of the exegetical bric-à-brac now current in Eliotic discussion became available. Thus Mr. Harding does
not discuss the identity of the ghost in part II of "Little Gidding,"
nor treat us to Dantescan analogies, but attempts to state clearly the
order of fact in which such pieces of information when we encounter
them must take their place, for instance that "the verse in this narrative passage, with its regular measure and insistent alliteration,
so effective for combining the macabre with the urbane and dreary,
is a way to indicate and a way to control the pressure of urgent
misery and self-disgust."

With the aid of a similar sense of relevance, Mr. Allen Tate in his
essay on *Ash-Wednesday* carries readers of poetry unscathed past the
question of doctrinal assent or dissent. Of the hundreds of essays
that take poems of Eliot's for their ostensible point of departure, a
surprising number focus on the congeniality or uncongeniality, for
the critic, of Eliot's "ideas." Against this tendency Mr. Tate's is an
early and largely unheeded protest. Mr. Blackmur's "In the Hope of
Straightening Things Out" is a late protest against the habit of treating Eliot's critical prose in a similar way. For the critical work was
empirical, discontinuous, devoted on one occasion or another to specific bodies of work, specific problems, amid circumstances mordantly
characterized in Ezra Pound's note *("in* the 'citta dolente' among the
unstill gibberings of 'fellow reviewers' . . . maggots living in or on
the mental activity of their time but contributing nothing to its
life"). Eliot mimicked these folk very knowingly, often with considerable comic effect; but once bound into autonomous collections, his
essays for that very reason simulate a pontifical unity which it is Mr.
Blackmur's business to take apart and assemble less formally. For
"the order in Eliot's criticism is that of conversation; and I mean
this, as I think he would take it, as a pleasing characteristic of a
critic so deeply concerned with matters of general order, and I believe
it is a characterization that leads to a sense of the unity of his mind."

It is a unity extending into the plays, which have been hardly
less haggled over, so informal do they seem against the illusion of
formality which we take from the critic and the lyric poet. Out of
dozens of articles on them, three are here selected. Mr. John Peter,
in the course of being irritated by the *succès d'estime* of *The Cocktail Party,* celebrates persuasively the virtues of *Murder in the Cathe-*

dral. Mr. Denis Donoghue in the course of a book on the problems of poetic drama in the twentieth century locates the point of advance marked by *The Cocktail Party,* not as an achieved classic, but as a provisional assault on those problems. And since neither essayist is centrally concerned with the radical difference between the verse of Eliot's plays and that of his poems, and since this difference is generally registered as a disappointing loss, the plays a spent poet's hobby, I include a brief review of *The Elder Statesman* which turns on this very point. None of the actors, deprived of fine lines to mouth, is allowed to affirm a vision centered on himself, as Othello does, as Hamlet does. And if they are deprived of that satisfaction, it is because the plays are about privacy, not affirmation. Shakespeare's is for better or worse a universe of actors, strutting and fretting; and so is the universe of *The Waste Land;* but the universe of Eliot's dramatic comedies is a universe of persons who learn to discard the satisfactions of the imprisoning role.

Donald Davie's valedictory essay may perhaps not be prophetic in the way he intends, but it is likely to prove prophetic none the less. For if Dr. Leavis, for instance, spoke for a generation which could not gainsay Eliot's contemporary relevance, and Mr. Mizener and Mr. Blackmur for a generation concerned with disentangling the work's enduring power from a very slightly perceptible obsolescence, Mr. Davie represents a still later body of serious readers for whom some Eliot poems at least (his example is "The Dry Salvages") simply do not work. And perceiving as he does in the entire fifty years' enterprise a working out, into necessarily desperate subtleties, of a post-symbolist poetic situation, he draws our attention finally to the self-sufficiency of the remarkable oeuvre which has cogent uses even for its own banalities and gaucheries.

Eliot's work, as he once noted of Shakespeare's, is in important respects one continuous poem; nor does this unity merely reflect the singleness of his life, for about 1929, when his critical attention circled back to Dante, we can detect him commencing a deliberate program of parallelling early poems with late ones ("Gerontion" with "A Song for Simeon"), and even one kind of late one with another (*Ash-Wednesday* with the alas unfinished *Coriolan*). Six years later he rounded off his Collected Poems with "Burnt Norton," an explicit half-size counterpart to *The Waste Land,* following so far as might be its every contortion of form, but devoted to the "heart of light" as the 1922 poem had been to the Heart of Darkness. These new-written poems do not replace their counterparts, any more than the 1947 Milton lecture replaces the differently directed essay of 1936 (in *On Poetry and Poets,* he pointedly printed them both, as Milton I and Milton II). Nor do the poems compete with one another. They complete one another; and *Four Quartets,* as Mr. Davie observes, carries this process of parts mutually supplementary to "a stage of such subtlety and intricacy in the post-symbolist tradition that it is impossible to think of its ever being taken a stage further."

Yeats wrote "Sailing to Byzantium" in the spirit of a ceremonious dialogue, across a century, with Keats' "Ode to a Nightingale" ("no hungry generations" . . . "those dying generations"; the immortal feathered bird "not born for death" and the crafted bird "of hammered gold and gold enamelling"); he allows us to suppose, even, that "Sailing to Byzantium" is such a poem as Keats might himself have written at sixty. (Yeats . . . Keats: did the man who filled a page of his notebook with "drums drums drums drums drums . . ." ponder the affinity of those numinous names?) But Eliot closes off the possibility of such a future trans-temporal dialogue, having written the counter-poems himself, and so left not an affirmation, partial and assertive, for some future voice to complete, but an equilibrium, Calder-like in its precarious mobility, for present and future to cherish or ignore. There is nothing for another poet to do but do otherwise; and that is presumably how Eliot would have it. There is not even a selection to make; he has virtually made it himself, in cannily declining to publish we cannot tell how many verses. This oeuvre has always strained toward completeness, the completeness implied by its own logic: spare, intent, chastened, building out of the wreckage of one lifetime, and often of "old stones that cannot be deciphered," a structure the very weight of whose keystones, seeking the ground, sustains them in the air. "Triumphal March," he called in 1931 his ironic vision of the busy world going somewhere, parodying as he did so the structural devices and documentary components of a busily contemporary poetry also concerned with going somewhere, into the dismally activist Thirties. In that title he echoed, with benevolent irony, the name of a wholly different order of artifact: the Arch which stands when the last marcher has left, and endures when the last centurion or sergeant-major is dust: stable, poised, not a building but the essential gesture of a building, very nearly at its inception a simulated ruin, testimony to the legions of gone things that have been and been done on this spot. The analogy is his, and so is the risk, calmly accepted, that the future may choose to do its building elsewhere.

To Meet Mr. Eliot

by Arthur Mizener

Nearly forty years ago, setting out to make a case for Ben Jonson, Mr. Eliot observed that "the reputation of Jonson has been of the most deadly kind that can be compelled upon the memory of a poet," and went on to describe that reputation as "the most perfect conspiracy of approval." For anyone who grew up with Mr. Eliot's poetry, responding to it profoundly and looking on its author almost with awe, it comes as a shock to find that a similar conspiracy against Mr. Eliot is beginning to be organized. Yet I think it has to be admitted that for many readers Mr. Eliot is beginning to seem an elder statesman of letters, a Great Man to whom the newspapers—as they did last spring—refer as a "68-year-old poet and playwright," almost as if he were another Poet among School Children, looked upon with uncomprehending respect as a man no longer expected to contribute anything the spectators care enough about to quarrel with.

This attitude is likely to seem an outrageous indignity to those of us for whom Mr. Eliot's poetry has always been an immediately moving experience. But we know from what happened, for example, to Tennyson's reputation that to meet history's conspiracy of approval with indignation will not do; it only makes matters worse. If we are to preserve the greatness of Mr. Eliot's poetry for readers who have not known the experience from which that greatness emerges, we are going to have to recognize that some of the elements in his poetry which seemed to appeal directly to our most private sentiments now sometimes persuade people that it is too much the poetry of a period's sentiment. For thirty years we have taken it pretty much for granted that every reader found himself in immediate touch with the moving center of Mr. Eliot's poetry and have devoted ourselves to sharpening the reader's awareness of what moved him. What is now beginning to be needed is an approach to Mr. Eliot's poetry which will be of use to readers who are separated from it by what he once called "the burden of respectability" its very success has imposed on it. When one can read "with pleasure and edification" even an address to Mr. Wilkinson's spade by Mr. Eliot, it is difficult to adopt the attitude this purpose requires; it asks of us some of the detachment Mr. Eliot himself has always cultivated, not least successfully in the comments on his own work in his most recent essay, "The Frontiers of Criticism." [1]

This acute "historical" sense of his own work goes back a long way with Mr. Eliot. As early as 1931 he was saying, "when I wrote a poem called *The Waste Land,* some of the more approving critics said I had expressed the 'disillusionment of a generation,' which is nonsense. I may have expressed for them their illusion of being disillusioned, but that did not form part of my intention." It is understandable that so serious a poet as Mr. Eliot was distressed to find himself confused with people like Aldous Huxley (whom he described at about that time as "a depressing life-forcer") and thought of as disillusioned in the way popular writers of the twenties were. Mr. Eliot's poetry did not, certainly, express this popular disillusionment, but it did speak to something in its age more potent than either that age's opinions—most of which Mr. Eliot disliked—or its sentimentalities; it achieved its greatness by penetrating to the very heart of its own times. If longing and terror, glory and horror, are permanent, they none the less exist for each age in its own dialect; Mr. Eliot's lifelong effort to preserve the dialect of the tribe has not been conducted in a foreign language.

The most striking characteristic of his verse has always been its relevance, and this relevance has been achieved by the constant submission of his fine perception to the discipline of his intelligence. His early criticism is deeply concerned with the nature of this kind of discipline and is insistent on the need for an unremitting cultivation of what he once called "the two forms of self-consciousness ["which must go together"], knowing what we are and what we ought to be." It is difficult not to believe that Mr. Eliot's main means for cultivating this self-consciousness—despite his expressed preference for a single regional culture—has been the deliberate movement from one urban culture to another.

But this is a guess. We know something of Mr. Eliot's history (there is a biographical note in F. O. Matthiessen's book), but very little of the kind of man he has been: the revealing indulgences of vanity in his career have been few and obscure and his friends have been remarkably discreet. There are a few glimpses of him as a young man, for instance, in Conrad Aiken's recollection of him as

> a singularly attractive, tall, and rather dapper young man; with a somewhat Lamian smile, who reeled out of the doorway of the Lampoon on a spring evening, and, catching sight of me, threw his arms about me. . . . "And that," observed my astonished companion, "if Tom remembers it tomorrow, will cause him to suffer agonies of shyness." And no doubt it did: for he *was* shy.

A couple of years later, we hear, he was going to Boston debutante parties as a discipline for this shyness, and for the same reason learning to box and—in his own phrase—"to swarm with passion up a rope." In another year or two he is writing Conrad Aiken from Oxford: "Come, let us desert our wives, and fly to a land where there are no Medici prints, nothing but concubinage and conversation. Oxford is very pretty, but I don't like to be dead." Not long after, we catch a few more glimpses of him as a young poet around London, smiling what Wyndham Lewis called his "Giaconda smile" in Pound's small, triangular sitting room, content, apparently, to listen while Pound talked.

There are certain things which stand out in these glimpses of what Mr. Eliot was like before he completed his public persona. There is the sensibility, so energetic that it constantly overflows into an extravagance for which he feels apologetic. There is the vigorous, disciplinary self-consciousness with which he strives to control both his extravagance and his temperamental shyness. And there is the repeated shift from one urban culture to another, from Harvard to the Sorbonne, from Marburg to Oxford, and the effort to make the sensibility grow up to and into it—"mixing memory and desire."

Mr. Eliot began his life in an environment which must have had some of the heightened consciousness of its cultural inheritance characteristic of exiled groups. As he himself pointed out in his introduction to his mother's poem, *Savonarola*, Charlotte Stearns brought with her from Boston its nineteenth-century compound of "Schleiermacher, Emerson, Channing, and Herbert Spencer." The Eliots' awareness of this tradition must have been intensified by the very different air of St. Louis, just as their awareness of that air must have been intensified by their Boston inheritance. Thus for Mr. Eliot, even "the penny world I bought/To eat with Pipit behind the screen" was not a simple one to be accepted without critical self-consciousness. The Harvard and Boston of his undergraduate years must have offered him a yet more complex conception of his tradition's memory to adapt desire to and a more imposing sense of the recalcitrance of the everyday world and our everyday selves. The process of adaption and complication of which we can catch glimpses here was to be deliberately repeated again and again in his life.

As a consequence his poems have always been constructed around the contrasts among different ways of life which he has possessed as experience. The young man who submitted himself to the discipline of Boston parties knew the world of "Cousin Nancy" Ellicott, who "smoked/And danced all the modern dances"; he also knew the world of "Matthew and Waldo guardians of the faith,/The army of unalterable law" which Cousin Nancy altered without even knowing it—*by* not knowing it. Whatever Charlotte Stearns' son may think of Nancy, she is his cousin and he knows from both propinquity and deliberately acquired experience the power she possesses. Most of Eliot's early poems know better the power of the Bleisteins than the ineffectuality of the Burbanks, are more acutely aware of "what we are" than hopeful of our ability to realize "what we ought to be." What can the poor old aunts, who "were not quite sure how they felt about it," do about Nancy's crude energy which leaves Matthew and Waldo on the shelf, unhonored sybils hanging in their basket, and leaves nowhere Meredith's assurance that the stars in their courses assert eternal providence? Let Prufrock walk among the lowest of the dead and Burbank meditate on his decayed house; Sweeney and Bleistein are up and doing, men not easily to be persuaded to consider the seven laws of architecture or the word others have found swaddled within the darkness of the world.

Thus, in a way fundamentally characteristic of American experience, the abyss between the idea and the reality of Mr. Eliot's world increased; as his sensibility was subdued to an increasingly complex conception of Western Culture, the world of his everyday experience appeared more monstrous and remote. No wonder he came to feel that "we live in an incredible public world and an intolerable private world." However reluctant a man may be to move toward such despair, this course appears to be nearly unavoidable for the gifted provincial writer who seeks to acquire the memory of his whole culture and to discipline desire to it. This feeling is as evident in such different poets as Hart Crane and Allen Tate as it is in Mr. Eliot. That Mr. Eliot faced it honestly and without sentimentality is a great triumph of intelligence and integrity; that he found an unaffected and effective way out of it is perhaps even a greater triumph.

At its responsible best, the repeated adaption of the feelings to a more complicated conception of tradition produces a sensibility different from that of either the original or the adopted culture. Mr. Eliot's perceptions characteristically have the precision and self-consciousness of a foreigner speaking a language nearly perfectly:

> Now the light falls
> Across the open field, leaving the deep lane
> Shuttered with branches, dark in the afternoon. . . .
> In a warm haze, the sultry light
> Is absorbed, not refracted, by grey stone.
> ("East Coker," I)

This is a man for whom what he sees has, for all its familiarity, some element of the alien about it, so that he notices still, almost with surprise, that the light "is absorbed, not refracted, by grey stone." Mr. Eliot's possession of his tradition has this same air. It has been acquired, as fully acquired as a fine intelligence and a powerful will can make it. But it is acquired, and it never becomes entirely habitual. As a result, Mr. Eliot's perceptions have a very special kind of brilliance.

Step by step, "by a continual surrender of himself as he [was] at the moment to something which [was] more valuable," Mr. Eliot committed himself to the fullest conception of Western Culture he could grasp. As he presently realized, with a care for emotional honesty that perhaps only the heir of American Unitarianism would have, this included Catholic Christianity. "Culture," as Mr. Eliot said, "after all, is not enough, even though nothing is enough without culture."

From the beginning of his career, Mr. Eliot's prose has given us a commentary of remarkable vividness on this process of adaption. As he himself observed in "The Frontiers of Criticism," "the best of my *literary* criticism . . . consists of essays on poets and poetic dramatists who had influenced me." The epigraph of the first essay in his first book of criticism—"Eriger en lois ses impressions personnelles, c'est le grand effort d'un homme s'il est sincère"—sums up his whole policy as a poet. In one of his earliest essays, "Tradition and the Individual Talent," he made the purpose behind that policy quite clear. "Poetry," he said, "is not a turning loose of emotion, but an escape from emotion; it is not the expression of a personality, but an escape from per-

sonality." "But, of course," he added, "only those who have personality
and emotions know what it means to want to escape these things."
Some odd combination of slyness and humility frequently leads Mr.
Eliot to treat the crucial point of his argument this way, as if it were
self-evident and could almost be thrown away. But the point here is
clear enough. The way to avoid being "laid waste by the anarchy of
feeling" is, in life, the discipline of an adequate culture. In verse, the
escape from this disorder is an adequate form, a form which provides
impersonal occasions and motives unrelated to the writer's for what
he wants to express. This is not a theory for writing poetry without
involving the personality and the emotions (as the term "escape" might
conceivably suggest); it is a theory for writing a poetry which makes
the best use of them by giving them the greatest formal and therefore
public order.

The ordering form of Mr. Eliot's verse derives immediately from
Ezra Pound's imagism. Pound's imagism is only one manifestation of
an almost mystical theory of perception which is one of the remarkable
phenomena of our time. From James's "represent" through Joyce's
"epiphanies" and Mr. Eliot's "objective correlative" to Hemingway's
"the way it was," our writers have been dominated by a belief that
every pattern of feelings has its pattern of objects and events, so
that if the writer can set down the pattern of objects in exactly the
right relations, without irrelevances or distortions, they will evoke in
the reader the pattern of feelings. Whatever the limitations of this
view—and we have hardly considered seriously yet what they may
be—it suited Mr. Eliot's talent, with its great powers of visual and
aural perception.

The early poems, in *Prufrock* and *Poems,* are either short lyrics or
dramatic monologues. As we read through the lyrics, we see Mr. Eliot
moving from the relatively simple contrasts of Cousin Nancy with
Arnold and Emerson to something more complicated. In "Sweeney
Erect," for example, we see Sweeney indifferently shaving while the
woman in his bed has an epileptic fit. The poem's judgment of
Sweeney's mode of life is implicit in Mr. Eliot's image of it. But he
reinforces this image, first with a reference to Emerson's "Self-Re-
liance," and then with an extravagant figure, a comparison of Sweeney
and Theseus:

> Display me Aeolus above
>   Reviewing the insurgent gales
> Which tangle Ariadne's hair
>   And swell with haste the perjured sails.

The full realized sorrow of romantic betrayal which is embodied in the Ariadne story gives us a further measure of the mean vanity of the ladies and Mrs. Turner, of Doris's inadequate goodheartedness, and of Sweeney's complacent and innocent confidence that he "knows the female temperament."

But the Ariadne story is not reality for us, or not the necessary whole of it, any more than is the language in which it is presented here. We notice the delicate emphasis on the original meanings of "reviewing" and "insurgent," the excessively verbal wit of the transferred epithet in the last line, the conventional tragic irony of the contrast between the wind's blowing Ariadne's lovely hair and Theseus' impatient ship. This is a pastiche of Jacobean verse, too skilful to be taken only as parody and too evidently artificial to be taken as wholly straightforward. Its point is reinforced by the poem's epigraph from *The Maid's Tragedy*. Mr. Eliot has always reluctantly admired Beaumont and Fletcher's skill and disapproved of what he considers their lack of integrity ("the blossoms of Beaumont and Fletcher's imagination . . . are cut and slightly withered flowers stuck into sand"). In *The Maid's Tragedy* the deserted heroine comes upon her waiting women at work on a tapestry of Ariadne's story. She assures them their Ariadne is not nearly pathetic enough, makes an eloquent speech offering herself as a model ("and behind me,/Make all a desolation. See, see, wenches," as the first quarto has it), and strikes a theatrically pathetic pose. Mr. Eliot's conviction that this scene is, for all its effectiveness, false is clear from the way he quotes the folio reading of Aspatia's remark out of context: "And behind me/Make all a desolation. Look, look, wenches!"

The world of Sweeney and his woman is brutally limited, almost apish, for all its humanity and "naturalness," but the dream of a world in which Theseus and Ariadne conduct themselves with tragic splendor has a way of turning artificially pretty. If there is in the Ariadne story at its best a suggestion of human possibilities which make Sweeney's world look brutish, there is in Sweeney's story an honesty about the primitive foundation of man's nature which makes very clear the affectations of the Ariadne story at its worst.

What Mr. Eliot does with the dramatic monologue can be illustrated with "Gerontion." "Gerontion" is an immensely skilful "impersonalizing" adaption of the Jacobean dramatic soliloquy. The weary old man who speaks it is a character remote from Mr. Eliot himself, and both this character, with his long memory and his imprisoning Pyrrhonism, and the form, with its convention of free association, are remarkably suited to the impersonal expression of Mr. Eliot's *impressions person-*

nelles, his sense of what has gone wrong with the human situation in his own time and must therefore have been what menaced it with greater or less success in other times. "Gerontion" is a powerful and moving expression of these emotions, and it gains a good deal, at least in a negative way, by not presenting them to us merely as the poet's opinions. It shows an astonishing awareness of the images of our world which evoke most powerfully its special kind of despair, and Mr. Eliot mixes these images with just the kind of endless speculation to which Gerontion's state of mind drives us—"These matters that with myself I too much discuss/Too much explain." The brilliance with which the poem exemplifies such speculations is evident if we compare the most famous of them, the passage which begins "After such knowledge, what forgiveness?" with the less effective expression of this thought the different requirements of "The Rock" led Mr. Eliot to write:

> All our knowledge brings us nearer to our ignorance,
> All our ignorance brings us nearer to death,
> But nearness to death no nearer to GOD.
> Where is the Life we have lost in living?
> Where is the wisdom we have lost in knowledge?
> Where is the knowledge we have lost in information?

"Gerontion" is a triumph of transforming a set of personal convictions into an expression which is valid for anyone in our time and perhaps valid for men in all times who have seen what always exists, the solid evidence that the human situation is not a very easy one.

But one does not have to share Professor Winters' feelings about pseudo-reference to feel that a dramatic monologue, deprived as it is of the defining context a soliloquy has, must create within its own limits a sharp impression of the speaker's character if the poet is to have all the benefits of his dramatic disguise. "Gerontion" does not do so. From the first lines, the poem carries such a burden of symbolic meaning that it is difficult to read as the speech of a realized character. Mr. Edmund Wilson has been taken to task for not recognizing that Mr. Eliot's poems are dramatic monologues and complaining that Mr. Eliot talked like an old man at forty. But the fact is that "Gerontion" is in large part only nominally dramatic, almost as if there were some deficiency in Mr. Eliot's sense of the ordinary, immediate reality of people, as if he saw them always as grotesques answering to names like Mrs. Phlaccus and Professor Channing-Cheetah. "The dramatist," he once said quite rightly, "need not understand people; but he must be exceptionally aware of them." Mr. Eliot, to use his own words, is often exceptionally aware only of "the reality of the moral synthesis . . . behind the motions of his personages."

In both subject and form *The Waste Land* is "Gerontion" writ large. It is Mr. Eliot's fullest and most eloquent presentation of the contrasting worlds of Burbank and Bleistein and of the despair the contemplation of that contrast induces; and it is a dramatic monologue with a speaker who is, as Mr. Eliot's note says, "not indeed a 'character' " who must none the less unite all the rest. But in *The Waste Land* Mr. Eliot is beginning to elaborate the seasonal image which appears sporadically in "Gerontion" and to substitute for the character of the speaker, which provides the structure for the conventional dramatic monologue, a pattern of reiterated images. This form is given its fullest development in the *Four Quartets* where it shows to greatest advantage.

With *The Waste Land* and "The Hollow Men" Mr. Eliot's career reached a crisis. The Tiresias who helplessly foresuffers all is the final term in a series which begins with Prufrock. Whether Bleistein and Sweeney know it or not, there is no further to go in this desert. But it was five years before Mr. Eliot began, in *Ash-Wednesday*, to find where else to go. If the speaker in *Ash-Wednesday* cannot yet discipline "the lost heart" that "stiffens and rejoices/In the lost lilac and the lost sea voices," even when he does not "wish to wish these things," he is now sure he knows what the right wish is ("Teach us to care and not to care/Teach us to sit still") and is freshly aware of that "Jansenism of the individual biography," as Mr. Eliot calls it in his essay on the *Pensées,* which may have led him to this echo of Pascal. Though *Ash-Wednesday* is also a dramatic monologue, its effects depend very little on the independent character of the speaker; insofar as they do, the coherence of the speaker's voice and manner are enough to support them.

Considering how deeply Mr. Eliot must have been personally involved in the emotions *Ash-Wednesday* is made of, its scrupulous honesty—after all the fundamental purpose for Mr. Eliot's "impersonality"—is a remarkable achievement. These bones sing as truly as they can, but their singing is "chirping/With the burden of the grasshopper" in the waste land, where desire shall fail because memory has. No more than the prophet can the poem say whether these bones shall live; but they can sit still, "forgetting themselves and each other, united/In the quiet of the desert."

It was nearly a decade before Mr. Eliot brought his whole personality and all his feelings under the control of this conception. This was the most formidable disciplining of the sensibility he had attempted and its cost must have been an effort of the imagination difficult to conceive. Its reward was the *Four Quartets*. Formally, too, the *Four Quartets*—despite the title's refusal to claim more than a loose coherence for them—is remarkable, both because the unobtrusive speaker of the poem has the whole of Mr. Eliot's public reputation behind him as definition and because his monologue's structure of reiterated ideas and images is dramatically convincing as meditation and deeply moving in meaning. The quiet, unostentatious, glowing intensity of the *Four Quartets* cannot be described but perhaps it can be illustrated.

This is the opening strophe of the first part of the final quartet, "Little Gidding."

> Midwinter spring is its own season
> Sempiternal though sodden towards sundown,
> Suspended in time, between pole and tropic.
> When the short day is brightest, with frost and fire,
> The brief sun flames the ice, on pond and ditches,
> In windless cold that is the heart's heat,
> Reflecting in a watery mirror
> A glare that is blindness in the early afternoon.
> And glow more intense than blaze of branch, or brazier,
> Stirs the dumb spirit: no wind, but pentecostal fire
> In the dark time of the year. Between melting and freezing
> The soul's sap quivers. There is no earth smell
> Or smell of living thing. This is the spring time
> But not in time's covenant. Now the hedgerow
> Is blanched for an hour with transitory blossom
> Of snow, a bloom more sudden
> Than that of summer, neither budding nor fading,
> Not in the scheme of generation.
> Where is the summer, the unimaginable
> Zero summer?

To this image of the seasonal world of time Mr. Eliot began to commit himself in *Ash-Wednesday*, not because the world of time is the whole of reality, but because "only through time time is conquered." What he is seeking is an image which will realize both the recognition that "in my beginning is my end" and the recognition that "in my end is my beginning." Only thus can he finally achieve "a sense of the timeless as well as of the temporal and of the timeless and temporal together," as he put it at the very beginning of his career.

This strophe is therefore first of all the description of a temporal occasion, what we sometimes call a spring*like* day in midwinter. But that language is false, for it recognizes only temporality, assumes that this is "really" only a midwinter moment that seems like spring. It is, of course, that; the *Quartets* do full justice to the world of time and recognize the intimacy within that world of man's life and nature's:

> Keeping the rhythm in their dancing
> As in their living in the living seasons
> The time of the seasons and the constellations
> The time of milking and the time of harvest
> The time of the coupling of man and woman
> And that of beasts. Feet rising and falling.
> Eating and drinking. Dung and death.

The modulation at the end of this passage from "East Coker" does not deny the reality of this life or its goodness; it only suggests the insufficiency of such a life.

If we recognize that the world of time is only a part of reality, then we recognize that this season is not merely spring*like*. Taken quite simply for what it appears, it is "its own season," namely, "midwinter spring." As such it is in fact "sempiternal"—only, to be sure, because time is real too, "sodden toward sundown." It is "suspended," but it is also "in time." The next two lines sustain this sense of the seasons' dual reality ("When the *short* day is *brightest*") and fix our attention on its special quality. This quality is hinted at by "Between pole and tropic"; it is made overt by "with frost and fire" and "The brief sun flames the ice."

But because men are always "living in the living seasons," this unseasonal season is, in both its temporality and its suspense, a season of the heart as well as a season of nature. "The brief sun flames the ice, on pond and ditches,/In windless cold that is the *heart's* heat." From this point on the strophe takes account of all these aspects of the season. For instance, "Reflecting in a watery mirror/A glare that is blindness in the early afternoon." This does complete justice to the temporal experience, the uneven reflecting surfaces of the ice, the merely uncomfortable glare of natural sunlight which, we remind ourselves, need be endured only for "the early afternoon." But it is also charged with an awareness that the uneven surface of man's

nature has reflected a flash of the blinding glow that has, in the words
of "Burnt Norton," "glittered out of the heart of light."

The emphasis in these first eight lines has been on the temporal
phenomenon; the human one is largely implicit. The next four lines
emphasize the human phenomenon, but keep the natural one before
us by using the season of nature as a metaphor for the season of the
heart ("Between melting and freezing/The soul's sap quivers"). The
next seven lines generalize the image further. "This *is* the spring
time," the spring time not of "time's covenant" but of timeless reality's, a spring which, if it stirs men's hearts more than the most
vivid temporal passion, is also icy cold. It is hotter than "East Coker's"
rustics leaping through their bonfire in a commodious celebration
of natural love but altogether without the smell of their mortality,
the earthly smell of "dung and death."

The last two lines intensify our awareness that this is no mere
description but an experience. In "Burnt Norton" the speaker had
been impatient of mere time ("Ridiculous the waste sad time/Stretch-
ing before and after"); in "East Coker" he was still thinking almost
entirely of "the intense moment/Isolated, with no before and after."
But by "The Dry Salvages" he was aware that "the point of inter-
section of the timeless/With time, is an occupation for the saint":
"for most of us, there is only the unattended/Moment, the moment
in and out of time." In the last two lines of this strophe his anguished
longing for the occupation of the saint reasserts itself. If midwinter
spring can be what he has just experienced, what must the "unimagi-
nable/Zero summer" be like, that inconceivable "time" when, simultaneously, midwinter has become zero weather and spring has become
full summer?

Perhaps this illustration will suggest something of the quiet magnificence with which Mr. Eliot has finally brought together in the
Four Quartets the two worlds which have lain apart in his imagination from the beginning of his career—the world of time and those
who, like Sweeney, keep its rhythm, and the brilliant, ordered world
of the disciplined imagination and those who, like the saints, keep
its stillness. Here are Mr. Eliot's very great gifts at their best; much
more, here is the reward for his having devoted a lifetime to the object he set himself at the beginning of his career, "to transmute his
personal and private agonies into . . . something universal and impersonal." If new readers are sometimes put off by the severity of
Mr. Eliot's manners (as Mr. Eliot is himself when he rereads his early
work) let them remember that without the intensity of will they

indicate Mr. Eliot would never have been able to mix the desire of a brilliant midwestern Unitarian with the central memory of Western Culture and so show his time, not perhaps what it is, but what it would be if its nature were fully realized.

Early London Environment

by Wyndham Lewis

The end of last month and of this month respectively (March and April namely) have been the deadline for articles I had agreed to write about two very old friends of mine. The circumstance attending the composition of these articles, in one respect at least, has been dramatic. For one of these friends is confined in a criminal asylum in America, but the other is among us here, a rarely honored member of his profession, dwelling in the bland atmosphere of general approbation.

As I took up my pen and addressed myself to these tasks, I could not help but wonder what qualities are conducive to one issue, what to the other: which are those that draw A down into such portentous shadows, which that thrust B up into so brilliantly sunlit a position? Need the Freudian machinery be invoked? For me I think the question tends to take no count of the climb up into the sun, but only the problem of what keeps anybody—A, B, C, or D—out of a madhouse.

This is not, however, an excursion into psychology nor psychiatry. What made the description of this rhetorical gesture of wondering enquiry almost essential, or something on similar lines, is the fact that I first met B (the subject of this article) at the home of A. And their two destinies at that early date, again, form so much one undistinguishable pattern—so that you could not speak of B without mentioning A, that their personalities, if not their literary reputations, would of necessity be discussed. A good opportunity presents itself at this point to observe that personalities, the "scene," not literary reputations, is to be the sole subject matter.

The task more particularly assigned me, as I understand it, is to

"Early London Environment." From *T. S. Eliot,* edited by March and Tambimuttu (London: Editions Poetry, 1948; Chicago: Henry Regnery Co., 1949). Reprinted by permission of Henry Regnery Co.

say something about the earliest phase of Mr. T. S. Eliot's life in London, or what I recall of it. There is, naturally, a scarcity of witnesses—it was a long time ago, and his movements as yet private and unprominent. So, on this most solemn occasion, I shall do my best.

I am much more of an authority on Mr. Eliot at a later date. The earlier Mr. Eliot about whom I am to write is a figure entering the portals—seated in the parlor—of Heartbreak House. He and war came together. Preparatory to going into the army I pressed on with the composition of *Tarr*—and also was not able to move about a great deal. What I have to tell will be, perhaps, a little like a portrait which is all accessories and not much figure—that is, if the author of the *Cantos* can be described as an accessory.

Well, Mr. Eliot swam into my ken in Ezra Pound's diminutive triangular sitting room, in which all Ezra's social life was transacted, since, although really absurdly tiny, it was the only room in the Pound flat where there was any daylight.

In the base of the triangle was the door. As I entered the room I discovered an agreeable stranger parked up one of the sides of the triangle. He softly growled at me, as we shook hands. American. A graceful neck I noted, with what elsewhere I have described as "a Gioconda smile." Though not feminine—besides being physically large his personality visibly moved within the male pale—there *were* dimples in the warm dark skin; undoubtedly he used his eyes a little like a Leonardo. He was a very attractive fellow then; a sort of looks unusual this side of the Atlantic. I liked him, though I may say not at all connecting him with texts Ezra had shown me about some fictional character dreadfully troubled with old age, in which the lines (for it had been verse) "I am growing old, I am growing old, I shall wear the bottoms of my trousers rolled"—a feature, apparently, of the humiliations reserved for the superannuated—I was unable to make head or tail of.

Ezra now lay flung back in typical posture of aggressive ease. It resembled extreme exhaustion. (Looking back, I believe he *did* over-fatigue himself, like an excitable dog, use his last ounce of vitality, and that he did in fact become exhausted.) However, he kept steadily beneath his quizzical but self-satisfied observation his latest prize, or discovery—the author of "Prufrock." The new collector's piece went on smiling and growling out melodiously his apt and bright answers to promptings from the exhausted figure of his proud captor. His ears did not grow red, or I am sure I should have noticed it. Ezra then gave us all some preserved fruit, of which it was his habit to eat a great deal.

The poem of which this was the author had, I believe, already been published. But Pound had the air of having produced it from his hat a moment before, and its author with it simultaneously, out of the same capacious headpiece. He blinked and winked with contemplative conceit and contentment, chewing a sugared and wonderfully shrunken pear: then removed his glasses to wipe off the film of oily London dust that might have collected—but really to withdraw, as it were, and leave me alone with Mr. Prufrock for a moment.

Then, that finished, Ezra would squint quickly, sideways, up at me —"granpa"-wise, over the rims of his glasses. With chuckles, and much heavy fun, in his screwed-up smiling slits of eyes, he would be as good as saying to me in the Amos and Andy patter of his choice: "Yor ole uncle Ezz is wise to wot youse thinkin. Waaal Wynd damn I'se tellin *yew,* he's lot better'n he looks!"

Contempt on my part was always assumed, because a mania like Pound's to act as a nursery and lying-in establishment—*bureau de renseignment* and unofficial agency for unknown literary talent did involve the successive presence of numbers of preposterous people. These I would find either groping around in the dark in the large middle room of the flat—even playing the piano there—or quite often seated where Mr. Eliot was now installed. The situation therefore was one for which a regular convention existed, of quizzical dumb-show on the part of the incorrigible host, and stony stares back from me.

This very small room, in which Mr. Eliot had alighted, and in which he sat placidly smiling, was, allowance made for the comic side of Ezra's manic herding of talent, a considerable place. Dorothy Shakespeare had become Dorothy Pound and of course was in this dwarf room, too, nodding, with a quick jerk of the head, unquestioning approval of Ezra's sallies, or hieratically rigid as she moved delicately to observe the Kensingtonian Tea ritual. (Long habit in the paternal mansion responsible, she was a good turncoat *bourgeoise,* who wore her red cockade with a grim pleasant gaucherie.) In any event, all social transactions were necessarily *intime.* One at a time was their rule for genius.

Mr. Eliot would presently be taken to a much larger place—where there would be more than just a crowded little triangle to sit in: not so important, yet an essential part of Ezra's exiguous social machine. For those not familiar with the hills and valleys of London, the event with which I opened took place practically at the foot of Notting Hill. Now almost at the top of that hill stood a squarish Victorian mansion, of no great size but highly respectable, within whose walls Ford Madox

Ford (known then as Hueffer) lived and entertained with Violet Hunt. A gate in a tall wall gave access to it, and standing in the center of a patch of grass, just visible from the pavement, was a large carving of Ezra by Brzeska. It was Ezra in the form of a marble phallus. Mr. Eliot would have to be taken here.

A number of people were to be met, certainly, belonging to the literary, theatrical, and occasionally monied, world at Hueffer's (as it is better to call him, rather than Ford): for he was unspeakably gregarious. But Mr. Eliot would be taken around there primarily to be shown to Hueffer. The latter gentleman in all probability thought he wrote poems like "Prufrock" just as well if not better himself. A sort of Wild West turn like Ezra, at whose hyperborean antics he could smile—that would be one thing. But it would be quite another for what was, as he saw it, a kind of Harvardian Rupert Brooke to make claims upon his tolerance. Such I imagine might be the situation arising from such a contact. But by South Lodge Mr. Eliot would have to pass, as part of the initiatory proceedings.

There is no more exact manner available to me of dating my first encounter with Mr. Eliot than by stating that before the first number of my magazine *Blast* I did not know him, and he was not known I think to others; but that before my second number I knew him. *Blast No. 1* was published in June 1914, *Blast No. 2* in July 1915. In *No. 2* I printed some poems of his—"Preludes" and "Rhapsody on a Windy Night." The last of the "Preludes" (No. 4) contains especially fine lines, which I have often seen quoted:

> I am moved by fancies that are curled
> Around these images, and cling:
> The notion of some infinitely gentle,
> Infinitely suffering thing.
> Wipe your hand across your mouth, and laugh;
> The worlds revolve like ancient women
> Gathering fuel in vacant lots.

It is no secret that Ezra Pound exercised a very powerful influence upon Mr. Eliot. I do not have to define the nature of this influence, of course. Mr. Eliot was lifted out of his lunar alleyways and *fin de siècle* nocturnes, into a massive region of verbal creation in contact with that astonishing didactic intelligence—that is all. "Gerontion" (1920) is a close relative of "Prufrock," certain matters filtered through an aged mask in both cases, but "Gerontion" technically is "school of Ezra."

The didactic vocation was exercised by Ezra, unfortunately, in the void (with the exception of such a happy chance as his association with his fellow countryman, Mr. Eliot)—in a triangular box, as we have seen, practically at the foot of Notting Hill. Between Hueffer and himself there was a solid bond. Ezra "believed in" Ford. Ford, who knew what he was talking about, praised the other's verses to the skies. And Ezra regarded it as typical—and very justly—that Hueffer should find no support in England for the *English Review*.

Degas's often quoted remark, made to another American, with whom publicity was second nature, "Whistler, you behave as if you had no talent," applies to this case. Ezra, the would-be master or teacher, often behaved "as if he had no talent."

It occurs to me that to some English ears these remarks and descriptions may appear wanting in reticence. That is not so at all. In the first place, we are public figures. A man becomes that of his own free will—in fact the becoming it entails quite a lot of work, frequently requiring many years of pretty close attention and solid labor. In the arts the personality is engaged; accordingly everything about this figure is public, or one day will be. Indeed, the more *publicity* the better pleased is every *public man*.

This is the number one consideration. In the second place, although I bring the scene to life in which Mr. Eliot at that stage of his career found himself, it is the scene, and not Mr. Eliot, I recreate.

Knowing the principal figures in it still so well does not make the re-creation easier—though you would perhaps suppose it would. Some of these figures do not change much; others do. For instance, in 1938 when I was painting Ezra (the picture is now in the Tate) he swaggered in, coattails flying, a malacca cane out of the Nineties aslant beneath his arm, the lion's head from the Scandinavian Northwest thrown back. There was no conversation. He flung himself at full length into my best chair for that pose, closed his eyes, and was motionless, just as a dog who has been taxing its strength to the full flings itself down and sleeps. Ezra was not haggard, he looked quite well, but was exhausted. He did not sleep, but he did not move for two hours by the clock.

"Go to it Wyndham!" he gruffled without opening his eyes, as soon as his mane of as yet entirely ungrizzled hair had adjusted itself to the cushioned chair top. A reference to my portrait of Mr. Eliot, painted some months earlier, produced the remark that now I had a "better subject to work from." A mild and not unpleasing example of the gasconade. But that was how I always found Ezra, full of bombast, germanic kindness, but *always* in appearance the Westerner in excelsis. On the tips of his toes with aggressive vitality, till he dropped, or as good as. (A note here I should like to add: I have had experience of Ezra for a long time: in some respects he does not forget the teaching of Chinese sages.)

With Mr. Eliot it has always been quite the opposite. Appearing at one's front door, or arriving at a dinner rendezvous (I am thinking of the late Thirties, not his more vernal years of course) his face would be haggard; he would seem at his last gasp. (Did he know?) To ask *him* to lie down for a short while at once was what I always felt I ought to do. However, when he had taken his place at a table, given his face a dry wash with his hands, and having had a little refreshment, Mr. Eliot would rapidly shed all resemblance to the harassed and exhausted refugee, in flight from some Scourge of God. Apparently a modest reserve of power, prudently set aside, would be drawn on. He would be as lively as ever he could be or any one need be—for of course it is not necessary to fly about on the tips of one's toes with one's scarf and coattails flying.

Immediately after World War I—I had not long left a military hospital and was restarting with a new studio—Mr. Eliot himself is, for me, much more distinct. For instance, we went to the Loire and Brittany together—that holiday involving a meeting, the first for both of us, with James Joyce in Paris; after that a stay at Saumur, and then the Breton coast in the Golfe de Vannes region. I hope I shall not be destroying some sentimental illusion if I record that to my surprise I remarked that my companion entered most scrupulously in a small notebook the day's expenses. This he would do in the evening at a café table when we had our nightcap. There was not much more he could spend before he got into bed.

The intermediate years—since he first sat in Pound's toy room—had greatly matured Mr. Eliot. The "Gioconda" period seemed a thing of the distant past; the saturnine vein was strongly fed with the harsh spectacle of the times. He was an American who was in flight from the same thing that kept Pound over here; and with what had he been delected, as soon as he had firmly settled himself upon this side of the water? The spectacle of Europe committing suicide—just that.

The Hollow Men (of 1925) is generally considered Mr. Eliot's most successful attempt to make the paralysis and decay concrete for his contemporaries, in drained-out cadences and desiccated vocables. The date of *The Hollow Men* takes one on to the times when I was often with Mr. Eliot at the Schiffs', in Cambridge Square or at Eastbourne, and in the relaxation of a household where we were very much spoiled by our hosts—for my part, the last time I saw Mr. Eliot in a mood that was very young. Even in the early Thirties, however, the haggard and exhausted mask of which I spoke earlier was seen nothing of. I must get back now without delay to the foot of Notting Hill, in the first twelve months after the "lights had gone out in Europe."

Pound possessed, in Miss Harriet Weaver, a very substantial auxiliary indeed. Her little office in Adelphi rather than South Lodge would be a place worth visiting for Mr. Eliot. Sympathy, as much as ambition, would cause him to prefer the active Quaker lady, editress, to the ineffectual ex-editor Ford Madox Hueffer.

The Egoist was Miss Weaver's paper, but at the period of which I speak you would rather have supposed that it belonged to Ezra Pound. *The Egoist* also on occasion published books (my novel *Tarr* for instance). And the old files of *The Egoist* contain much work of Mr. Eliot's. This, I should suppose, was the first place where his work appeared in England. The way was also smoothed by Pound for "Prufrock's" début in book form. So, for all his queerness at times— ham publicity of self, misreading of part of poet in society—in spite of anything that may be said Ezra is not only *himself* a great poet, but has been of the most amazing use to other people. Let it not be forgotten for instance that it was he who was responsible for the all-important contact for James Joyce—namely Miss Weaver. It was *his* critical understanding, *his* generosity, involved in the detection and appreciation of the literary genius of James Joyce. It was through him that a very considerable sum of money was put at Joyce's disposal, at the critical moment.

Such is the career side of Mr. Eliot's association with Ezra Pound. But he met in his company Imagists and others, several of those who at a later time wrote for him in *The Criterion*—Gould Fletcher, Aldington, Flint. And when I spoke of Ezra *transacting* his social life, there was nothing social for him that did not have a bearing upon the business of writing. If it had not it would be dull. He was a man of letters, in the marrow of his bones and down to the red-rooted follicles of his hair. He breathed Letters, ate Letters, dreamt Letters. A very rare kind of man. To fall into the clutches of this benevolent mentor was not the making of Mr. Eliot—for he had already begun *making himself,* after quite a distinct fashion, in "Prufrock" and other pieces. Here was a stiffening. Here were a variety of transformations, technical and otherwise, which it is not my specifically non-critical function to indicate.

Had it not been the very earliest period of Mr. Eliot's life in literary circles in England, some account of which was required of me, the background would not have been dominated by one figure, as in this article certainly has been the case. It always seems to be in the little triangular room, practically at the foot of Notting Hill, that I see Mr. Eliot. I recall entering it, for example, when on leave (a *bombadier*). Mr. Eliot was there—in the same place as the first time (there was nowhere else to sit however). After a little while I found him examining me, his head on one side. I asked him what there was about me that puzzled him. He was wondering, he answered, whether the short hair suited me or not. (Before the army it had been thick and long.) My point is forcibly brought out by the fact that I had no idea where Mr. Eliot lived. He appeared—he often was to be found—in the triangle, the supreme figure of Ezra a few feet away of course. I am not displeased, nor I am sure will Mr. Eliot be, that the dictates of my commission led me perforce to write quite a lot about this old friend of ours.

Bradley

by Hugh Kenner

J. Alfred Prufrock is a name plus a Voice. He isn't a "character" cut out of the rest of the universe and equipped with a history and a little necessary context, like the speaker of a Browning monologue. We have no information about him whatever; even his age is ambiguous (the poet once referred casually to Prufrock in a lecture as a *young* man). Nor is he an Everyman, surrounded by poetic effects: the range of "treatment" is excessive. Everyman's mind doesn't teem with allusions to Hesiod, Hamlet, Lazarus, Falstaff, entomology, eschatology, John the Baptist, mermaids. What "Prufrock" is, is the name of a possible zone of consciousness where these materials can maintain a vague congruity; no more than that; certainly not a person. You are not, in allowing their intermodulations to echo in your mind, deepening your apprehension of an imagined character, such as Hamlet, or discerning his boundaries; Prufrock is strangely boundless; one doesn't affirm at a given point with certainty, "Here is where his knowledge would have stopped," or "These are subtleties to which he would not have aspired." Like the thing you look at when you raise your eyes from this page, he is the center of a field of consciousness, rather yours than his: a focussing of the reader's attention, in a world made up not of cows and stones but of literary "effects" and memories prompted by words.

Prufrock is in all these respects the generic Eliot character; Gerontion, say, is one of his metamorphoses, another Voice with no ascertainable past and no particularized present: not even a shadowy apparatus of streets and stairs and rooms full of talking women, but a "dry month" which we take to be metaphoric and a "decayed house" whose tenants turn out to be the thoughts of his brain. The extreme case of the Eliotic pseudo-person is Tiresias in *The Waste Land*: "the most important personage in the poem," yet "a mere spectator," a congeries of effects, who is only presented personally in a footnote. "What Tiresias *sees,* in fact, is the substance of the poem"; and what Tiresias *is*—so far as he can be said to exist for the reader—is what he sees: the whole disparate poem, ravelling out boundlessly into literary echoes and mythological traditions as old as the human race. He is, once more, the name of a possible zone of consciousness where the materials which he is credited with being aware of can coexist; and what else, we seem to hear the author ask, what else, unless a delimited shadow like "the young man carbuncular," can a developed human consciousness be said to be?

As that question implies, a quality inherent in all incantatory poetry, poetry that eschews the statement and evokes the unspoken mood, is being deliberately pressed by Eliot into the service of a corresponding view of things. Other poets have used the method, and they are comparatively innocent of the deliberate view of things the method implies. They took it as it came to them from predecessors in a literary tradition: Tennyson from Coleridge, Coleridge from Bowles and Cowper; and if the method's grip on human personality is slight, if Coleridge can project only moods of himself and Tennyson (more rashly ambitious) only a few tones, variegated by unexceptionable reflections and labelled "Arthur" or "Lancelot," that is a disability with which they put up or of which they remain unaware. It is as true of Arthur as of Prufrock that he is a name plus a Voice, surrounded by every possible vagueness, blurring into the highly literary tapestry of which he is an unemphatic feature; but what is a defect of Tennyson's intention would seem to be the thoroughly deliberated focal point of Eliot's. Eliot has achieved, for one thing, the most *generalizing* style in English literature, capable, as Marshall McLuhan has pointed out, of summing up all possible relevant case histories in an imaged "state."

> For example, the initial situation in "Prufrock" or "Gerontion" is inclusive of every mode of metamorphosis or schizophrenia from the shaman to the medium and the poet, on one hand, and of every possible combination of ultimate disappointment and rage, on the other hand. The number of possible case histories of people having such experience is the number of possible "explanations" of the state of Prufrock and Gerontion. . . . Mr. Eliot . . . is not interested in plots or case histories which trace by cause and effect the stages leading to a particular situation. He is interested in the situation which exhausts

all such causes and effects and includes further levels of analogical perception.[1]

This capacity for generalization, latent in any "verbalist" poetic, or in any poetry descended from an efflorescent poetic drama, is brought to fruition by Mr. Eliot under the auspices of an idealist philosophy, much meditated during his student years, for which a person is continuous with τὸ πᾶν.

It is true that a poetry brewed out of the sounds and implications of words is not a medium in which to think; but as Mr. Eliot has frequently implied, he makes no pretence of thinking *in* his verse. "The poet who 'thinks,' " he has written, "is merely the poet who can express the emotional equivalent of thought"; and this, he implies, is something that Tennyson and Browning could not do but that Shakespeare and Donne could do. "Tennyson and Browning are poets, and they think; but they do not feel their thought as immediately as the odour of a rose. A thought to Donne was an experience; it modified his sensibility." A thought to Donne, however, was not necessarily something he originated; it was quite likely something he picked up from his ambience. (Eliot once found it "quite impossible to come to the conclusion that Donne believed anything.") "I can see no reason for believing that either Dante or Shakespeare did any thinking on his own"; it is not the poet's job to think; his job is "to express the greatest emotional intensity of his time, based on whatever his time happened to think."

It seems not to have been asked, what thoughts modified Eliot's sensibility. He tells us, here and there, pretty clearly: the thoughts of Francis Herbert Bradley.

The intellectual world of Francis Herbert Bradley (1846-1924) apparently occupied Mr. Eliot's close attention for a longer period than that of anyone else, not a poet, in whom he has professed an interest, and began to occupy him, moreover, during his late twenties, at the time when his own intellectual stuff was most malleable. "Prufrock" was composed in 1911. The Houghton Library, Harvard, contains an unpublished doctoral dissertation, "Experience and the Objects of Knowledge in the Philosophy of F. H. Bradley," dated 1916; "but external evidence points to the possibility that Eliot completed most, if not all of it, before that time. He was prevented by the war from returning to this country to submit his thesis at Harvard."[2] In 1915 he was in residence at Bradley's Oxford College,

---

[1] "Mr. Eliot's Historical Decorum," *Renascence* (Autumn, 1949), 13-14.
[2] R. H. Church in the *Harvard Advocate*, CXXX (December 1938), 24.

Merton. The next year he made his début in London not as a poet or literary critic but as an impecunious reviewer of philosophic books; immediately we find the signature of T. Stearns Eliot appended to an eleven-page essay in the Leibniz Bicentennial issue of *The Monist*: "Leibniz's Monads and Bradley's Finite Centers" (1916). In 1922, adding notes to *The Waste Land*, he included, more in an anthologist's than an exegete's spirit, a vivid paragraph from Bradley's *Appearance and Reality* that might have been composed by a disciplined Prufrock:

> My external sensations are no less private to myself than are my thoughts or my feelings. In either case my experience falls within my own circle, a circle closed on the outside; and, with all its elements alike, every sphere is opaque to the others which surround it. . . . In brief, regarded as an existence which appears in a soul, the whole world for each is peculiar and private to that soul.

In 1927 he wrote for the *Times Literary Supplement* a tribute to Bradley's greatness disguised as a review of the reprinted *Ethical Studies*; the reference to Bradley's "polemical irony and his obvious zest in using it, his habit of discomfiting an opponent with a sudden profession of ignorance, of inability to understand, or of incapacity for abstruse thought" suggests a model for some of the polemic gestures of the critic who scored a point against Shelley by claiming not to understand some stanzas from the "Skylark," and has repeatedly evaded quibbles concerning his more abstrusely based positions by claiming amateur status and incapacity for pursuing the abstruse.

By the time of that 1927 essay, Eliot's active interest in Bradley would seem to have been fading; he cites texts, but with an opportunist's interest in their usefulness for discomfiting Matthew Arnold. From his mid-twenties till his late thirties, however, he appears to have kept his knowledge of the philosopher's books in repair, and the 1916 thesis, a closely argued and widely documented account and defense of Bradley's position concerning "immediate experience," is evidence for his unqualified ingestion of certain perspectives of Bradley's which one does not discover him ever to have repudiated. It would be surprising if this transient closeness of identification between himself and the English philosopher had not left an ineradicable stain on his mind; and it is precisely as a stain, imparting color to all else that passes through, that Bradley is most discernible in Eliot's poetic sensibility.

He was uniquely equipped to exert that sort of tonal influence on a disciple; he is not the sort of philosopher who can be tied, rhetorically, to a cause. It is as a coloring, not as a body of doctrine, that he stays in the mind; partly because such doctrines as he professes are so little detachable from their dry and scrupulous expression by him, modified by the exact context in which he chooses to expound them. They exist, indeed, more in Bradley's prose than in the mind; paraphrase them, and they become the commonplace dancing bears from which he is at such ironic pains to distinguish them. In 1924 Eliot presented him to the reading publics of France and America as a potential influence "upon the sensibility of one or two or more literary generations," whose philosophy, borrowing "none of the persuasiveness of science and none of the persuasiveness of literature," has none of the "meretricious captivation" of, say, Bergson's "exciting promise of immortality," and can operate, therefore, only "upon the sensibility through the intellect." [3] It cannot even be believed in; to believe in the deliverances of a mind not your own, you must simplify them to a set of propositions that command assent without reference to the initial fragrance.

> But Bradley is wholly and solely a philosopher. . . . Philosophy may be futile or profitable, he seems to say, but if you are to pursue it at all, you must work with such and such data—which are neither literature nor science. All we can do is to accept these data and follow our argument to the end. If it ends, as it may well end, in zero, well, we have at least the satisfaction of having pursued something to the end, and of having ascertained that certain questions which occur to men to ask, are unanswerable or meaningless. Once you accept his theory of the nature of the judgment, and it is as plausible a theory as any, you are led by his arid and highly sensitive eloquence . . . to something which, according to your temperament, will be resignation or despair: the bewildered despair of wondering why you ever wanted anything and what it was that you wanted, since this philosophy seems to give you everything that you ask and yet to render it not worth wanting.

"Why should the aged eagle stretch its wings?" What Eliot's readers have frequently taken for a mood, the *Waste Land* tone, what I. A. Richards grandiloquently called "the disillusionment of a generation," is actually Bradley's deeply thought out *metaphysical* scepticism; and at the bottom of Eliot's frequent disavowals of capacity for abstruse thought lies ultimately not a polemical strategy but Bradley's unsettling conviction that abstruse thought, carried on for deter-

---

[3] In the *Nouvelle Revue Française* and *Vanity Fair*.

minate ends, is meretricious. Eliot's strategy (for strategy remains present) employs the ironic intimation that other and more ardently active people have not been brought to this realization, of how principles invoked in the press of practical disputation thereby turn into slogans, losing what little integrity they have, that of standpoints in an evasive whole of perception, and how one must therefore defend practical judgments by reference to one's impressions alone. One of the most important deposits of Bradleyism in Eliot's sensibility is visible in the disarmingly hesitant and fragmentary way in which he makes a point or expresses a conviction, doubting that he is quite the man to undertake the job in hand, or devoting an entire volume to "notes towards the definition" of a single word.

Naturally, a few odds and ends of what the plain reader of Bradley would call Bradleyan "doctrines" do turn up in Eliot's writings. This passage from *Appearance and Reality* has a very Eliotic ring:

> For whether there is progress or not, at all events there is change; and the changed minds of each generation will require a difference in what has to satisfy their intellect. Hence there seems as much need for new philosophy as there is for new poetry. In each case the fresh production is usually much inferior to something already in existence; and yet it answers a purpose if it appeals more personally to the reader. What is really worse may serve better to promote, in certain respects and in a certain generation, the exercise of our best functions.

Assaying this for traces of irony presents a characteristic difficulty; as we shall see, its most Bradleyan qualities lie less in its frontal claim than in its more elusive implications. There is no difficulty however in assigning the filiation of such Eliotisms as "Art never improves, but . . . the material of art is never quite the same"; or "Sensibility alters from generation to generation, whether we will or no; but expression is only altered by a man of genius"; or even the 1927 remark that "Christianity will continue to modify itself into something that can be believed in." It is very Bradleyan, also, to argue that "The whole of Shakespeare's work is *one* poem"; so that "what is 'the whole man' is not simply his greatest or maturest achievement, but the whole pattern formed by the sequence of plays: . . . we must know all of Shakespeare's work in order to know any of it"; or more generally, substituting the mind of Europe for that of Shakespeare, to assert that "No poet, no artist of any art, has his complete meaning alone. His significance, his appreciation, is the appreciation of his relation to the dead poets and artists"; or finally, to argue that as we change, so does the literature of the past change; we cannot read the Shakespeare Dr. Johnson read; "for order to persist after the subvention of novelty, the *whole* existing order must be, if ever so slightly, altered."

All these formulations deprive us of a simple rigid object to stare at, dangling in front of a cardboard frieze labelled "context" which we may use to make measurements from or disregard as we choose; and deprive us likewise of our assured impartial sense that we who stare are delicate but inviolable perceiving-machines, correcting our grandfathers and instructing our posterity, feeding data into our memories to be consulted when relevant. For memory is to perception as the pool to the ripples: the whole of Bradley's metaphysic emanates from his assertion that the dichotomy of observer and observed is simply a late and clumsy abstraction, of limited usefulness, crassly misrepresenting the process of knowing. The streets, the yellow fog, the drains, the coffee-spoons are Prufrock; the "evenings, mornings, afternoons" are Prufrock, as much so as the voice which says, "I have known them all already, know them all."

"In feeling the subject and object are one," states Eliot flatly in his 1916 thesis, paraphrasing Bradley's description of "immediate experience." "At any time," writes Bradley, "all that we suffer, do, and are forms one psychical totality. It is experienced all together as a coexisting mass, not perceived as parted and joined even by relations of coexistence. It contains all relations, and distinctions, and every ideal object that at that moment exists in the soul." Hence, to reproduce the quality of immediate experience, there is exacted of verse a blending suavity, not an assured rattle of subjects and predicates, nor images standing in explicable analogy to one another.

> Among the smoke and fog of a December afternoon
> You have the scene arrange itself—as it will seem to do—
> With, "I have saved this afternoon for you";
> And four wax candles in the darkened room,
> Four rings of light upon the ceiling overhead,
> An atmosphere of Juliet's tomb
> Prepared for all the things to be said, or left unsaid.
>   ("Portrait of a Lady")

What seems to be a salient verb, in line 2, is virtually cancelled later in the same line; for the rest, we have participles and relative clauses related to nothing, the gestures of verbs rather than their commitments, syntax not abolished but anaesthetized. Juliet's tomb, the

smoke and fog, the candles, the imminent conversation form, precisely "one psychical totality, experienced all together as a coexisting
mass." What syntax will specify the infusion, into your experience of
reading this book now, of the place in which you are half-aware of
yourself reading it?

So "Prufrock" begins somewhere in its own epigraph, and uncoils
through adverbial clauses of dubious specificity past imperatives of
uncertain cogency to a "do not ask." One function of the epigraphs
is to blur the beginnings of the poems; they open not with the éclat
of some syntactic gesture—"Of Man's first Disobedience . . ."—but
with an awakened dubiety about the scope of a quotation. *The Waste
Land's* initial firm show of business dissolves on inspection into a
throbbing of participles attached to a furtive copula: an indeterminate breeding, mixing, stirring, covering, feeding, that invisibly
smothers Chaucer's Aprille with the vibrations of the Sibyl's "I want
to die."

Such writing is far from what is called in classrooms "orderly,"
because our criteria of orderliness were developed, late in the seventeenth century, at the behest of a smartly diagrammatic view of the
world. A famous passage in Sprat's *History of the Royal Society*
(1667) celebrates "the primitive purity, and shortness, when men
deliver'd so many things, almost in an equal number of words."
This argues an atomistic view of *things*; they lie in great numbers
opaquely before the mind, awaiting arrangement and selection. The
mind, on the other hand, is wholly separate from them; it is the busy
finger that arranges and selects. Identities, resemblances, and differences are noted; there is nothing else to note. The archetypal
statement is the equation; this fish is indistinguishable from that
one; $a = b$. Hence "a close, naked, natural way of speaking: positive
expressions; clear senses; a native easiness: bringing all things as near
the Mathematical plainness, as they can."

Since that age it has been characteristically assumed that because
things can be clearly and distinctly separated from our continuous
experience of them, therefore clear statements about the identity
and difference of things underlie whatever colors, complications, and
aids to persuasion are affixed by any writer not merely confused.
Thus A. E. Housman stated that metaphor and simile were "things
inessential to poetry": either accessories employed "to be helpful,
to make his sense clearer or his conception more vivid," or else orna-
ments possessing "an independent power to please." It is but a step,
in this climate, to the familiar assumption that a self-evident separation between *me* and *what I experience* governs all thought, or that

what I experience is made up of self-evident component parts, this object and that one, actions with beginnings, middles and ends mimed by sentences with subjects, verbs, and predicates, the starts and stops of sentences and paragraphs corresponding to perceived divisions in the action being chronicled. The classical rhetoricians who saw that all writing is radically artificial were discarded as inciters to artifice; and it became unfashionable to note how a simple sentence like "Jack threw the ball to Will" imposes a symmetrical shape and three grammatical categories upon a bit of spontaneous play. To a reader situated in that universe of schematic diagrams, naturally Eliot's prose and verse seem obscure.

For Bradley, on the other hand, "At every moment my state, whatever else it is, is a whole of which I am immediately aware. It is an experienced non-relational unity of many in one." "Non-relational" is the key phrase, here as in much of Bradley's metaphysical writing. It is Bradley's shorthand for his untiring contention that this immediate awareness in which my sentience (to call it "mine") proceeds, is not reducible to parts in a certain relation, notably myself confronting what is not myself, or these things in this manner related to those. Nor can it be imaged by relating a subject to a predicate, both duly chamfered with modifiers.

> At any moment my actual experience, however relational its contents, is in the end non-relational. No analysis into relations and terms can ever exhaust its nature or fail in the end to belie its essence. What analysis leaves for ever outstanding is no mere residue, but is a vital condition of the analysis itself. Everything which is got out into the form of an object

—(for you are starting to simplify experience drastically the minute you say "tree")—

> implies still the felt background against which the object comes, and, further, the whole experience of both feeling and object is a non-relational immediate felt unity. . . .

It was statements like these, and their implications, that Eliot pondered for many years. Their importance, for a poet situated in the early twentieth century, is obvious; what they do, once their implications have been watchfully distilled, is ally the realities of everyday experience with the vocabulary of poetic effects out of which Tennyson and Swinburne, Verlaine and Poe, brewed a phantasmagoria of nuances. Romantic poetry had postulated a special world because the normal one had been usurped by an orderliness which was profoundly sensed to be wrong, but which in the absence of systematic grounds for that uneasy sense could only be ignored. In the prose world feeling was nascent or disorderly thought, something to be burnished away. From the poetic world, thought was exorcised as a merely calculated schematizing. And this "dissociation of sensibility, from which we have never recovered," cut poetry off from serious intellectual activity. "Jonson and Chapman," Eliot notes, "were notably erudite, and were notably men who incorporated their erudition into their sensibility: their mode of feeling was directly and freshly altered by their reading and thought." They are superseded by, say, Tennyson and Browning, who "are poets, and they think; but they do not feel their thought as immediately as the odor of a rose"; or by, say, Shelley, who incorporated his erudition into his writing, but not into his sensibility. "Sensibility" is Eliot's term for a scrupulous responsiveness to the Bradleyan "immediate experience": a responsiveness that precedes, underlies, and contains any degree of analysis. In the Shelleyan apostrophe to the West Wind—

> Thou on whose stream, mid the steep sky's commotion
> Loose clouds like earth's decaying leaves are shed
> Shook from the tangled boughs of heaven and ocean,

we can explain these mysterious tangled boughs as an attempted incorporation into the verse of known facts about the origin of clouds, forcibly subdued to a logic postulated by the simile of the leaves That clouds are drawn up from the ocean by solar heat and d posited at altitudes where condensation renders them visible is a fa gleaned from books; but knowledge of these facts has not modifie Shelley's apprehension of clouds, it merely complicates the imag under which he regards them, the same under which he would hav regarded them had no books of meteorology existed.[4] "The tangle boughs of heaven and ocean" is a construction of words, attemptin under the cover of rhythmic propulsiveness to adequate itself t known but intractable fact. Verse spends a half century ridding itsel of this radical defect; Swinburne abandons himself to words entirely Swinburne abandons, that is, "immediate experience" for a universe

---

[4] Cf. "The majority of verse writers are contented with *approximation* to meaning, an approximation which in many contemporary verse writers takes the deceptive form of a thumping scientific precision."—T. S. Eliot, 1935.

of language where the inclusiveness and continuity, but not the felt
truth, of immediate experience can be mimed.

> When you take to pieces any verse of Swinburne, you find always that
> the object was not there—only the word. Compare
>
>> Snowdrops that plead for pardon
>> And pine for fright
>
> with the daffodils that come before the swallow dares. The snowdrop
> of Swinburne disappears, the daffodil of Shakespeare remains.

This leads Eliot to a confident affirmation of considerable scope:

> Language in a healthy state presents the object, is so close to the object
> that the two are identified. They are identified in the verse of Swin-
> burne solely because the object has ceased to exist, because the mean-
> ing is merely the hallucination of meaning, because language, uprooted,
> has adapted itself to an independent life of atmospheric nourishment.
> In Swinburne, for example, we see the word "weary" flourishing in
> this way independent of the particular and actual weariness of flesh
> or spirit. The bad poet dwells partly in a world of objects and partly
> in a world of words, and he never can get them to fit. Only a man of
> genius could dwell so exclusively and consistently among words as
> Swinburne.

Swinburne, that is, had purchased at great cost an air of poetic inclusiveness which there could, in 1908, be no question of abandoning.
"The question was, where do we go from Swinburne?" Unfortunately,
Swinburne marked not only the fullest achievement of romantic inclusiveness, but the final phase of a decadence. "The answer appeared
to be, nowhere."

Bradley, of course, didn't solve Eliot's initial poetic problem; there
is no evidence that Eliot paid him any attention until after he had
written "Prufrock" and "Portrait of a Lady." (He did not buy his
own copy of *Appearance and Reality* until mid-1913.) The study of
Bradley, however, may be said to have done three things for a poet
who might otherwise not have passed beyond the phase of imitating
Laforgue. It solved his *critical* problem, providing him with a point
of view toward history and so with the scenario for his most comprehensive essay, "Tradition and the Individual Talent"; it freed him
from the Laforguian posture of the ironist with his back to a wall.

by emphasizing the artificiality of *all* personality including the one we intimately suppose to be our true one, not only the faces we prepare but the "we" that prepares; and it released him from any notion that the art his temperament bade him practice was an eccentric art, evading for personal and temporary reasons a more orderly, more "normal" unfolding from statement to statement. A view of the past, a view of himself and other persons, a view of the nature of what we call statement and communication; these delivered Eliot from what might well have been, after a brilliant beginning, a cul-de-sac and silence. Want of a liberating view of history had misled more than a century of poetic activity into prizing either explosive "originality" or equally sterile "traditionalism." Want of some radical insight into "personality" had led a Wordsworth to eliminate people, except as vivid apparitions or passing shadows, a Byron to dissipate energy in an endless dialectic of self-expression, mask after mask, a Dickens or a Browning to equate the personal with the arresting, and reduce persons to accumulations of flashy effects. Want of a view of poetry that could bypass the dichotomies posed by talk about "communication" had condemned the French symbolists and their English heirs of the Nineties to the status of literary experimenters, never at their most vigorous free from the imputation of creating or delimiting a "special" world with which alone poetry can concern itself. Baudelaire, it is true, elevated "imagery of the sordid life of a great metropolis" to the *first intensity*—

> On voit un chiffonnier qui vient, hochant la tête
> Buttant, et se cognant aux murs comme un poète—

but the old ragpicker remains subordinated to an "on voit," a piquant item in the landscape of "poetic" perception. No one, however, who had allowed the Bradleyan phenomenology to invade his mind would (except in makeshift prose) compel a presentation to dangle from "one sees," unless to throw ironic light on the perceiver ("I should have lost a gesture and a pose."). Contrast Eliot's metropolitan landscape:

> Under the brown fog of a winter dawn,
> A crowd flowed over London Bridge, so many,
> I had not thought death had undone so many.
> Sighs, short and infrequent, were exhaled. . . .
> ("The Burial of the Dead")

The unobtrusive "I" neither dominates nor creates this scene, being itself subordinated to a barely grammatical subordination, and in any case embedded in a quotation from Dante; the very exhalation is impersonal; and a definite article deprives "the brown fog" of unique reported status, consigning it to that cooperatively constructed world (made up of London, Dante, crowds, sighs, you, and I) in which brown fogs pass without undue remark.

If Eliot's sense of poetry, of personality, and of history are all congruent with Bradley's philosophy, that is largely because the man who developed those views also found Bradley congenial. For that matter, Laforgue no doubt drew his attention to Schopenhauer, who was interested in Buddhism and wished men to recognize their true condition: each one alone in an illusory world. Laforgue, too, presumably sponsored Eliot's famous two-year sojourn in Oriental mazes. But in helping him develop his sense of the past, Bradley's was the active role. "Tradition and the Individual Talent" (1919) concludes a train of thought which can be traced through earlier *Egoist* articles to its origins in the Bradley thesis three years earlier. It follows from Bradley's denial of any separation "of feeling from the felt, or of the desired from desire, or of what is thought from thinking," that our attempt to separate the past from our knowledge of it, what really happened from the way we imagine things to have been, is ultimately meaningless. Early in his Bradley thesis Eliot notes that for a geologist to conceive of the development of the world, he must present it as it would have looked had he, with his body and his nervous system, been there to see it. It follows that we cannot conceive of a past indifferent to us; obversely, that all that we know of the past is part of our experience now. And it follows that "the conscious present is an awareness of the past in a way and to an extent which the past's awareness of itself cannot show."

Eliot's poems differ from reader to reader to an unusual degree, posed between meaning nothing and meaning everything, associating themselves with what the reader thinks of, and inclines to wonder whether Eliot was thinking of. So he despatches, perhaps, a genetic query to London—does the end of "Prufrock" contain an allusion to Donne's "Teach me to hear mermaids sing?" and is no doubt informed that if Donne did indeed enter into the composition of those lines, his presence must have been quite unconscious. He is present, of course, if you find it helpful to think of him; the nature of this poetry is to appropriate anything that comes near. In chapter II of *The Great Gatsby* we read of "a valley of ashes," a "gray land" above which brood "the eyes of Doctor T. J. Eckleburg," blue and gigantic, their retinas one yard high. There is no point in asking Mr. Eliot whether this is a source for *The Hollow Men,* because *The Hollow Men* was finished just before *The Great Gatsby* existed for Eliot to read. Nevertheless *The Hollow Men* appropriates the valley of ashes and the eyes of Doctor Eckleburg once the two works have entered the same consciousness, and become members of our present, which is an awareness of things that were never aware of each other.

A book is a set of words; it is we who give them life; and it is our life that we give them. So every author we read becomes as we read him a more or less alien contemporary, but a contemporary whose own sense of the past is imperfect compared to ours. The author of *Hamlet* is by definition a poet who has never heard of Pope or Byron, who has read nothing published subsequent to 1601. This consideration leads Eliot to one of his most pregnant epigrams:

> Some one said: "The dead writers are remote from us because we *know* so much more than they did." Precisely, and they are that which we know.

Every age, furthermore, is an age of transition; we are not to be misled by the look of Augustan stability, or by the convenient parentheses within which literary historians enclose several decades of serial activity. Nor is even, say, "Shakespeare"—let alone "The Elizabethan drama"—a fixed point, for the Shakespeare who wrote *Romeo and Juliet* was not the Shakespeare we think of, but a Shakespeare who had not written *Hamlet.* If Shakespeare at any moment thought that he had at length achieved a plateau and an identity, Shakespeare was deceived;

> The knowledge imposes a pattern and falsifies,
> For the pattern is new in every moment
> And every moment is a new and shocking
> Valuation of all we have been.
> ("East Coker," II)

This brings us to the "person," of whom Bradley notes that "the usual self of one period is not the usual self of another."

> It is impossible to unite in one mass these conflicting psychical contents. Either then we accept the man's mere history as his self, and if so why call it one? Or we confine ourselves to periods, and there is no longer any single self.

And if the present self is evasive, the past one is illusory:

> My past self is arrived at only by a process of inference. . . . We are
> so accustomed each to consider his past self as his own, that it is worth
> while to reflect how very largely it may be foreign. My own past is,
> in the first place, incompatible with my own present, quite as much as
> my present can be with another man's. . . . I may regard it even with
> a feeling of hostility and hatred. It may be mine merely in the sense
> of a persisting incumbrance, a compulsory appendage, joined in conti-
> nuity and fastened by an inference. . . .

"Who are you now?" the Unidentified Guest asks Edward Chamber-
layne in *The Cocktail Party*.

> You don't know any more than I do,
> But rather less. You are nothing but a set
> Of obsolete responses. The one thing to do
> Is to do nothing. Wait.

The next day Edward learns that his wife is to come back "from the
dead."

> EDWARD: That figure of speech is somewhat . . . dramatic,
> As it was only yesterday that my wife left me.

> UNIDENTIFIED GUEST: Ah, but we die to each other daily.
> What we know of other people
> Is only our memory of the moments
> During which we knew them. And they have changed since then.
> To pretend that they and we are the same
> Is a useful and convenient social convention
> Which must sometimes be broken. We must also remember
> That at every meeting we are meeting a stranger.

The roots of this exchange are in a comment Eliot wrote on Bradley
more than thirty years before. Someone else, he notes, may call my
view of the world "subjective," a merely personal appendage of "me";
I, however, cannot call it subjective, because to call it subjective would
be to separate me from it; and my experience is inseparable from the
conviction that the three things my interlocutor would separate—I,
the objective world, and my feelings about it—are an indissoluble
whole. It is only in social behavior, Eliot concludes, in the conflict

and readjustment of what Bradley calls "finite centers," that feelings
and things are torn apart: "we die to each other daily."

The meaning of the term "finite center" is less important than the
process by which Bradley arrives at it. Let us try the experiment of
asking him who Prufrock is (his own gambit was to pose the question,
What is the real Julius Caesar?). If you ask him what is Mr. Prufrock's
essential self, he will first discard "essential" as implying that of which
Prufrock himself is self-consciously and therefore distortedly aware;
and reply at some length that the real Prufrockian focus of consciousness (he will not say the real Prufrock, any more than he will
say the real you) is a finite center. ("The finite Center," writes Eliot,
"so far as I can pretend to understand it, *is* immediate experience.")
Further than that Bradley is evasive. If you look at a finite center the
gaze of your mind's eye corrupts it, or you start thinking things into
it. So Bradley shrinks from discussing it directly, though he will
invoke it with his own peculiar tentative confidence while discussing
something else. His ultimate answer to the question about Julius
Caesar was that, Caesar's experience of himself being as inaccessible,
and as irrelevant, as a geranium's experience of itself, the "real Julius
Caesar" cannot be less than—for us—every impression, every sentiment, that attracts itself to that name, and every effect that can be
attributed to it. In the same way J. Alfred Prufrock exists only while
someone is reading or remembering the poem, and exists only *as* each
particular reader experiences him.

Julius Caesar, being dead, is of course like Prufrock a tradition and
a literary character. Who or what is my real dinner companion? is
a more difficult question; since the cheese and the jugged hare presumably figure in his immediate experience as they do in mine. I
figure in it also. "A self," Eliot noted, describing Bradley's episte-
mology in *The Monist,*

> is an ideal and largely practical construction, one's own self as much
> as others. My self remains "intimately one thing with that finite center
> within which my universe appears. Other selves on the contrary are
> for me ideal objects." The self is a construction in space and time. It
> is an object among others, a self among others, and could not exist
> save in a common world.

As for an object,

> For Bradley, I take it, an object is a common intention of several souls,
> cut out (as in a sense are the souls themselves) from immediate experi-

ence. The genesis of the common world can only be described by admitted fictions . . . on the one hand our experiences are similar because
they are of the same objects, and on the other hand the objects are only
"intellectual constructions" out of various and quite independent experiences. So, on the one hand, my experience is in principle essentially public. My emotions may be better understood by others than by myself; as
my oculist knows my eyes. And on the other hand everything, the whole
world, is private to myself. Internal and external are thus not ad-
jectives applied to different contents within the same world; they are
different points of view.

A reader in quest of formulae for mediating between the mental
landscapes of Prufrock, Gerontion, or Tiresias and the thoughts and
feelings of their author would be wise to approach his problem
through that paragraph, where according to his temperament he will
either find what he wants or be discouraged from seeking it. And
beneath the malaise of Prufrock, the rage of Gerontion whose voice
is that of twenty poets, or the hysteria of the man in *The Family
Reunion* who cannot even call his crime his own, one may also feel
throbbing Eliot's extra-curricular response to this world in which
Bradley compelled him to believe, where the soul has no structure,
perhaps no identity, and presumably no means of extricating itself
from its own history. It is not a passionless response. Bradley must
sometimes have smiled through Eliot's dreams like the bearer of news
from the Pit, and Eliot must more than once have felt as did Kurtz in
Conrad's *Heart of Darkness* when he gazed long into his own dissolving interior and spoke the words which were later affixed as epigraph
to the original draft of *The Waste Land*: "The horror! The horror!"
    Bradley has an attractive mind, though he has perhaps nothing to
tell us. He is an experience, like the taste of nectarines or the style
of Henry James; to rethink him is to recall with labor a landscape
once seen in a dream; he is like a vivid dream in that, as Eliot said,
he modifies the sensibility. Since the physical world, he writes, is
a state of my brain, and my brain is part of the physical world,

> the physical world is an appearance; it is phenomenal throughout. It is
> the relation of two unknowns, which, because they are unknown, we can-
> not have any right to regard as really two, as related at all. It is an
> imperfect way of apprehension, which gives us qualities and relations,
> each the condition of and yet presupposing the other.

These are not elements of a vision; they are statements about the im-
possibility of framing a vision in which the imagination may repose.

They underwrite, however, poetry Eliot had already written when he began to pay them attention, and dissolve any temptation not to continue writing in a similar mode. Whoever ponders such statements will see how a poet who deeply pondered them could not regard "things" as subject matter, or "images" in a poem as references to substantiality. Images, consequently, are absorbed into literary tradition, as the bones in Part II of *Ash-Wednesday* occupy simultaneously Ezekiel's vision, a tale of the Grimms, and the area of association implied by the *Ash-Wednesday* context of three leopards, a juniper-tree, and a Lady. Subject matter, similarly, is absorbed into states of feeling, as in the third part of *Ash-Wednesday* it is equally meaningless to say that the ascent of the stairs is or is not an actual imagined happening, dissolving as it does, under a kind of inspection irrelevant to the experiencing of the poetry, into Dante's purgatorial stairs, the Eliotic stairs of "Prufrock" and "La Figlia che Piange," and some still more nebulous suggestion of a tradition of psychic ascent. The poem is a continuum in which the perceiving mind, intent on the quality of its own feelings, constantly adjusts the scope and emphasis of its perception.

Such a description fits *Appearance and Reality* as well; and *Four Quartets*, with their drily intense opening abstractions

> . . . If all time is eternally present,
> All time is unredeemable . . .

modulated without desertion of the abstract plane, into the injunction to

> . . . be still and still moving
> Into another intensity
> For a further union, a deeper communion. . . .
> ("East Coker," V)

The method of the *Quartets* bears a close resemblance to that of the book which begins with the apparently suicidal remark that "Metaphysics is the finding of bad reasons for what we believe upon instinct, but to find these reasons is no less an instinct," but which later, without alteration of its essential tone or modus, can speak of "that absolute self-fruition that comes only when the self bursts its limits, and blends with another finite self." There are even resemblances of detail, as when Bradley speaks of an Absolute which

. . . is timeless, but it possesses time as an isolated aspect, an aspect which, in ceasing to be isolated, loses its special character. It is there, but blended into a whole which we cannot realize;

and Eliot of an unmoving Love,

> Timeless, and undesiring
> Except in the aspect of time
> Caught in the form of limitation
> Between un-being and being.
>   ("Burnt Norton," V)

Bradley, again, states that Science

. . . quite ignores the existence of time. For it habitually treats past and future as one thing with the present . . . The character of an existence is determined by what it has been and by what it is (potentially) about to be. But if these attributes, on the other hand, are not present, how can they be real? . . .

Which is perhaps the germ of the *Burnt Norton* opening:

> Time present and time past
> Are both perhaps present in time future
> And time future contained in time past.
> If all time is eternally present
> All time is unredeemable.
> What might have been is an abstraction
> Remaining a perpetual possibility
> Only in a world of speculation.
> What might have been and what has been
> Point to one end, which is always present.

When we have done contrasting the spareness dominated by Eliot's taut verse rhythms with the loosening effect of Bradley's constant scrupulousness of qualification, we may note one quality this prose and this verse have in common: an eschewal of eloquence. It is the absence of ornament, of blur and ready satisfaction, of otiose diction—

> Life, like a dome of many-coloured glass
> Stains the white radiance of Eternity
> Until Death tramples it to fragments . . .

that confers on Eliot's maturest verse that tension which, until Eliot had achieved it, no one would have thought to include among the possible modes of poetry; and it is a comparable quality of Bradley's argument, neither dissolving into whimsical sub-predications like a philosophical Henry James, nor like Plato choosing the short cut of myth and peroration, that permits him to include feeling without engendering it, and rise, in his predications of an Absolute where all contradictions are reconciled, into an exciting tautness of implication. *Appearance and Reality* is a great triumph of style, style that never deserts its proper business of completing and clarifying the deliverances of the intellect. Though he has no message to deliver, he fills the mind; yet each time we want to see with what he fills it, we must reread the book. No aftertaste lingers with which we may solace ourselves, only the satisfaction of having pursued the sinuosities of a memorably adequate performance. With perhaps the sole exception of the paragraph quoted in the notes to *The Waste Land,* no quotations survive the whole. This chaconne for unaccompanied violin has no extra-philosophical attractions; Eliot has noted how by contrast "Bergson's exciting promise of immortality" has "a somewhat meretricious captivation," and how a Rousseau "has proved an eternal source of mischief and inspiration," whereas Bradley, with "the melancholy grace, the languid mastery, of the late product" has "expounded one type of philosophy with such consummate ability that it will probably not survive him." This man who lacked "the permanence of the pre-Socratics, of all imperfect things," exerted his permanent fascination for Eliot's temperament precisely through his ability to touch every aspect of thought and feeling that concerned his endeavor while remaining within the proper limits of prose; the purple patch is a confession of insufficiency. If he remains on the thin ice of phenomenology, he is phenomenology's most accomplished skater, producing a book conformed, in everything but its mode of organization, to the most austere canons of art: like Brancusi's *Bird in Flight* which is made out of polished bronze and contains no hint of a compromise with feathers.

It was not unnatural, in a world which contained so satisfying a book, to resolve that it was not the poet's business to think; not only because Bradley had nullified all trenchant thought as abrupt and partial, but because he had disqualified "responsible" thought for poetry by demonstrating that like poetry it is a fulltime occupation, leading not to apothegms but to a decantation of verbal substances that will satisfactorily fill up the voids in mental existence, though with a different filler than the poet's. The philosopher does not start,

Bradley insists, with certain axioms from which he reasons downward
toward the familiar; he starts, like the poet in Eliot's account, with
a want to be satisfied, for him a theoretical want, a desire "to find
a way of thinking about facts in general which is free from contradiction."

> It is assumed that, if my thought is satisfied with itself, I have, with
> this, truth and reality. But as to what will satisfy I have, of course, no
> knowledge in advance. My object is to get before me what will content
> a certain felt need, but the way and the means are to be discovered only
> by trial and rejection.

Bradley's way is the way of satisfying *those* needs; the needs a poet
sets out to satisfy are different needs, needs that will be satisfied by
the existence of the unique particular poem toward which he is ob-
scurely impelled. For either one to borrow from the other's methods
is to avail himself of an illegitimate short cut: illegitimate because
he will take satisfaction in the result only by a perpetuated self-deceit.
The radical criticism of *Adonais* is that it fails to exercise that kind
of intelligence "of which an important function is the discernment
of exactly what, and how much, we feel in any given situation."

We can learn from Bradley's drily impassioned style that he took
the model of clarity to be not a mathematical process but an impersonal human being talking. One may profitably contrast *Appearance
and Reality* with the Whitehead and Russell *Principia Mathematica,*
a book to be worked through rather than read. (Eliot worked far
enough through it to find the pronouncement with which he once
startled a hasty correspondent in *The Athenaeum*.[5] Nor on the other
hand does his method at all resemble that of Santayana, whose extra-
philosophic impulses not only begat a novel, but suffused his essays
with personality. Bradley disciplined philosophy until it gave his
powers full satisfaction. He arrives at no conclusions, at no incitements
to action. As late as 1924 Eliot supposed that his influence would grow
and spread, with that of Henry James and Sir James Frazer, in a future
whose characteristic sensibility might be "infinitely more disillusioned"

---

[5] This man deserves notice as a pioneer in the dangerous game of supposing
that Eliot's informality of critical organization bespeaks a genteel indifference to
logic. He objected that an Eliotic generalization was belied by Eliot's own practice, and was picked off his limb by a nicely aimed citation of Whitehead and
Russell on the paradox of the Cretan liar. The moral is clearly that the next man
who wishes to make that particular protest will have to outflank the entire *Principia Mathematica* first, but this moral has not been heeded.

than that of Shaw, or Thomas Hardy, or Anatole France, perhaps "harder and more orderly: but throbbing at a higher rate of vibration with the agony of spiritual life." Alas, he was insufficiently disillusioned to guess that the "one or two or more literary generations" on whose behalf he prophesied would find Freud and Marx more to their taste.

Irregular Metaphysics

by R. P. Blackmur

For the purpose of this lecture it is almost enough to begin by saying that where the great novelists of our times have dealt with the troubles caused by the new knowledges (and the erosion of some of the old ones) in a kind of broad and irregular psychology, so the poets have been led to deal with them (or to repel them, or rival them) in a kind of irregular and spasmodic, but vitalized metaphysics. Both have done so in terms of the charge of maintaining the health and the possibilities of language under the conditions of our knowledge. One of those conditions is the relative disappearance of generally accepted (if only for argument) systematic metaphysics that bears on daily life, the life of our own adventure, in which we have by no means lost our interest. Thus the poet and the literary man generally find themselves in the very irregular task of doing what they can by literary means to adjust the new and old relations of our knowledges to life. This is, I think, why Eliot began his early critical work by remarking on the dissociation of ideas which marks our times almost with stigmata. Thus it is that Paul Valéry could ask: "Whenever you think do you not feel you are disarranging something?" And thus, in writing about Valéry, Elizabeth Sewell could observe that "Words are the only defense of the mind against being possessed by thought or dream." [. . .]

Shelley wrote, in one of those sentences struck off late at night, which yet last in the day by their own light, "All the authors of revolutions of opinion are not only necessarily poets as they are inventors, nor even as their words unveil the permanent analogy of things by images which participate in the life of truth; but as their periods are harmonious and rhythmical, and contain in themselves the ele-

"Irregular Metaphysics." From *Anni Mirabiles 1921-1925* by R. P. Blackmur (Washington, D.C.: The Library of Congress, 1956), pp. 26-32. Excerpted and abridged, with the author's consent, from a lecture only partially concerned with Eliot.

ments of verse; being the echo of the eternal music." Here is the whole program of modern poetry and the gist of half its achievement. One would repeat, as text for everything wanted here to be said: The poets' words "unveil the permanent analogy of things by images which participate in the life of truth." The rest would be important if we were talking about prosody, but we are talking only about irregular metaphysics. The permanent analogy of things in images which participate in the life of truth, will do us very well. [. . .]

Analogy is exactly the putting of things side by side. In poetry they are bound together by rhythm, sped by meter, united by vision, experienced by music, said in voice. In analogy we get the relation of attributes, not substances; we get the *form* of reality as if form were itself a kind of action. If we think of the Greeks, we would say that the Oedipus of Sophocles is the more nearly logical, and that the Heracles of Euripides is the more nearly analogical; and it is for this reason that we have only lately begun to grasp the form of Euripides. Analogy is also the deep form of reminding that there is always something *else* going on: the identity which is usually a mystery apprehended in analogy; what is lost in "mere" logic, but is carried along in the story.

Analogy is like the old notion of underplot, or second plot in Elizabethan drama. Sometimes these underplots were only two logics, sometimes one and sometimes another; but sometimes they were a multiplying process. One times one equals one, but a one which is also a third thing, which is fused in the mind, in the looking of one working on the other. Emotions can be like plot and underplot. If we put two emotions of the established sorts in association (like love and hate) we get an artistic emotion differing from either but with attributes common to both. In association, emotions are fruitful, and we get a sense of living action where there had been sets of abstraction: as in the Mass. Feelings are even more fruitful than emotions. When Robert Frost comes to the end of his poem "Stopping by Woods on a Snowy Evening"—

> The woods are lovely, dark and deep,
> But I have promises to keep,
> And miles to go before I sleep,
> And miles to go before I sleep.

When he has got to the end, he has made a revelation in feelings; what you cannot otherwise touch; only *so;* and the analogies multiply and deepen into surds of feeling.

Analogy is indeed the very name for our characteristic poetic logics. No doubt the attraction of analogy for us is in the fragmentation of faith and the diversity of logics and the divisiveness of our minds generally. These fragments, says Eliot, I have shored against my ruins. For two gross of broken statues, says Pound, for a few thousand battered books. What shall I do for pretty girls, says Yeats, now my old bawd is dead? And so on. One should remember that the attraction of analogy for the medieval mind (to which we so much and so diversely resort) was just the opposite. To the medieval mind the unity of things was insistently present, and had to be interpreted; to us unity is what we only seek by all the machineries of desperation and longing, sometimes longing without hope; and the means of our search is by analogy or collateral form.

The reason why "Prufrock" is *now* a popular poem (though it was a very difficult poem for most people for its first twenty years of life) is that the analogies with which it is composed have had time to sink in. This, too, is how poems change and grow and even sometimes disappear: in relation to our apprehension of what is in analogy, where the elements go on working. The obscurity is like that of the womb. Collateral or analogical form is as near as we are likely to come to the organic. Dialectic (in the modern sense) only excites the passion for analogy in the creative sense. We can say for poetry that only in analogy are the opposites identical; and it was a similar perception that led St. Augustine to say that in every poem there is some of the substance of God.

My point had perhaps better be pushed a little further and by an analogy taken from mathematics and physics thought of besides poetry and morals. In mathematics it is not necessary to know what one is talking about; in physics it is, since the test is in knowledge. Yet the mathematics (creating out of the rigor of formal relations) generates the physics, and often does so without being itself understood. Mathematics is theoretic form for the *feeling* of the relation of things.

Poetry is like mathematics, morals like physics; and it is sometimes "true" that poetry creates the morals in the sense that poetry creates the felt relations of things which unite the substance and the problems of morals. Poetry is the rebelliousness and the pang of what is alive; poetry gives, as Dante says, the war of the journey and of the pity: creates the story of them. Poetry takes action in morals as mathematics does in physics.

There is a sense in which knowledge, when we have given it form, is creation—all knowledge, including revelation. Mathematics created the physics of the modern world, created the terms and released the powers of all our troubles. It is only an exaggeration, then, to say that poetry created the morals of the modern world, and sets in action the modes of human love and all the other heroic or rebellious modes of human behavior.

In this analogy, mathematics confronted the old physics; poetry confronted the old morals. Out of each confrontation comes the response either of a rival creation or an increment to creation, and in each case the relations between the two are likely to be irregular. The old physics and the old morals still tyrannize those parts of us and of the universe which do not conform—and because of truth or vitality—to the new powers and pangs. A firm rational view is possible in either field, but the poetic impulse is rather towards creation just as our behavior springs from the "enormous lap of the actual," and just because we believe in most, and find most precious, what of the actual we ourselves create. I do not say that this is what modern poetry "really" does, but that this is sometimes its operative ambition and its saving illusion. It is a course in which we have not—and cannot—reach the extreme. Even as our minds create new knowledge, we are still God's spies. Every new form of knowledge, or of the human, is monstrous until it is made a part of the acknowledgment of reason. Reason likes the finished job; poetry *likes* the new job—the living process rather than the vital purpose.

It is not surprising that an enterprise of this order—combining as it does, in intention, all the reach of the senses and all the norms of the mind—should have produced the first learned poetry in England since Milton, with the singular difference that it is also and deliberately irrational in its processes—is indeed an effort to erode the rational for metaphysical purposes. This is because the metaphysics was itself expressionistic, arising out of personal warrant and with a distrust of existing forms, whether intellectual or aesthetic. Many of these metaphysical poets rejected much of their traditional craft and syntax and quivered with horror at all statements not drawn from dreams. Expressionistic metaphysics has often paraded in a masquerade of painful unlearning, and a special kind of illiteracy goes with the learnedness where it remains. It knows its own fragmentariness and must reject every system as a deceit, and must therefore erect systems known to be inadequate.

Of all that has been said so far of the contours of this ambitious form of the poetic mind, there is no livelier illustration than *The Waste Land*. I say nothing here of what I hope to exemplify at the end of these remarks: the dramatic sensuality of the thought in the poem. Here I am concerned with the structures of the poem as they can be easily separated, the structures with which Eliot protects his poem from the ravages of its subject. Like the *Ulysses* of James Joyce, only less so, *The Waste Land* affords and requires a maximum of structures, and requires it in the effort to do the job of reason in the absence of effective predictive form. Reason had above all to do the labor of making the form all over again, for it had the labor of associating the elements of a sensibility believed to be dissociated empirically. This, if you like, was reason in madness, operating and drawing from madness; it was reason controlling madness. Let us list a few of the elements of this structure, and let us begin with the epigraph about the Cumean Sibyl hanging forever in a cage because she had forgotten the need for regeneration in the mere lust to endure. When, when, *when,* WHEN will the sands run out? She is perhaps the heroine of the poem, and the boys, acolytes, choirboys, scamps can only help her by jeering at her, and she can answer them only in Greek: I wish to die. She is the heroine of all that is stupid and clutching in life, if you like of all that survives, and is a little outside the poem, suspended over it in a cage. Against her, within the poem, is Tiresias, the hero of all that is numinous and comes from the godhead, but in the poem bored as well as tragic; he is the perspective and fate, of all that was created and made. He is the blind foreseer, the man who was woman. He is the hero of all our meanings that are beyond safety, the very peril of vision. Between the Sibyl and Tiresias—between the two forms of prophecy and their enactments—come the up and down and all-around-the-town of the poem: everything that goes with the actions of this poem and its frames, all that has to do with the Tarot pack of cards, with Christ, the Holy Grail, and Buddha. Through all these, in the walls and ceilings and floors as stringers and uprights, run various other structural elements. There is the liberating force of "literary" religion and the liberating force of "literary" anthropology (what comes from Jessie Weston and Frazer), and the preserving force of "allegorical" understanding. I do not know which of these has been more misinterpreted, and I would for myself only suggest that we accept them as part of Eliot's means of giving the weight of various intellectual orders of his poem, much as we have done with the merely "literary" references in the details of the text—all the better when we have not recognized them.

Here are two sentences that bear, taken from Basic Willey's *The Seventeenth Century Background* (Anchor edition, p. 72):

It is hard to say which is the more misleading—the "fundamentalist" reading which mistakes mythology for history, or the Alexandrian, which sees allegory where none was intended. In both there is a lack of capacity to distinguish between what is "statement" and what is emotive speech, a deficiency which not only affected scriptural interpretation, but rendered impossible any satisfactory theory of poetry for very many centuries.

So with the interpretation of Eliot and Yeats. In these various orders which Eliot has used there is no recognizable principle of composition. Even the Sibyl and Tiresias are not enough. The reason would not have been able to take up her task of poetic thought had not the psyche (one's private share of the Numen) brought in the compulsive force of images, of the obsessions of dreams, and of the force of dramatic mimesis to set up and reveal the hidden analogies of things. Thus it was that those of us who knew the least in the intellectual sense, in the first instance understood the poem best.

To reveal the hidden analogies of things; Shelley's insight was Eliot's task as poet; he has in his images to remind reason of its material, to remind order of its disorder, in order to create a sane art almost insane in its predicament. He had to make a confrontation of the rational with the irrational: a deliberate reversal of roles.

Here is part IV of *The Waste Land,* "Death by Water":

> Phlebas the Phoenician, a fortnight dead,
> Forgot the cry of gulls, and the deep sea swell
> And the profit and loss.
> > A current under sea
> Picked his bones in whispers. As he rose and fell
> He passed the stages of his age and youth
> Entering the whirlpool.
> > Gentile or Jew
> O you who turn the wheel and look to windward,
> Consider Phlebas, who was once handsome and tall as you.

This, as you will remember, is all there is to this section of the poem; it is a lyric interlude put in to remind you what the rest of the poem is about. Here the Reason and the Psyche together make a *poetic* rival creation, and make it in analogous symbolism, not logical allegory. The analogy moves wherever you wish it and wherever it wishes to move you. Here again are Valéry's question and Miss Sewell's comment. "Whenever you think do you not feel you are disarranging something?"—"Words are the only defense of the mind against being possessed by thought or dream." It is the words working on each other that make the life and the identity in the analogy. [. . .]

Lewis Carroll and T. S. Eliot
as Nonsense Poets

by Elizabeth Sewell

He thought he saw a Banker's Clerk
Descending from a bus:
He looked again, and found it was
A Hippopotamus.
                    (Sylvie and Bruno)
I saw the 'potamus take wing.
        ("The Hippopotamus")

It was Chesterton, that man of marvellous perception and often perverse practice, who announced in 1904 that Nonsense was the literature of the future. It was a brilliant guess. Even now, however, when it is clear that he was right, when the trials in Wonderland and the Snark have become prototypes of real trials from Reichstag to McCarthy, and much of our literature—poetry and criticism—and most of our philosophy is shaped on Nonsense principles, people are slow to recognize its importance, or that of Lewis Carroll. Carroll is no *lusus naturae* but a central figure, as important for England, and in the same way, as Mallarmé is for France. Nonsense is how the English choose to take their Pure Poetry, their *langage mathématique* or *romances sans paroles:* their struggle to convert language into symbolic logic or music. It is a serious struggle, but taken this way it need not appear so. Nonsense? A mere game, of course. This

"Lewis Carroll and T. S. Eliot as Nonsense Poets." From *T. S. Eliot, A Symposium for His Seventieth Birthday*, edited by Neville Braybrooke (London: Rupert Hart-Davis Ltd., 1959; New York: Farrar, Straus & Cudahy, 1959). Copyright © 1958 by Neville Braybrooke. Reprinted by permission of the author and Neville Braybrooke.

is characteristic of us. We like, you might say, to play possum in these matters.

The genre or game of Nonsense has strict rules. The aim is to construct with words a logical universe of discourse meticulously selected and controlled; within this playground the mind can then manipulate its material, consisting largely of names of things and numbers. The process is directed always towards analysing and separating the material into a collection of discrete counters, with which the detached intellect can make, observe and enjoy a series of abstract, detailed, artificial patterns of words and images (you may be reminded of the New Criticism), which have their own significance in themselves. All tendencies towards synthesis are taboo: in the mind, imagination and dream; in language, the poetic and metaphorical elements; in subject matter, everything to do with beauty, fertility and all forms of love, sacred or profane. Whatever is unitive is the great enemy of Nonsense, to be excluded at all costs.

The pure practice of Nonsense demands a high degree of asceticism, since its very existence in the mind depends on limitation and infertility. Nonsense is by nature logical and anti-poetic. The Nonsense poet, therefore, faces a constant paradox of self-denial. Something of the effects of this can be seen in the work of three great Nonsense practitioners, Mallarmé, Carroll, and Mr. T. S. Eliot.

Mallarmé devoted his life, at great cost, to this paradox, becoming in the course of it an ascetic, atheistic, secular saint of letters. Neither Carroll nor Mr. Eliot was content to do this, and in their attitude and literary production they can be seen to resemble one another, their progressions describing similar curves, perhaps characteristic of great Nonsense men: they begin with strict Nonsense of a high order, but then, chafing at the game's restrictions, they desire to include some or all of those elements of real life—human relationships, the body, sex, love, religion, growth and development in the natural world—which Nonsense rules out. The desire is noble but it disintegrates the game. Mallarmé in the end cunningly escapes the paradox by progressing to thinking about thinking, in *Un Coup de Dés,* allowing himself a dangerously beautiful if shadowy ship and ocean and a sudden miraculous precipitation of stars, yet keeping the overall figure of dice-play, which is numbers and a game, and so could be Nonsense still. The Eliot-Mallarmé connection is close, Mr. Eliot himself providing clues to it in "Lines for an Old Man" and "Little Gidding"; but the Eliot-Carroll connection is closer. With Carroll we move from pure Nonsense in the *Alices* through *The Hunting of the Snark* to *Sylvie and Bruno,* and with Mr. Eliot from *The Waste Land* and the poems of the Sweeney period through the *Four Quartets* to the late plays. Carroll is the best interpreter we have for Mr. Eliot, and *Old Possum's Book of Practical Cats,* Mr. Eliot's overt Nonsense work, is not a chance production, the master in a lighter mood. It is integral to the whole body of his work, and a key to his poetry and his problem.

Mr. Eliot couches his own autobiography in Nonsense terms, but at one remove, for he parodies Lear's *Autobiography* into "How unpleasant to meet Mr. Eliot!" He is an extensive parodist as Carroll was, and in each case this is a device for handling what might otherwise be dangerous for Nonsense. It is a matter of affirming and denying, and in his autobiography Mr. Eliot affirms and denies Nonsense in its relation to himself. He has told us that he drew from *Alice in Wonderland* that rose-garden with which the first of the *Four Quartets* opens, leading into the image of the rose which pervades and closes the last of them. In his 1929 essay on the Dante he so greatly reveres he says that we have "to pass through the looking-glass into a world which is just as reasonable as our own. When we have done that we begin to wonder whether the world of Dante is not both larger and more solid than our own." Nonsense goes deep in Mr. Eliot. One does not describe one's life, even ironically, construct an image system in serious poetry, nor interpret an honored poet in terms of something one considers trivial. It is we who would be at fault in seeing Nonsense so. What Mr. Eliot is doing here is working at the dilemma of his vocation as a Nonsense poet. The *Four Quartets* epitomize the problem. They are religious poems; yet one of their main images comes from classical Nonsense, the Wonderland rose which becomes the *Paradiso* rose drawn in its turn from a poet to understand whom, according to Mr. Eliot, we have to go through the looking-glass. And Nonsense as a pure systematic art form of mind and language excludes both poetry and religion.

Lewis Carroll, much less of a poet than Mr. Eliot but no less devoted a churchman, faces the same problem. He had, however, two advantages: first, he had an official status in the matter; second, he was luckier in his period. He had a triple identity, as the Reverend Charles Dodgson, as a professional mathematician and symbolic logician, and as a Nonsense writer. The last two, closely allied as they are, were allowed to meet; the first was sealed off, at least up till the *Sylvie and Bruno* period. And the age in which he lived, a pre-Freudian era in which more modern meanings of "repressions" or "integration" were unknown, made possible such a separation and that which resulted from it—the perfection of the *Alices*. (The *Snark* is already much more ambiguous.) It is a pattern that Mr. Eliot might almost envy, if only for its true Nonsense quality. He, in his Nonsense autobiography, describes his own features as being "of clerical cut," and it is remarkable how character after character in the plays is impelled towards Holy Orders.[1] Harry in *Family Reunion* departs for "a stony sanctuary and a primitive altar"; Celia in *The Cocktail Party* joins an order, "a very austere one," and is martyred; Eggerson in *The Confidential Clerk* announces that Colby Simpkins will soon be entering the Church; and in *Murder in the Cathedral* the protagonist is archbishop, saint, and martyr already. Mr. Eliot's difficulty is that nowadays religion and other such vital subjects cannot conveniently be affirmed and then closed off. One has to be Nonsense man, poet, and churchman all at once. Carroll's hippopotamus, secure in its Nonsense bounds, can remain of the earth, earthy; but Mr. Eliot's has got into the poetry and has somehow to be got into heaven. Yet despite the superficial differences between them, to us readers it is a great help to have one such quadruped by which to measure a second, and Carroll is the best point of reference we have for understanding Mr. Eliot.

Anyone interested in drawing minor parallels between earlier Eliot poems and the *Alices* will find material ready to hand: the reminiscence of the Frog Footman in "Portrait of a Lady" ("I shall sit here . . ."); the executioner who haunts *Sweeney Agonistes* among the playing cards as he does the Queen's croquet game; the echo, also in *Sweeney*, of the riddle of the Red King's dream ("If he was alive then the milkman wasn't"); the reversals or full stops of time in the two writers; the endless tea party, interminable as the Hatter's, in "Prufrock," "Portrait of a Lady," "Mr. Apollinax," "Hysteria," "A Cooking Egg," *The Waste Land* where the typist comes home at tea time, the first scene of *Family Reunion*, Skimbleshanks in *Old Possum*, till only the tea leaves are left in "The Dry Salvages"; and so on. These are not uninteresting, but they are very minor affairs. It is in the major poems, as it should be, that Carroll and Nonsense begin to be really helpful.

The Waste Land is comparable to the *Alices* and to them alone, as Mr. Eliot's nearest approach to pure Nonsense practice. He admits certain elements into his subject matter—myth, love, the poetry and beauty of the past—which are dangerous, but he employs classic Nonsense techniques to control them. Thus the fragmentation in the poem is not to be regarded, in this light, as a lament on our modern

[1] Ezra Pound in the Cantos refers to Mr. Eliot as either "the Rev. Eliot," or "Old Possum," as if he, too, saw the dilemma of the connection.

condition. It is the Nonsense poet's way of analyzing his subject matter into discrete parts, "one and one and one" as the Red Queen says, to make it workable in Nonsense terms.[2] The same is true of the sterility the poem deals with. This, too, is the Nonsense poet carefully setting up the conditions necessary for the exercise of his special art. To hold the whole poem together, the two classic Carroll frameworks are employed, playing cards and chess, the digits and moves of a game substituted for those dangerous and un-Nonsense entities, human relationships. The Nonsense rules procure the necessary working conditions—detachment of mind from subject matter, analysis of material, manipulation of patterns of unfused images. Into this careful systematics, highly intellectual as Nonsense is, even potentially subversive material can be fitted and held, and the result is probably Mr. Eliot's masterpiece.

With the *Four Quartets,* the situation is made more difficult by what is now the poet's increasing emphasis upon unitive subjects, particularly love and religion. We need here, as points of reference, the *Alices* and the *Snark,* with a glance forward to *Sylvie and Bruno.* The over-all Nonsense control of *The Waste Land* has gone; in its place we have Nonsense procedures still operating, but used now as defenses against particular dangers. We will consider four of these: poetry, words in their nonlogical functions, and the two central images, roses and dancing.

Traditional forms of poetry are admitted into the *Quartets* from time to time, with their complement of metaphor and nonlogical speech so antithetical to Nonsense. When they appear, however, they tend, as in the *Alices,* to be pounced on and immediately subjected to critical analysis. See Part II of "East Coker," for instance, where the passage "What is the late November doing" is followed at once by

> That was a way of putting it—not very satisfactory.
> A periphrastic study in a worn-out poetical fashion.

So Alice says to the Caterpillar after repeating some verses, "Not quite right, I'm afraid. . . . Some of the words have got altered," and receives the reply, "It is wrong from beginning to end." Poetry is dangerous to Nonsense, even if unsatisfactory, even if parodied,

---

[2] For the end of the poem particularly, the Baker in *The Hunting of the Snark* is also a helpful commentator: "I said it in Hebrew, I said it in Dutch,/I said it in German and Greek," etc.

and it is as well to reduce it to criticism at once. No one interested in the present hypertrophied condition of literary criticism should overlook the importance of the Caterpillar and Humpty Dumpty as spiritual ancestors of this development.

Words, the materials of poetry with their aura of figures and dreams, are perilous, too. Mr. Eliot's description of his own conversation, restricted so nicely to What Precisely, acknowledges the Nonsense rule: words must be rigorously controlled lest dream and poetry creep in. So "Burnt Norton" says that words decay with imprecision, will not stay in place, will not stay still, to which Humpty Dumpty adds, "They've a temper, some of them, particularly verbs." In "East Coker" comes the phrase "the intolerable wrestle with words and meanings," and the complaint that one has only learnt to get the better of words for the thing that one no longer has to say; but the obligation is to master the words, as Humpty confirms, "The question is, which is to be master, that's all." A poet may be in part at least subject to his words; a Nonsense poet never. Only at the end of "Little Gidding" are the words allowed out to dance, and even then they have to be formal, exact, precise. So we come to dancing and roses, the two great Dante images for heaven which are also Nonsense images in Carroll and Eliot poetry.

A rose is about as dangerous an image for Nonsense as could be imagined. It implies an immense range of living company—beauty, growth, the body, sex, love. Roses in Nonsense will need special treatment, and Carroll begins to operate on his immediately, with pots of paint wielded by playing-card people or animated numbers. Mr. Eliot adopts a different but no less effective technique, sterilizing his rose in his turn, at the beginning and end of "Little Gidding," with ice and fire which cancel one another out and wipe away with them the living notion of the rose, leaving only a counter or cipher, suitable for Nonsense, behind.

Lastly, there is the dance, a dangerously living and bodily image, too. Carroll's attitude to it is always insecure. The cavorting Mock Turtle and Gryphon are clumsy and tread on Alice's feet; three times round the mulberry bush is enough for Tweedledum and Tweedledee. Carroll's most revealing dance occurs in one of his letters, where he compares his own dancing to a rhinoceros and hippopotamus executing a minuet together. Carroll is the reluctant dancing hippo. Mr. Eliot is a reluctant dancer also in the *Quartets,* even though dancing is the way to heaven. The dance is constrained: "At the still point, there the dance is," restricted as the circling round the Mad Hatter's table or the crocodile walking up his own forehead in *Sylvie and Bruno*. The best comment on this inhibition of free movement comes in the *Snark*. "In my beginning is my end or say that the end precedes the beginning"; it runs in "East Coker" and "Burnt Norton," and the Bellman, familiar with this condition, describes it as being "snarked," a state when "the bowsprit got mixed with the rudder sometimes." Movement in Nonsense is admitted only to be annulled, if the control and pattern are to be preserved.

Where then can we go now? It seems only towards *Sylvie and Bruno, The Cocktail Party, The Confidential Clerk*. There is already a surprising similarity between Part II of "The Dry Salvages,"

> Where is there an end of it, the soundless wailing,
> The silent withering of autumn flowers

and so on, and the prose poem with which *Sylvie and Bruno* ends, with its chilly mists and wailing gusts over the ocean, its withered leaves of a blighted hope, and the injunction, to the hero sailing for India, "Look Eastward!" as the Eliot poem bears us on to Krishna and Arjuna. Yet this is not Mr. Eliot's last word as Nonsense poet. He will talk about love and God and heaven in the later *Quartets* and plays, as Carroll does in *Sylvie and Bruno Concluded,* but this is not the answer, nor the way in which the hippopotamus can enter heaven. Mr. Eliot's answer is more direct and much more surprising; one hesitates, with any writer calling his book *Old Possum,* to suggest that it seems also largely unconscious. He implies that the way for a Nonsense poet to reach heaven is by Nonsense itself; and so we have *Old Possum's Book of Practical Cats*.

Cats and Nonsense writers agree well together, in life and in books. Cats are images for the body and for woman (so Grishkin) but in appeasable form. It is possible that cats are also images for God, in miniature. Mr. Empson suggests that the Cheshire Cat represented God, and I believe that the GREAT RUMPUSCAT (Mr. Eliot's capitals) might do so, too. "Gerontion," after all, speaks openly of Christ the tiger. But here there is no menace, Mr. Eliot can permit himself liberties Carroll never took, and sly theological eddies wander through the Possum book, in "Old Deuteronomy," or the cat's three names, one of which is ineffable. In this so-called minor work can be found all the love and charity which cause Mr. Eliot, as Nonsense poet, so much trouble in the rest of his poetry, but released and reconciled. Here, too, sin is behovely ("I could mention Mungojerrie, I could mention Griddlebone") but all shall be well; and there is set moving in "The Song of the Jellicles," at long last and in despite of all impediments and far beyond any of the supposedly more poetic works, a dance so free and loving and joyful, yet quiet and half secret, that it is a clear image of heaven, and an invitation thither.

Since there is in any case a ball in preparation here, and it seems the merest accident that Mr. Eliot left one thing out of this his most beautiful Nonsense poem, may I make the omission good, and offer, in recognition and gratitude, a rose for the Jellicles.

Eliot and Tennyson

by S. Musgrove

In a brief review article published in 1926 under the title "Whitman and Tennyson," Eliot says next to nothing about Whitman as a poet, but deals with him as a figure of his time.[1] The interest of the article lies largely in the comparisons it makes; but, before we discuss these, we may pause to notice the rather curious tone of the opening sentences:

> This book is in no way a critical examination of Whitman's work; it has nothing to say—thank God!—about Whitman's influence upon *vers libre* and contemporary American verse; it is silent about Whitman's present standing in American literature . . . Mr. Holloway's subject is "Whitman the Man" and his environment, and he keeps to the matter in hand. The book is written in an artless style, which ends by pleasing; and in the end we think of all the things the book might have been and is not, and give the author thanks.

Is it over-fanciful to hear a faint exhalation of relief in this passage? Allowing for—and even sympathizing with—Eliot's frequently asserted impatience with mere "literary criticism," one cannot avoid the feeling that there is an excess of gratitude in the paragraph. To thank both God and the author for the absence of a critical enquiry into a matter of verse technique—a subject which has always interested Eliot—suggests the presence of some personal factor.

"Eliot and Tennyson." From *T. S. Eliot and Walt Whitman* by S. Musgrove (Wellington; London and New York: Cambridge University Press), pp. 36-47. Copyright 1954 by the University of New Zealand Press. Reprinted by permission of the author and the University of New Zealand Press.

[1] Review of *Whitman: An Interpretation in Narrative,* by E. Holloway, *The Nation and Athenaeum,* XL, No. 11 (December 18, 1926), 426.

The article, however, proceeds quite objectively. It asserts that Whitman must be seen in the perspective of the America of his time, which is the America of *Martin Chuzzlewit*. Then follows, as the main body of the article, the comparison with Tennyson—one of these provoking comparisons with which Eliot delights to tease settled literary opinion. Despite surface differences, there is a "fundamental resemblance" between the two, and it lies in the fact that each is, in his own way, the voice of the nineteenth century, of its progressivism, its optimism, above all, of its satisfaction with itself. The two men were essentially "satisfied—too satisfied—with things as they are."

> Whitman succeeds in making America as it was, just as Tennyson made England as it was, into something grand and significant . . . They had the facility—Whitman perhaps more prodigiously than Tennyson—of transmuting the real into an ideal . . . (Whitman's) "frankness" about sex . . . did not spring from any particular honesty or clearness of vision: it sprang from what may be called either "idealization" or a faculty for make-believe, according as we are disposed. There is, fundamentally, no difference between the Whitman frankness and the Tennyson delicacy . . .

And, to sum up the whole:

> Both were conservative, rather than reactionary or revolutionary; that is to say, they believed explicitly in progress, and believed implicitly that progress consists in things remaining much as they are.

This comparison Eliot underlines by means of a contrast: against these two is set, by a neat juxtaposition of dates and titles (*Leaves of Grass*, 1856, *Les Fleurs du Mal*, 1857) the figure of Baudelaire. Against the "satisfaction" of Whitman and Tennyson, he cites Baudelaire's "je m'ennuie en France, où tout le monde ressemble à Voltaire"; and against their faculty for making believe that real and ideal are one, the "chasm between the real and the ideal" which "opened before the horrified eyes" of the French poet.

The introduction of these two new terms into the equation makes for interesting complications. If my estimate of Eliot's relationship with Whitman is right, corresponding relationships should exist with Baudelaire and Tennyson: that is to say, Eliot's own "ideology" (if the word be permitted), as well as his poetical method, should be identifiable to a large degree with that of Baudelaire; and towards Tennyson he should reveal the same kind of philosophical distrust as he shows towards Whitman, while being nevertheless attracted to certain features of his poetical method and perhaps carrying away from him certain verbal memories. In other words, what we have is a quartette: Whitman and Tennyson matched against Baudelaire and Eliot.

There is no need of any lengthy analysis to expose the likenesses between Eliot and Baudelaire. The two essays "Baudelaire" and "Baudelaire in our Times" contain plenty of evidence to show how intimately Eliot identifies himself with Baudelaire.[2] In summary, it amounts to this: Baudelaire is above all a "serious and Catholic Christian," even his Satanism being but a way of "affirming belief"; he "rejects always the purely natural and the purely human . . . in other words, he is neither 'naturalist' nor 'humanist' "; and (like Eliot himself, most explicitly in *The Rock*) in "an age of bustle, programmes, platforms, scientific progress, humanitarianism and revolutions which improved nothing, an age of progressive degradation" (that is, the age of "Song of the Exposition" and of "Locksley Hall") he "perceived that what really matters is Sin and Redemption." As for his poetry, he is (like Eliot) a "poet in a romantic age" and therefore can be a "classical" poet only "in tendency"; yet his "renovation of language," as of traditional versification, his discovery of new poetical material, of imagery drawn from the life of "a great metropolis," enable him to "express with individual differences the general state of mind" of his age, and yet also to remain himself, "essentially a Christian, born out of his due time, and a classicist, born out of his due time." Almost every sentence here might be a description, not of Baudelaire, but of Eliot; the essay is an excellent instance of the point already made, that all Eliot's criticism issues from the problems which are personal to him as poet and thinker.

The evidence in the case of Tennyson is to be found in the essay "In Memoriam," [3] which again cites Baudelaire as a figure of contrast; but matters are here a little more complicated, because Eliot is particularly interested in the conflict of feeling and intellect in Tennyson, in a nature which, while distrusting so much in the contemporary world, none the less was constrained to exalt and uphold it. He was often "opposed to the doctrine that he was moved to accept and to praise," being, like Virgil, "the most instinctive rebel against the society in which he was the most perfect conformist." Yet, for all these inner reservations, the qualities of thought most evident in

[2] *Selected Essays*, pp. 371 ff.; *Essays Ancient and Modern*, pp. 63-75.
[3] *Selected Essays*, pp. 286-295.

Whitman are evident in Tennyson also: his mind, unlike Baudelaire's, was "not at all" that of the "theologian"; his creed had only
a "hazy connexion with . . . the Incarnate God"; his hope was for
"the gradual and steady improvement of this world"; he was strongly
interested in "contemporary science"; in other words he was the
"naturalist" and "humanist" rejected by Baudelaire and Eliot alike.[4]
All this is obvious enough, and needs no comment. There is more
interest in pursuing our second prognostication, by which we judged
that Eliot should show an admiration for certain poetical qualities
in Tennyson, and that his poetry should contain verbal memories of
Tennyson's imagery and content. Both requirements are satisfied. As
for the first point, the whole of the opening part of the essay is taken
up by praise of Tennyson's technical mastery, especially his metrics;[5]
Tennyson is "a great poet, for reasons that are perfectly clear." The
second point needs a more detailed examination. I have not attempted to search the whole of Tennyson's writings for verbal resemblances, but have concentrated on those poems quoted or cited by
Eliot in his essay, with certain others associated closely with them.

The selection of poems which Eliot makes in praising Tennyson is
interesting, and at times somewhat curious. *Maud,* he says, "consists"
for him only "of a few very beautiful lyrics"; and he names "O let
the solid ground," "Birds in the high Hall-garden," and "Go not,
happy day." The first choice, with its brilliant verbal economy, is
acceptable; but one would hardly have suspected in Eliot a readiness
to admire either

> I kiss'd her slender hand,
>   She took the kiss sedately;
> Maud is not seventeen.
>   But she is tall and stately.

or even

> Rosy is the West,
>   Rosy is the South,

---

[4] Compare the 1916 review of Balfour: "Mr. Balfour's ethics are a sort of
Tennysonian naturalism" (*International Journal of Ethics,* XXVI [Jan. 1916], 287.
This bald statement, made without any other reference to Tennyson, shows how
Eliot sees him as a type of nineteenth century thought.

[5] I suspect that Eliot's early series of quatrain poems may owe something to
Tennyson's mastery in the various quatrain forms, as well as to the seventeenth
century poets to whom credit is usually given [see, e.g., Helen L. Gardner, *The
Art of T. S. Eliot* (London: Cresset Press, Ltd., 1949), p. 19], but I have not investi-
gated the point in detail.

> Roses are her cheeks,
> And a rose her mouth.

It seems likely that Eliot's nomination of these particular lyrics has been influenced, and even directed, by a memory of an earlier time when his younger tastes revelled in such passages of sensuous modesty. We may, in fact, explain his selection by remembering his confession of an "adolescent course" in the romantic poets;[6] and we may also suppose that it is not entirely a coincidence that "Go not, happy day" contains an American reference:

> Till the red man dance
> By his red cedar-tree,
> And the red man's babe
> Leap, beyond the sea.

The impression that his admiration for Tennyson is deeply rooted in youthful memory is fortified by an examination of the other poems named or quoted by him. He dwells more particularly on the group of early lyrics, whose rich melody and thick colouring would be especially likely to appeal to a young reader. It is therefore encouraging to find, in "Burbank with a Baedeker," a deliberately ironical use of a line from one of the poems of this group (though not one named by Eliot in the essay). The line

> They were together, and he fell.

is meant to recall a line from "The Sisters."

> They were together, and she fell—

is, in fact, a conscious and destructive inversion of a romantic situation such as we shall find over and over again in his echoes of Whit-

---

[6] The only critic known to me who has observed any connection between Eliot's work and that of the nineteenth century romantics is Louis MacNeice, who remarks ("Eliot and the Adolescent," in *T. S. Eliot*, edited by March and Tambimuttu [Chicago: Henry Regnery Company, 1949], p. 147) "The images, and the rhythms, and the hypnotic, incantatory repetitions of *The Hollow Men* were not too alien to anyone brought up on the Bible and on Shakespeare's Tragedies and even on the autumnal Victorians. In the same way, the pockmarked moon of 'Rhapsody on a Windy Night' fell naturally into place beside Shelley's 'dying lady.' "

man. The poems mentioned in the essay begin with a stanza from
"The Song of the Sisters," but this we may put on one side, since it
is not printed in editions of Tennyson normally available and is
quoted by Eliot only for its metrical skill; the others are "the two
Mariana poems, 'The Sea-Fairies,' 'The Lotos-Eaters,' 'The Lady of
Shalott'" and some others unnamed. From "Mariana" he quotes (as
evidence that with the advent of Tennyson "something important
has happened" in English poetry) these lines:

> All day within the dreamy house,
>   The doors upon their hinges creak'd;
> The blue fly sung in the pane; the mouse
>   Behind the mouldering wainscot shriek'd,
> Or from the crevice peer'd about.

Readers of Eliot will feel at once a stirring of memory, recalling
decaying houses and shuttered rooms from more than one poem;
above all those of "East Coker":

> Houses live and die: there is a time . . .
>   . . . for the wind to break the loosened *pane*
> And to shake the *wainscot* where the field-*mouse* trots . . .[7]

(The "wind," incidentally, is in the two stanzas of "Mariana" before
and after the one quoted). They will recall also the dead house of
"Little Gidding":

> Dust inbreathed was a house—
> The wall, the *wainscot* and the *mouse*.

But this is not all. The houses of "East Coker" also "rise and fall" and
return "to the earth": a phrasing that suggests another early poem
of Tennyson's, "The Deserted House":

> The house was builded of the *earth*,
> And shall *fall* again to ground.

Another decayed house in Eliot is that of "Gerontion," and from this
we may add a further detail: the "old man" in the "draughty house,"

---

[7] This parallel is noticed by Miss Gardner (footnote 5), pp. 54-5, though she considers that "the sources are completely unimportant" for a poetical appreciation of
Eliot.

the "decayed house," thinks of those who were "bitten by *flies.*" "Gerontion," in fact, yields an even richer harvest than "East Coker"; it is not by chance, apparently, that both it and "Mariana" are introduced by quotations from one and the same play, *Measure for Measure.* To begin with, there is a connection between "Gerontion" and "The Deserted House": Tennyson writes of "Life and *Thought*" as "Careless Tenants," while Eliot makes the *"thoughts"* of the old man *"Tenants* of the house." Furthermore, the opening and closing phrases of "Gerontion"—

> . . . waiting for rain . . .
> Thoughts of a *dry brain* in a dry season—

are matched in Tennyson's "Fatima" where, in a "burning drouth," the lady "thirsted for the brooks, the showers," while swooning in her *"dry brain."* But the most convincing likeness is in the phrase standing next to the mention of flies already quoted:

> . . . *knee-deep* in the *salt* marsh . . .

This takes us to "Mariana in the South" (again, a poem of a lonely house) and to the lines

> On stony drought and steaming *salt:*
> Till now at noon she slept again,
> And seem'd *knee-deep* in mountain grass.

The "mountain grass" is not in "Gerontion," but it reappears, again in close association with a deserted, windowless building, in *The Waste Land,* as

> In this decayed hole among the mountains
> . . . the grass is singing.

There are, in fact, many resemblances both of detail and of general atmosphere between Eliot's landscapes and those of the early poems of Tennyson. In both are deserts and stagnant waters, droughts and glaring lights, though the details are combined in a different order. Thus, the "marsh" of "Gerontion" (and also the "moss" which follows a few lines later) may come from the "marish-mosses" of "Mariana," or perhaps from the "waste enormous marsh" (next to a "lowly

cottage") of the "Ode to Memory." [8] Then, in *The Waste Land*, near
to the mountain-grass passage already quoted, is

> . . . the cicada
> And dry grass singing

with, in the next line, a "sound of water"; which recalls, from
"Mariana in the South,"

> At eve a *dry cicada sung,*
> There came a *sound as of the sea.*

Associated by imagery and tone with *The Waste Land* is the short
poem "The Wind Sprang Up," where the phrase "the surface of the
blackened river" recalls "Mariana's" "sluice with blacken'd water";
and in *The Rock* another water passage—

> The light that *slants* upon our *western* doors at evening,
> The twilight over stagnant pools at *batflight*—

recalls from "Mariana" not only the "flitting of the *bats*," but

> the day
> Was *sloping* toward his *western* bower.

In the line preceding these in "Mariana" is "the thick-moted sun-
beam," which in turn recalls, once again, the close of "Burnt
Norton":

> Sudden in a shaft of sunlight
> Even while the dust moves,

and also the "dust in the air suspended" of the dead house of "Little
Gidding."

---

[8] I am inclined to find in this passage an origin for the closing lines of "Burnt
Norton": "Ridiculous the waste sad time Stretching before and after." The "waste
enormous marsh" of Tennyson "stretches wide and wild," and near it the
"trenched waters run from sky to sky," as "emblems of infinity." In the next
line is a "garden bower'd close," as in Eliot's adjacent line is the laughter of children "in the foliage," which, as the opening of the poem makes clear, is also a
garden. In Tennyson, of course, this is fen country.

Both poets make easy transitions from their deserted houses to the sea, and, as will be remembered, among the early poems of Tennyson praised by Eliot is "The Sea-Fairies." I should be inclined, however, to look for the origin of Prufrock's elusive mermaids rather in "The Merman" and "The Mermaid"; and, if it be urged that both in Eliot and Tennyson the mermaids behave merely as mermaids will, to point also to section II of *The Waste Land*, where, in a passage that remembers "Those are pearls that were his eyes" and before a "sea-wood" fire, the lady, seated like Tennyson's mermaid on a throne—though with acknowledgments also to Cleopatra—brushes her hair, threatens to rush out into the street with her "hair down, so"—Tennyson's more poetical mermaid wears it "low adown"—and plays a neurotic version of the mermaid's innocent game of "Who is it loves me? Who loves not me?": a version close enough to the original to yield at least a rhythmical equivalent in the line "What shall I do now? What shall I do?" Moreover, as in Eliot's dark room, with its "seven*branched* candelabra,"

> staring forms
> *Leaned out,* leaning, hushing the room enclosed

so, in Tennyson, among the "*branching* jaspers,"

> All things that are forked, and horned, and soft
> Would *lean out* from the hollow sphere of the sea,
> All looking down for the love of me.

Some of these likenesses may be fortuitous; but not all. The two groups of poems are too alike in their essential subject for that. The early Tennysonian lyrics are, almost all of them, about enchanted and deserted ladies left to mourn in empty houses for the infidelity or insufficiency of their lovers. This is also Eliot's subject; although setting and atmosphere are no longer romantic, having been transferred from the moated grange to the cosmopolitan salon, the plight of the ladies in *The Waste Land*, in "Portrait of a Lady" and in "Prufrock" remains the same, while "Gerontion" envisages an inversion of the situation in male terms. There is even a certain likeness in the geographical setting; for throughout the Tennyson group, not merely in "Mariana in the South," there is a constant suggestion of southern lands and southern skies, which is expressed directly in the lines

> . . . I seek a warmer sky,
> And I will see before I die
> The palms and temples of the South.

One recalls, from *The Waste Land,*

> I read, much of the night, and go south in the winter,

and more clearly, from *The Family Reunion* (where Wishwood is but one more version of the decayed house of childhood)

> I would follow the sun, not wait for the sun to come here.
> I would go south in the winter, if I could afford it.

Similarly, the lines which follow a little later in the same play

> Harry, Harry, you are very tired
> And overwrought . . .
> You are unused to our foggy climate
> And the northern country

send us back to Tennyson's opening stanza:

> You ask me, why, tho' ill at ease,
>   Within this region I subsist,
>   Whose spirits falter in the mist,
> And languish for the purple seas.

The relationship between the two poets is not difficult to reconstruct. One may imagine an early intoxication with the heady languor and the heavy sensuousness of the Tennysonian lyrics, and a fascination at a typically romantic situation; perhaps one should also add personal memories of old houses known in childhood. Later, though the maturing mind turns away dissatisfied from the deceptions of romance, there yet remains a lingering trace of that early sweetness. The consequence is that while poems like "Prufrock" are at pains to overturn the whole romantic apple-cart and to propound the situation of the deserted lady only in order to expose its falsehood, a detail here or a phrase there betrays the half-remembered origin.

To return to Eliot's essay. The links between his poetry and *In*

Memoriam itself are rarer; which is but natural, since *In Memoriam* is a poem less likely than the lyrics to fascinate an adolescent reader. Eliot selects for particular praise the remarkable seventh section:

> Dark house, by which once more I stand
>   Here in the long unlovely street,
>   Doors, where my heart was used to beat
> So quickly, waiting for a hand,
>
> A hand that can be clasp'd no more—
>   Behold me, for I cannot sleep,
>   And like a guilty thing I creep
> At earliest morning to the door.
>
> He is not here; but far away
>   The noise of life begins again,
>   And ghastly thro' the drizzling rain
> On the bald street breaks the blank day.

Nobody will dispute Eliot's judgment that this is great poetry; yet it is but accurate to observe, once more, that the material of it is of a kind used frequently in his own poetry. Again, we are led to the dark house, to the "doors" and through the "streets" which form the landscape of so many of his early poems. As commentary on Tennyson's street-scene, a few passages out of many similar ones will serve:

> And when all the world came back
> And the light crept up between the shutters . . .
> You had such a vision of the street
> As the street hardly understands.
>
> The showers beat
> On broken blinds and chimney-pots,
> And at the corner of the street
> A lonely cab-horse steams and stamps.
>
> . . . returning as before
> Except for a slight sensation of being ill at ease
> I mount the stairs and turn the handle of the door
> And feel as if I had mounted on my hands and knees.
>
> Four o'clock,
> Here is the number on the door.
> Memory!

The link here is so obvious that there is no surprise for us in Eliot's remark that this vision of Tennyson's "gives me the shudder that I fail to get from anything in *Maud*." It is of interest also that the adjoining sections in *In Memoriam* contain again the situation of the deserted lover—in one case a woman, in the other a man— which has fascinated Eliot so often:

> O! somewhere, meek, unconscious dove,
>   That sittest ranging golden hair:
>   And glad to find thyself so fair,
> Poor child, that waitest for thy love! . . .

> A happy lover who has come
>   To look on her that loves him well,
>   Who lights and rings the gateway bell,
> And learns her gone and far from home . . .

(One notices how often the detail of the dressing of the hair recurs in both poets.) Furthermore, in the tenth section there is something that looks like a common memory of Sappho. Where Tennyson has

> Thou bring'st the sailor to his wife,
>   And travell'd men from foreign lands . . .

Eliot, in *The Waste Land,* announces the evening hour, which

> . . . brings the sailor home from sea.

What is particularly interesting about this echo is that we shall find yet another use of it, and in a very suggestive context, in Whitman.

The other passages from *In Memoriam* quoted by Eliot are given as illustrations of Tennyson's philosophical beliefs, and therefore show less connection with his own work. None the less, it is not impossible to scent Sweeney in the line

> No longer half-akin to brute,

or even "Rachel *née* Rabinovitch," as she "tears at the grapes with murderous paws" in

> Nature, red in tooth and claw.

How then, do these memories of Tennyson link up with those from Whitman? They are less extensive and, I think, go less deep than those from the American poet, being more purely "literary" memories; at least one echo, and perhaps more, is conscious and deliberately ironical. Yet they are of a kind which explains the identification of Whitman and Tennyson made by Eliot in the article from which this part of our enquiry began. Both Whitman and Tennyson are men of an older generation who have, each in his different way, fascinated the awakening poet in Eliot. Both he has later come to distrust; but fragments from the poetry of each have remained embedded in his memory, to work their way to the surface when a common subject or a common situation calls them forth.

"Marie, Marie, Hold on Tight"

by George L. K. Morris

As a rented house in Provence provided somewhat sparse reading matter, I took up a volume with the unpromising title *My Past,* by a Countess Marie Larisch. To my surprise, it proved thoroughly engrossing. Perhaps it was a book which everybody read when it was first published (1916). T. S. Eliot was certainly one who read it, and before he wrote *The Waste Land.*

For a variety of reasons, the book should have created a sensation. To begin with, Countess Larisch was a niece and confidante of the Austrian Empress Elizabeth, who was famous in her time for a glamorous combination of good looks and neurasthenia; secondly, the author had been the unwilling go-between for the Archduke Rudolph and Maria Vetsera, and was blamed by almost everyone for the tragedy at Mayerling; and thirdly, she was endowed with a surprising gift for vivid characterizations.

Anyone familiar with Eliot's poem does not read very far before coming upon a similarity of names and places that can hardly be fortuitous. We have seen that the Countess' name was Marie.[1] Moreover her home was on the Starnberger-See (*Waste Land,* line 8). Marie's family, the Wittelsbachs—which included the Empress and their cousin, the "mad king" Ludwig—occupied various castles around the Bavarian lake. "The archduke my cousin" (lines 13-14 of the poem): Marie had several archduke cousins, but Rudolph was her first cousin;

" 'Marie, Marie, Hold on Tight.' " From *Partisan Review,* XXI (March-April, 1954), 231-233. Copyright 1954 by *Partisan Review*. Reprinted by permission of the author and *Partisan Review*.

[1] It might be noted that *Marie* is a most unusual name in Central Europe; the German form is customarily *Maria.*

although they always disliked each other cordially, they had been
forced to associate since childhood—and each unknowingly brought
about the other's downfall. Marie went "south in winter" (line 18)—
Menton, to be specific; and—to clinch matters—she frequently observed that only in the mountains she felt free (line 17); when the
Mayerling catastrophe caused her to leave Vienna, it was to the
mountains that she retired for good. Richard Wagner had a humorous
rendezvous with Marie when she was a girl; in the poem he intrudes
only through a stanza of *Tristan*.

The *Waste Land* décor, moreover, bears kinship to certain passages
in Countess Larisch's book. The opening lines of Part IV echo an
account of the Empress' dressing room, with its notable combination
of magnificence and ennui. And the "Chapel Perilous" of Part V
curiously resembles the tumbledown chapter-house at Heiligenkreuz,
to which the uncles of Maria Vetsera carried her mangled remains,
through the windy night with a pale moon; the police allowed only
a moment for the burial, and no time at all to say a prayer.

On another level we can find more subtle points of contact between
the book and poem. I know few autobiographies that encompass so
many violent deaths—notably death by drowning and death by fire.
And, as we might expect, there was considerable superstition and
fortune-telling in the Hapsburg wasteland. The most noteworthy
"death-by-drowning" episode concerns the suicide of the Bavarian king
in the Starnberger-See. Of all her relatives, it was to Ludwig that the
imaginative Empress always felt most closely drawn. A striking chapter
gives Elizabeth's account of his reappearance several nights after his
death, and the apparition she always insisted was not at all in a dream.
She was awakened by the drip-drip of water in her room, and saw
Ludwig standing by her bed, his hair and clothes drenched and hung
with sea-weed. He foretold that her sister (who had been his fiancée)
would join him before long, and already he saw her surrounded by
flames and smoke. She was later burnt to death at the Bazar de la
Charité fire in Paris. And he added that she herself would follow,
after a death that would be "short and painless." The Empress was
assassinated the following year, while boarding a steamer on Lac
Leman ("by the waters of Leman I sat down and wept").[2]

As I seem to have intruded into these pages in the guise of detective,
I have no business to be reviewing a forty-year-old book. But I find
it difficult to close without paying homage to some of the more preposterous characters who accompany the narrative. My favorite was an

[2] Eliot commentators have ascribed the curious Lac Leman reference variously,
from the League of Nations to a medieval word for "lover."

Archduchess who thought she'd swallowed a sofa which had become permanently lodged in her head, and she refused to leave her room for fear that the ends would stick in the door-jambs. A quick-witted attendant performed a miraculous cure, by gaining admission to one of Her Highness' frequent bilious attacks, and slipping a doll's sofa into the basin. And in more serious vein, there was the noble Archduke John of Tuscany, whom Marie links with Rudolph in a plot to overthrow Franz-Joseph and to build a democratic Hungary. She hints that its failure was the real motive behind Rudolph's suicide. John of Tuscany was drowned in a shipwreck off Cape Horn.

It will be understood, I hope, that there has been no intent here to detract from the formidable merits of Eliot's work. On the contrary, I find an added interest if one of the monuments of modern literature should be connected with a source so unexpected. And some day, perhaps, the copious *Waste Land* notes—always diligent in their tributes to Dante, Shakespeare, and Miss Jessie Weston—will also put in a word for Marie Larisch.

The Waste Land

by F. R. Leavis

It was *The Waste Land* that compelled recognition for
the achievement. The poem appeared first in the opening number
of *The Criterion* (October 1922). The title, we know, comes from Miss
J. L. Weston's book, *From Ritual to Romance,* the theme of which is
anthropological: the Waste Land there has a significance in terms of
Fertility Ritual. What is the significance of the modern Waste Land?
The answer may be read in what appears as the rich disorganization of
the poem. The seeming disjointedness is intimately related to the erudition that has annoyed so many readers[1] and to the wealth of literary
borrowings and allusions. These characteristics reflect the present state
of civilization. The traditions and cultures have mingled, and the historical imagination makes the past contemporary; no one tradition can

[1] "I don't like his erudition-traps," said a very distinguished author to me once.
And this, from *Gallion's Reach* (pp. 35-36), by H. M. Tomlinson, is representative:
"His grin broadened. 'All I can say is, my dear, give me the old songs, though
I can't sing them, if they're the new. What does poetry want with footnotes about
psycho-analysis and negro mythology?'

"'Suppose,' someone asked him, 'that you don't know anything about them?'

"'Well, I couldn't get them out of footnotes and the poetry all at one stride,
could I? But Doris, they were very clever and insulting poems, I think. Sing a
song of mockery. Is that the latest? But it was a surprising little book, though
it smelt like the dissection of bad innards.' "
The novelist, with a certain subtle naïveté, clearly identifies himself with the
attitude, and he clearly means the reader to do the same. And there is every reason
to suppose that he would not object to the reader's supposing that he had Mr.
Eliot in mind. The First Edition of *Gallion's Reach* is valuable.

digest so great a variety of materials, and the result is a breakdown of forms and the irrevocable loss of that sense of absoluteness which seems necessary to a robust culture. The bearing of this on the technique developed in "Burbank" and "A Cooking Egg" does not need enlarging upon.

In considering our present plight we have also to take account of the incessant rapid change that characterizes the Machine Age. The result is a breach of continuity and the uprooting of life. This last metaphor has a peculiar aptness, for what we are witnessing today is the final uprooting of the immemorial ways of life, of life rooted in the soil. The urban imagery that affiliates Mr. Eliot to Baudelaire and Laforgue has its significance; a significance that we touched on in glancing at the extreme contrast between Mr. Eliot and Hardy. We may take Mr. T. F. Powys today as the successor of Hardy: he is probably the last considerable artist of the old order (he seems to me a great one). It does not seem likely that it will ever again be possible for a distinguished mind to be formed, as Mr. Powys has been, on the rhythms, sanctioned by nature and time, of rural culture.

The spirit of *Mr. Weston's Good Wine* could not be described as one of traditional faith; all the more striking, then, is the contrast in effect between Mr. Powys's and Mr. Eliot's preoccupation with "birth, copulation and death." [2] Mr. Powys's disillusion belongs to the old world, and the structure and organization of his art are according. There is no need to elaborate the comparison.

The remoteness of the civilization celebrated in *The Waste Land* from the natural rhythms is brought out, in ironical contrast, by the anthropological theme. Vegetation cults, fertility ritual, with their sympathetic magic, represent a harmony of human culture with the natural environment, and express an extreme sense of the unity of life. In the modern Waste Land

> April is the cruellest month, breeding
> Lilacs out of the dead land,

[2]   . . . .

Nothing at all but three things

DORIS.   What things?

SWEENEY.   Birth, and copulation, and death.
              That's all, that's all, that's all, that's all.
              Birth, and copulation, and death.

DORIS.   I'd be bored

SWEENEY.   You'd be bored.
              Birth, and copulation, and death.
                    ("Fragment of an Agon.")

but bringing no quickening to the human spirit. Sex here is sterile, breeding not life and fulfilment but disgust, accidia, and unanswerable questions. It is not easy today to accept the perpetuation and multiplication of life as ultimate ends.

But the anthropological background has positive functions. It plays an obvious part in evoking that particular sense of the unity of life which is essential to the poem. It helps to establish the level of experience at which the poem works, the mode of consciousness to which it belongs. In *The Waste Land* the development of impersonality that "Gerontion" shows in comparison with "Prufrock" reaches an extreme limit: it would be difficult to imagine a completer transcendence of the individual self, a more complete projection of awareness. We have, in the introductory chapter, considered the poet as being at the conscious point of his age. There are ways in which it is possible to be too conscious; and to be so is, as a result of the breakup of forms and the loss of axioms noted above, one of the troubles of the present age (if the abstraction may be permitted, consciousness being in any case a minority affair). We recognize in modern literature the accompanying sense of futility.

The part that science in general has played in the process of disintegration is matter of commonplace: anthropology is, in the present context, a peculiarly significant expression of the scientific spirit. To the anthropological eye beliefs, religions and moralities are human habits—in their odd variety too human. Where the anthropological outlook prevails, sanctions wither. In a contemporary consciousness there is inevitably a great deal of the anthropological, and the background of *The Waste Land* is thus seen to have a further significance.

To be, then, too much conscious and conscious of too much—that is the plight:

> After such knowledge, what forgiveness?

At this point Mr. Eliot's note on Tiresias deserves attention:

> Tiresias, although a mere spectator and not indeed a "character," is yet the most important personage in the poem, uniting all the rest. Just as the one-eyed merchant, seller of currants, melts into the Phoenician Sailor, and the latter is not wholly distinct from Ferdinand Prince of Naples, so all the women are one woman, and the two sexes meet in Tiresias. What Tiresias *sees,* in fact, is the substance of the poem.[3]

[3] Note to line 218 of *The Waste Land.*

If Mr. Eliot's readers have a right to a grievance, it is that he has not given this note more salience; for it provides the clue to *The Waste Land*. It indicates plainly enough what the poem is: an effort to focus an inclusive human consciousness. The effort, in ways suggested above, is characteristic of the age; and in an age of psychoanalysis, an age that has produced the last section of *Ulysses*, Tiresias —"venus huic erat utraque nota"—presents himself as the appropriate impersonation. A cultivated modern is (or feels himself to be) intimately aware of the experience of the opposite sex.

Such an undertaking offers a difficult problem of organization, a distinguishing character of the mode of consciousness that promotes it being a lack of organizing principle, the absence of any inherent direction. A poem that is to contain all myths cannot construct itself upon one. It is here that *From Ritual to Romance* comes in. It provides a background of reference that makes possible something in the nature of a musical organization.[4] Let us start by considering the use of the Tarot pack. Introduced in the first section, suggesting, as it does, destiny, chance and the eternal mysteries, it at once intimates the scope of the poem, the mode of its contemplation of life. It informs us as to the nature of the characters: we know that they are such as could not have relations with one another in any narrative scheme, and could not be brought together on any stage, no matter what liberties were taken with the Unities. The immediate function of the passage introducing the pack, moreover, is to evoke, in contrast with what has preceded, cosmopolitan "high life," and the charlatanism that battens upon it:

> Madame Sosostris, famous clairvoyante,
> Had a bad cold, nevertheless
> Is known to be the wisest woman in Europe,
> With a wicked pack of cards.

Mr. Eliot can achieve the banality appropriate here, and achieve at the same time, when he wants it, a deep undertone, a resonance, as it were, of fate:

>   . . . and this card,
> Which is blank, is something he carries on his back,
> Which I am forbidden to see. I do not find

[4] Mr. I. A. Richards uses the analogy from music in some valuable notes on Mr. Eliot that are printed in an appendix to the later editions of *The Principles of Literary Criticism*.

> The Hanged Man. Fear death by water.
> I see crowds of people, walking round in a ring.

The peculiar menacing undertone of this associates it with a passage in the fifth section:

> Who is the third who walks always beside you?
> When I count, there are only you and I together
> But when I look ahead up the white road
> There is always another one walking beside you
> Gliding wrapt in a brown mantle, hooded
> I do not know whether a man or a woman
> —But who is that on the other side of you?

The association establishes itself without any help from Mr. Eliot's note; it is there in any case, as any fit reader of poetry can report; but the note helps us to recognize its significance:

> The Hanged Man, a member of the traditional pack, fits my purpose in two ways: because he is associated in my mind with the Hanged God of Frazer, and because I associate him with the hooded figure in the passage of the disciples to Emmaus in Part V.

The Tarot pack, Miss Weston has established, has affiliations with fertility ritual, and so lends itself peculiarly to Mr. Eliot's purpose: the instance before us illustrates admirably how he has used its possibilities. The hooded figure in the passage just quoted is Jesus. Perhaps our being able to say so depends rather too much upon Mr. Eliot's note; but the effect of the passage does not depend so much upon the note as might appear. For Christ has figured already in the opening of the section (see "What the Thunder Said"):

> After the torchlight red on sweaty faces
> After the frosty silence in the gardens
> After the agony in stony places
> The shouting and the crying
> Prison and palace and reverberation
> Of thunder of spring over distant mountains
> He who was living is now dead
> We who were living are now dying
> With a little patience

The reference is unmistakable. Yet it is not only Christ; it is also the Hanged God and all the sacrificed gods: with the "thunder of spring" "Adonis, Attis, Osiris" and all the others of *The Golden Bough* come in. And the "agony in stony places" is not merely the Agony in the Garden; it is also the agony of the Waste Land, introduced in the first section: ("The Burial of the Dead," ll. 19 ff.).

> What are the roots that clutch, what branches grow
> Out of this stony rubbish? Son of man,
> You cannot say, or guess, for you know only
> A heap of broken images, where the sun beats,
> And the dead tree gives no shelter, the cricket no relief,
> And the dry stone no sound of water.

In "What the Thunder Said" the drought becomes (among other things) a thirst for the waters of faith and healing, and the specifically religious enters into the orchestration of the poem. But the thunder is "dry sterile thunder without rain"; there is no resurrection or renewal; and after the opening passage the verse loses all buoyancy, and takes on a dragging, persistent movement as of hopeless exhaustion—

> Here is no water but only rock
> Rock and no water and the sandy road
> The road winding above among the mountains
> Which are mountains of rock without water

—the imagined sound of water coming in as a torment. There is a suggestion of fever here, a sultry ominousness—

> There is not even solitude in the mountains

—and it is this which provides the transition to the passage about the hooded figure quoted above. The ominous tone of this last passage associates it, as we have seen, with the reference (ll. 55-56) to the Hanged Man in the Tarot passage of "The Burial of the Dead." So Christ becomes the Hanged Man, the Vegetation God; and at the same time the journey through the Waste Land along "the sandy road" becomes the Journey to Emmaus. Mr. Eliot gives us a note on the "third who walks always beside you":

The following lines were stimulated by the account of one of the Antarctic expeditions (I forget which, but I think one of Shackleton's): it was related that the party of explorers, at the extremity of their strength, had the constant delusion that there was *one more member* than could actually be counted.

This might be taken to be, from our point of view, merely an interesting irrelevance, and it certainly is not necessary. But it nevertheless serves to intimate the degree of generality that Mr. Eliot intends to accompany his concrete precision: he is both definite and vague at once. "Just as the one-eyed merchant, seller of currants, melts into the Phoenician Sailor, and the latter is not wholly distinct from Ferdinand Prince of Naples"—so one experience is not wholly distinct from another experience of the same general order; and just as all experiences "meet in Tiresias," so a multitude of experiences meet in each passage of the poem. Thus the passage immediately in question has still further associations. That same hallucinatory quality which relates it to what goes before recalls also the neurasthenic episode (ll. 111 ff.) in "A Game of Chess" (the second section):

> "What is that noise?"
>> The wind under the door.
> "What is that noise now? . . ."

All this illustrates the method of the poem, and the concentration, the depth of orchestration that Mr. Eliot achieves; the way in which the themes move in and out of one another and the predominance shifts from level to level. The transition from this passage is again by way of the general ominousness, which passes into hallucinated vision and then into nightmare:

> —But who is that on the other side of you?
>
> What is that sound high in the air
> Murmur of maternal lamentation
> Who are those hooded hordes swarming
> Over endless plains, stumbling in cracked earth
> Ringed by the flat horizon only
> What is the city over the mountains
> Cracks and reforms and bursts in the violet air
> Falling towers

Jerusalem Athens Alexandria
Vienna London
Unreal.

The focus of attention shifts here to the outer disintegration in its
large, obvious aspects, and the references to Russia and to post-war
Europe in general are plain. The link between the hooded figure of
the road to Emmaus and the "hooded hordes swarming" is not much
more than verbal (though appropriate to a fevered consciousness),
but this phrase has an essential association with a line (56) in the
passage that introduces the Tarot pack:

> I see crowds of people, walking round in a ring.

These "hooded hordes," "ringed by the flat horizon only," are not
merely Russians, suggestively related to the barbarian invaders of
civilization; they are also humanity walking endlessly round in a
ring, a further illustration of the eternal futility. "Unreal" picks up
the "Unreal city" of "The Burial of the Dead" (l. 60), where "Saint
Mary Woolnoth kept the hours," and the unreality gets further
development in the nightmare passage that follows:

> And upside down in air were towers
> Tolling reminiscent bells, that kept the hours
> And voices singing out of empty cisterns and exhausted wells.

Then, with a transitional reference (which will be commented on
later) to the theme of the Chapel Perilous, the focus shifts inwards
again. "Datta," "dayadhvam," and "damyata," the admonitions of
the thunder, are explained in a note, and in this case, at any rate,
the reliance upon the note justifies itself. We need only be told once
that they mean "give, sympathize, control," and the context preserves
the meaning. The Sanscrit lends an appropriate portentousness, inti-
mating that this is the sum of wisdom according to a great tradition,
and that what we have here is a radical scrutiny into the profit of life.
The irony, too, is radical:

> *Datta:* what have we given?
> My friend, blood shaking my heart
> The awful daring of a moment's surrender

> Which an age of prudence can never retract
> By this, and this only, we have existed

—it is an equivocal comment. And for comment on "sympathize" we have a reminder of the irremediable isolation of the individual. After all the agony of sympathetic transcendence, it is to the individual, the focus of consciousness, that we return:

> Shall I at least set my lands in order?

The answer comes in the bundle of fragments that ends the poem, and, in a sense, sums it up.

Not that the *poem* lacks organization and unity. The frequent judgments that it does betray a wrong approach. The author of "The Lyric Impulse in the Poetry of T. S. Eliot," [5] for instance, speaks of "a definitely willed attempt to weld various fine fragments into a metaphysical whole." But the unity of *The Waste Land* is no more "metaphysical" than it is narrative or dramatic, and to try to elucidate it metaphysically reveals complete misunderstanding. The unity the poem aims at is that of an inclusive consciousness: the organization it achieves as a work of art is of the kind that has been illustrated, an organization that may, by analogy, be called musical. It exhibits no progression:

> I sat upon the shore
> Fishing, with the arid plain behind me

—the thunder brings no rain to revive the Waste Land, and the poem ends where it began.

At this point the criticism has to be met that, while all this may be so, the poem in any case exists, and can exist, only for an extremely limited public equipped with special knowledge. The criticism must be admitted. But that the public for it is limited is one of the symptoms of the state of culture that produced the poem. Works expressing the finest consciousness of the age in which the word "highbrow" has become current are almost inevitably such as to appeal only to a tiny minority. [6] It is still more serious that this minority should

---

[5] In *Scrutinies*, II, collected by Edgell Rickword.

[6] This matter is discussed at length by the present author in *Mass Civilisation and Minority Culture* (reprinted in *Education and the University* by F. R. Leavis).

be more and more cut off from the world around it—should, indeed, be aware of a hostile and overwhelming environment. This amounts to an admission that there must be something limited about the kind of artistic achievement possible in our time: even Shakespeare in such conditions could hardly have been the "universal" genius. And *The Waste Land,* clearly, is not of the order of *The Divine Comedy* or of *Lear.* The important admission, then, is not that *The Waste Land* can be appreciated only by a very small minority (how large in any age has the minority been that has really comprehended the masterpieces?), but that this limitation carries with it limitations in self-sufficiency.

These limitations, however, are easily overstressed. Most of the "special knowledge," dependence upon which is urged against *The Waste Land,* can fairly be held to be common to the public that would in any case read modern poetry. The poem does, indeed, to some extent lean frankly upon *From Ritual to Romance.* And sometimes it depends upon external support in ways that can hardly be justified. Let us take, for instance, the end of the third section, "The Fire Sermon":

> la la

> To Carthage then I came

> Burning, burning, burning, burning
> O Lord Thou pluckest me out
> O Lord Thou pluckest

> burning

It is plain from Mr. Eliot's note on this passage—"The collocation of these two representatives of eastern and western asceticism, as the culmination of this part of the poem, is not an accident"—that he intends St. Augustine and the Buddha to be actively present here. But whereas one cursory reading of *From Ritual to Romance* does all (practically) that is assigned as function to that book, no amount of reading of the *Confessions* or *Buddhism in Translation* will give these few words power to evoke the kind of presence of "eastern and western asceticism" that seems necessary to the poem: they remain, these words, mere pointers to something outside. We can only conclude that Mr. Eliot here has not done as much as he supposes. And so with the passage (ll. 385 ff.) in "What the Thunder Said" bringing in the theme of the Chapel Perilous: it leaves too much to Miss

Weston; repeated recourse to *From Ritual to Romance* will not invest it with the virtue it would assume. The irony, too, of the

Shantih   shantih   shantih

that ends the poem is largely ineffective, for Mr. Eliot's note that " 'The Peace which passeth understanding' is a feeble translation of the content of this word" can impart to the word only a feeble ghost of that content for the Western reader.

Yet the weaknesses of this kind are not nearly as frequent or as damaging as critics of *The Waste Land* seem commonly to suppose. It is a self-subsistent poem, and should be obviously such. The allusions, references and quotations usually carry their own power with them as well as being justified in the appeal they make to special knowledge. "Unreal City" (l. 60), to take an extreme instance from one end of the scale, owes nothing to Baudelaire (whatever Mr. Eliot may have owed); the note is merely interesting—though, of course, it is probable that a reader unacquainted with Baudelaire will be otherwise unqualified. The reference to Dante that follows—

> A crowd flowed over London Bridge, so many,
> I had not thought death had undone so many

—has an independent force, but much is lost to the reader who does not catch the implied comparison between London and Dante's Hell. Yet the requisite knowledge of Dante is a fair demand. The knowledge of *Antony and Cleopatra* assumed in the opening of "A Game of Chess," or of *The Tempest* in various places elsewhere, no one will boggle at. The main references in *The Waste Land* come within the classes represented by these to Dante and Shakespeare; while of the many others most of the essential carry enough of their power with them. By means of such references and quotations Mr. Eliot attains a compression, otherwise unattainable, that is essential to his aim; a compression approaching simultaneity—the co-presence in the mind of a number of different orientations, fundamental attitudes, orders of experience.

This compression and the methods it entails do make the poem difficult reading at first, and a full response comes only with familiarity. Yet the complete rout so often reported, or inadvertently revealed—as, for instance, by the critic who assumes that *The Waste Land* is meant to be a "metaphysical whole"—can be accounted for only by a wrong approach, an approach with inappropriate expectations. For the general nature and method of the poem should be obvious at first reading. Yet so commonly does the obvious seem to be missed that perhaps a little more elucidation (this time of the opening section) will not be found offensively superfluous. What follows is a brief analysis of "The Burial of the Dead," the avowed intention being to point out the obvious themes and transitions: anything like a full analysis would occupy many times the space.

The first seven lines introduce the vegetation theme, associating it with the stirring of "memory and desire." The transition is simple: "April," "spring," "winter,"—then

> Summer surprised us, coming over the Starnbergersee
> With a shower of rain . . .

We seem to be going straight forward, but (as the change of movement intimates) we have modulated into another plane. We are now given a particular "memory," and a representative one. It introduces the cosmopolitan note, a note of empty sophistication:

> In the mountains, there you feel free.
> I read, much of the night, and go south in the winter.
> [Cf. "Winter kept us warm"]

The next transition is a contrast and a comment, bringing this last passage into relation with the first. April may stir dull roots with spring rain, but

> What are the roots that clutch, what branches grow
> Out of this stony rubbish?

And there follows an evocation of the Waste Land, with references to Ezekiel and Ecclesiastes, confirming the tone that intimates that this is an agony of the soul ("Son of man" relates with the Hanged Man and the Hanged God: with him "who was living" and "is now dead" at the opening of "What the Thunder Said"). The "fear"—

> I will show you fear in a handful of dust

—recurs, in different modes, in the neurasthenic passage (ll. 111 ff.) of "A Game of Chess," and in the episode of the hooded figure in "What the Thunder Said." The fear is partly the fear of death, but still more a nameless, ultimate fear, a horror of the completely negative.

Then comes the verse from *Tristan und Isolde,* offering a positive in contrast—the romantic absolute, love. The "hyacinth girl," we may say, represents "memory and desire" (the hyacinth, directly evocative like the lilacs bred out of the Waste Land, was also one of the flowers associated with the slain vegetation god), and the "nothing" of the Waste Land changes into the ecstasy of passion—a contrast, and something more:

> —Yet when we came back, late, from the Hyacinth garden,
> Your arms full, and your hair wet, I could not
> Speak, and my eyes failed, I was neither
> Living nor dead, and I knew nothing,
> Looking into the heart of light, the silence.

In the Waste Land one is neither living nor dead. Moreover, the neurasthenic passage referred to above recalls these lines unmistakably, giving them a sinister modulation:

> "Speak to me. Why do you never speak. Speak.
>   "What are you thinking of? What thinking? What?
> "I never know what you are thinking. Think."
>
>   .   .   .   .
>
>   "Do
> "You know nothing? Do you see nothing? Do you remember
> "Nothing?"

The further line from *Tristan und Isolde* ends the passage of romantic love with romantic desolation. Madame Sosostris, famous clairvoyante, follows; she brings in the demimonde, so offering a further contrast—

> Here is Belladonna, the Lady of the Rocks,
> The lady of situations

—and introduces the Tarot pack. This passage has already received some comment, and it invites a great deal more. The "lady of situations," to make an obvious point, appears in the "Game of Chess." The admonition, "Fear death by water," gets its response in the fourth section, "Death by Water": death is inevitable, and the life-giving water thirsted for (and the water out of which all life comes) cannot save. But enough has been said to indicate the function of the Tarot pack, the way in which it serves in the organization of the poem.

With the "Unreal City" the background of urban—of "megalo-politan"—civilization becomes explicit. The allusion to Dante has already been remarked upon, and so has the way in which Saint Mary Woolnoth is echoed by the "reminiscent bells" of "What the Thunder Said." The portentousness of the "dead sound on the final stroke of nine" serves as a transition, and the unreality of the City turns into the intense but meaningless horror, the absurd incon-sequence, of nightmare:

> There I saw one I knew, and stopped him, crying: "Stetson!
> "You who were with me in the ships at Mylae!
> "That corpse you planted last year in your garden,
> "Has it begun to sprout? Will it bloom this year? . . ."

These last two lines pick up again the opening theme. The corpse acquires a kind of nightmare association with the slain god of *The Golden Bough,* and is at the same time a buried memory. Then, after a reference to Webster (Webster's sepulchral horrors are robust), "The Burial of the Dead" ends with the line in which Baudelaire, having developed the themes of

> La sottise, l'erreur, le péché, la lésine

and finally *L'Ennui,* suddenly turns upon the reader to remind him that he is something more.

The way in which *The Waste Land* is organized, then, should be obvious even without the aid of notes. And the poet's mastery should be as apparent in the organization as in the parts (where it has been freely acclaimed). The touch with which he manages his difficult transitions, his delicate collocations, is exquisitely sure. His tone, in all its subtle variations, exhibits a perfect control. If there is any instance where this last judgment must be qualified, it is perhaps here (from the first passage of "The Fire Sermon"):

> Sweet Thames, run softly till I end my song,
> Sweet Thames, run softly, for I speak not loud or long.
> But at my back in a cold blast I hear
> The rattle of the bones, and chuckle spread from ear to ear.

These last two lines seem to have too much of the caricature quality of "Prufrock" to be in keeping—for a certain keeping is necessary (and Mr. Eliot commonly maintains it) even in contrasts. But even if the comment is just, the occasion for it is a very rare exception.

The Waste Land, then, whatever its difficulty, is, or should be, obviously a poem.[7] It is a self-subsistent poem. Indeed, though it would lose if the notes could be suppressed and forgotten, yet the more important criticism might be said to be, not that it depends upon them too much, but rather that without them, and without the support of *From Ritual to Romance,* it would not lose more. It has, that is, certain limitations in any case; limitations inherent in the conditions that produced it. Comprehensiveness, in the very nature of the undertaking, must be in some sense at the cost of structure: absence of direction, of organizing principle, in life could hardly be made to subserve the highest kind of organization in art.

But when all qualifications have been urged, *The Waste Land* remains a great positive achievement, and one of the first importance for English poetry. In it a mind fully alive in the age compels a poetic triumph out of the peculiar difficulties facing a poet in the age. And in solving his own problem as a poet Mr. Eliot did more than solve the problem for himself. Even if *The Waste Land* had been, as used to be said, a "dead end" for him, it would still have been a new start for English poetry.

[7] "It is a test (a positive test, I do not assert that it is always valid negatively), that genuine poetry can communicate before it is understood."—T. S. Eliot, "Dante." *Selected Essays,* p. 200.

T. S. Eliot, 1925-1935

by D. W. Harding

This new volume [*Collected Poems, 1909-1935*] is an opportunity, not for a review—for "The Poetry of T. S. Eliot" begins to
have the intimidating sound of a Tripos question—but for asking
whether anything in the development of the poetry accounts for
the change in attitude that has made Mr. Eliot's work less *chic* now
than it was ten years ago. Perhaps the ten years are a sufficient ex-
planation—obvious changes in fashionable feeling have helped to
make the sort-of-communist poets popular. But on the other hand
it may be that these poets gratify some taste that Mr. Eliot also
gratified in his earlier work but not in his later. If so it is surely a
taste for evocations of the sense of protest that our circumstances
set up in us; for it seems likely that at the present time it is expressions of protest in some form or other that most readily gain a poet
popular sympathy. And up to *The Waste Land* and *The Hollow Men*
this protest—whether distressed, disgusted, or ironical—was still the
dominant note of Mr. Eliot's work, through all the subtlety and
sensitiveness of the forms it took. Yet already in these two poems
the suggestion was creeping in that the sufferers were also failures.
We are the hollow men, but there are, besides,

> Those who have crossed
> With direct eyes, to death's other Kingdom

And in all the later work the stress tends to fall on the regret or
suffering that arises from our own choices or our inherent limitations,
or on the resignation that they make necessary. Without at the

"T. S. Eliot, 1925-1935." From *Scrutiny*, V (September, 1936), 171-176. First pub-
lished in America in *The Importance of Scrutiny* by Eric Bentley (George W.
Stewart, Inc., 1948; Grove Press, 1957). Reprinted by permission of the author, F. R.
Leavis, and Eric Bentley.

moment trying to define the change more closely one can point out certain characteristics of the later work which are likely to displease those who create the fashions of taste in poetry today, and which also contrast with Mr. Eliot's earlier work. First it is true that in some of the poems (most obviously in the Choruses from *The Rock*) there are denunciation and preaching, both of which people like just now. But there is a vital difference between the denunciation here and that, say, in *The Dog Beneath the Skin*: Mr. Eliot doesn't invite you to step across a dividing line and join him in guaranteed rightness—he suggests at the most that you and he should both try, in familiar and difficult ways, not to live so badly. Failing to make it sound easy, and not putting much stress on the fellowship of the just, he offers no satisfaction to the craving for a life that is ethically and emotionally *simpler*.

And this characteristic goes with a deeper change of attitude that separates the later work from the earlier. Besides displaying little faith in a revolt against anything outside himself, Mr. Eliot in his recent work never invites you to believe that everything undesirable in you is due to outside influences that can be blamed for tampering with your original rightness. Not even in the perhaps over-simple "Animula" is there any suggestion that the "simple soul" has suffered an avoidable wrong for which someone else can be given the blame. Mr. Eliot declines to sanction an implicit belief, almost universally held, which lies behind an immense amount of rationalization, self-pity and childish protest—the belief that the very fact of being alive ought to ensure your being a satisfactory object in your own sight. He is nearer the more rational view that the process of living is at its best one of progressive dissatisfaction.

Throughout the earlier poems there are traces of what, if it were cruder and without irony and impersonality, would be felt at once as self-pity or futile protest: for example,

> Put your shoes at the door, sleep, prepare for life.
> The last twist of the knife.
> ("Rhapsody on a Windy Night")

or,

> Wipe your hand across your mouth, and laugh;
> The worlds revolve like ancient women
> Gathering fuel in vacant lots.
> ("Preludes," IV)

or again,

> The nightingales are singing near
> The Convent of the Sacred Heart,
>
> And sang within the bloody wood
> When Agamemnon cried aloud,
> And let their liquid siftings fall
> To stain the stiff dishonoured shroud.
>   ("Sweeney Among the Nightingales")

Obviously this is only one aspect of the early poetry, and to lay much stress on it without qualification would be grotesquely unfair to "Gerontion" especially and to other poems of that phase. But it is a prominent enough aspect of the work to have made critics, one might have thought, more liable to underrate the earlier poems than, with fashionable taste, the later ones. For there can be no doubt of the greater maturity of feeling in the later work:

> And I pray that I may forget
> These matters that with myself I too much discuss
> Too much explain
> Because I do not hope to turn again
> Let these words answer
> For what is done, not to be done again
> May the judgment not be too heavy upon us
>   (*Ash-Wednesday*, I)

This may be called religious submission, but essentially it is the submission of maturity.

What is peculiar to Mr. Eliot in the tone of his work, and not inherent in maturity or in religion, is that he does *submit* to what he knows rather than welcoming it. To say that his is a depressed poetry isn't true, because of the extraordinary toughness and resilience that always underlie it. They show, for instance, in the quality of the scorn he expresses for those who have tried to overlook what he sees:

> . . . the strained time-ridden faces
> Distracted from distraction by distraction
> Filled with fancies and empty of meaning

> Tumid apathy with no concentration
> Men and bits of paper . . .
>
>   ("Burnt Norton," III)

But to insist on the depression yields a half-truth. For though acceptance and understanding have taken the place of protest the underlying experience remains one of suffering, and the renunciation is much more vividly communicated than the advance for the sake of which it was made. It is summed up in the ending of *Ash-Wednesday*:

> Blessèd sister, holy mother, spirit of the fountain, spirit
>   of the garden,
> Suffer us not to mock ourselves with falsehood
> Teach us to care and not to care
> Teach us to sit still
> Even among these rocks,
> Our peace in His will
> And even among these rocks
> Sister, mother
> And spirit of the river, spirit of the sea,
> Suffer me not to be separated
>
> And let my cry come unto Thee.

This is the cry of the weaned child, I suppose the analysts might say; and without acquiescing in the genetic view that they would imply one can agree that weaning stands as a type-experience of much that Mr. Eliot is interested in as a poet. It seems to be the clearer and more direct realization of this kind of experience that makes the later poems at the same time more personal and more mature. And in the presence of these poems many who liked saying they liked the earlier work feel both embarrassed and snubbed.

However, all of this might be said about a volume of collected sermons instead of poems. It ignores Mr. Eliot's amazing genius in the use of words and rhythms and his extraordinary fertility in styles of writing, each "manner" apparently perfected from the first and often used only once (only once, that is, by Mr. Eliot, though most are like comets with a string of poetasters laboriously tailing after them). One aspect of his mastery of language may perhaps be commented on here because it reaches its most remarkable expression in the latest of the poems, "Burnt Norton." Here most obviously the poetry is a linguistic achievement, in this case an achievement in the creation of concepts.

Ordinarily our abstract ideas are over-comprehensive and include too wide a range of feeling to be of much use by themselves. If our words "regret" and "eternity" were exact bits of mosaic with which to build patterns much of "Burnt Norton" would not have had to be written. But

> . . . Words strain,
> Crack and sometimes break, under the burden,
> Under the tension, slip, slide, perish,
> Decay with imprecision, will not stay in place,
> Will not stay still.

One could say, perhaps, that the poem takes the place of the ideas of "regret" and "eternity." Where in ordinary speech we should have to use those words, and hope by conversational trial-and-error to obviate the grosser misunderstandings, this poem is a newly-created concept, equally abstract but vastly more exact and rich in meaning. It makes no statement. It is no more "about" anything than an abstract term like "love" is about anything: it is a linguistic creation. And the creation of a new concept, with all the assimilation and communication of experience that that involves, is perhaps the greatest of linguistic achievements.

In this poem the new meaning is approached by two methods. The first is the presentation of concrete images and definite events, each of which is checked and passes over into another before it has developed far enough to stand meaningfully by itself. This is, of course, an extension of a familiar language process. If you try to observe introspectively how the meaning of an abstract term—say "trade"—exists in your mind, you find that after a moment of blankness, in which there seems to be only imageless "meaning," concrete images of objects and events begin to occur to you; but none by itself carries the full meaning of the word "trade," and each is faded out and replaced by another. The abstract concept, in fact, seems like a space surrounded and defined by a more or less rich collection of latent ideas. It is this kind of definition that Mr. Eliot sets about here—in the magnificent first section for instance—with every subtlety of verbal and rhythmical suggestion.

And the complementary method is to make pseudo-statements in highly abstract language, for the purpose, essentially, of putting forward and immediately rejecting ready-made concepts that might have seemed to approximate to the concept he is creating. For instance:

> Neither from nor towards; at the still point, there the dance is,
> But neither arrest nor movement. And do not call it fixity.
> Where past and future are gathered. Neither movement from nor
>   towards,
> Neither ascent nor decline.

Or

> Not the stillness of the violin, while the note lasts,
> Not that only, but the co-existence,
> Or say that the end precedes the beginning,
> And the end and the beginning were always there
> Before the beginning and after the end.
>
> And all is always now.

In neither of these methods is there any attempt to state the meaning by taking existing abstract ideas and piecing them together in the ordinary way. Where something approaching this more usual method is attempted, in the passage beginning "The inner freedom from the practical desire," it seems a little less successful; admirable for the plays, where the audience is prominent, it fails to combine quite perfectly with the other methods of this poem. But it is Mr. Eliot himself who, by the closeness of his approach to technical perfection, provides a background against which such faint flaws can be seen.

T. S. Eliot's Later Poetry

by F. R. Leavis

"The Dry Salvages" (pronounced to rhyme with *assuages*)
is the third member to appear of a sequence that began with "Burnt
Norton," continued with "East Coker," and, one gathers, is to be
completed in a fourth poem.[1] Each member is a poem in itself, as
the separate publication intimates, but it is plain now, with three
of the four to hand, that the sequence is to be a real whole; a total
context which each constituent poem needs for its full significance.
Now, too, with this new poem before him, the literary critic finds
himself once more turning over the principle that poetry is to be
judged as poetry—turning it over and wondering what it is worth
and how far it will take him. May there perhaps be a point at which
literary criticism, if (as he must believe) there is, or ought to be,
such a thing, finds itself confronting the challenge to leave itself behind and become another thing? Is, in any case, the field of literary
criticism so delimitable as to exempt him from the theological equip-
ment he can lay no claim to?

In overcoming this last uneasiness he will have found encourage-
ment in the performances of commentators who have not needed to
share it: it will have been so clear that their advantage has not been altogether an advantage, but has tended to disqualify them for appre-
ciating the nature of the poet's genius. They are apt to show too
great an alacrity in response; to defeat his essential method by jump-
ing in too easily and too happily with familiar terms and concepts.

"T. S. Eliot's Later Poetry." From *Education and the University* (London, 1943;
New York, 1948). Copyright 1943 by Chatto & Windus Ltd. First published in
Scrutiny, XI, No. 1 (Summer, 1942), 60-71. Reprinted by permission of the author
and Chatto & Windus Ltd. All rights reserved.
[1] This was of course written before the appearance of "Little Gidding."—H.K.

This is the method that is carried to an experimental (and hardly successful) extreme in *Family Reunion,* where, if I understand rightly, Mr. Eliot aims at bringing his public, assumed for the purpose to be pagan, face to face with the Christian position or view of life without invoking Christian dogma, or such familiar concepts and symbols as would fall comfortably in with the lethargy of custom. In the poetry, of course, there is no pretense that the sensibility is not Christian; but it is not for nothing that D. W. Harding described "Burnt Norton," which doesn't stand apart from the body of Eliot's religious verse, as being concerned with the creation of concepts.[2] The poet's magnificent intelligence is devoted to keeping as close as possible to the concrete of sensation, emotion, and perception. Though this poetry is plainly metaphysical in preoccupation, it is as much poetry, it belongs as purely to the realm of sensibility, and has in it as little of the abstract and general of discursive prose, as any poetry that was ever written. Familiar terms and concepts are inevitably in sight, but what is distinctive about the poet's method is the subtle and resourceful discipline of continence with which, in its exploration of experience, it approaches them.

Of course, the sensibility being Christian, they lie behind the poetry, as well as being in front of it (so to speak) as something to be re-created; but they are never taken up as accepted instruments for getting to work with. We might apply here some adaptation of the poet's critical dictum: "(Tradition) cannot be inherited, and if you want it you must obtain it by great labour." Well-equipped commentators would do well, for a simple illustration of the kind of dangers and temptations awaiting them, to consider how Eliot uses Dante in *Ash-Wednesday,* and how easy it would be with the aid of a Dante primer to work out an illuminating commentary that would save grateful readers the trouble of understanding the poem.

The poetry from *Ash-Wednesday* onwards doesn't say, "I believe," or "I know," or "Here is the truth"; it is positive in direction but not positive in that way (the difference from Dante is extreme). It is a searching of experience, a spiritual discipline, a technique for sincerity—for giving "sincerity" a meaning. The preoccupation is with establishing from among the illusions, evanescences and unrealities of life in time an apprehension of an assured reality—a reality that, though necessarily apprehended in time, is not of it. There is a sustained positive effort—the constructive effort to be "conscious":

---

[2] See his extraordinarily interesting and penetrating review of *Collected Poems, 1909-1935,* in *Scrutiny* for September, 1936. It seems to me pre-eminently the note on Eliot to send people to. [See pages 104-109 of the present volume.—H.K.]

> Time past and time future
> Allow but a little consciousness.
> To be conscious is not to be in time
> But only in time can the moment in the rose-garden.
> The moment in the arbour where the rain beat,
> The moment in the draughty church at smokefall
> Be remembered; involved with past and future.
> Only through time time is conquered.
>
> ("Burnt Norton," II)

With these "moments" is associated "the sudden illumination":

> The moments of happiness—not the sense of well-being,
> Fruition, fulfilment, security or affection,
> Or even a very good dinner, but the sudden illumination—
> We had the experience, but missed the meaning,
> And approach to the meaning restores the experience
> In a different form, beyond any meaning
> We can assign to happiness.
>
> ("The Dry Salvages," II)

"Illumination," it will be seen, is no simple matter, and *Ash-Wednesday,* where the religious bent has so pronounced a liturgical expression, is remarkable for the insistent and subtle scrupulousness of the concern manifested to guard against the possibilities of temptation, self-deception, and confusion that attend on the aim and the method.

Perhaps the way in which the sense of an apprehended higher reality, not subject to the laws of time and mundane things, is conveyed is most simply illustrated in "Marina," that lovely poem (a limiting description) with the epigraph from Seneca. There, in the opening, the enchanted sense of a landfall in a newly discovered world blends with the suggestions (to be taken up later on in the poem) of "daughter"—the "daughter" being associated by the title of the poem with the Shakespearean heroine who, lost at sea, was miraculously found again, for the father an unhoped-for victory over death:

> What seas what shores what grey rocks and what islands
> What water lapping the bow
> And scent of pine and the woodthrush singing through the fog
> What images return
> O my daughter.

The images that follow in the next paragraph bring in the insistently recurring "Death" after each line, and they are evoked in order that we may find that they now

> Are become unsubstantial, reduced by a wind,
> A breath of pine, and the woodsong fog
> By this grace dissolved in place.

It may be remarked that the mundane actuality, the world of inescapable death, is elsewhere in the poems of the phase less easily dismissed; its reduction to unreality is a different affair, having nothing of enchantment about it, and the unreality is not absence. And perhaps it should be noted, too, as an associated point that "grace," in its equivocal way, is the one explicitly religious touch in "Marina."

The evocation of the apprehended reality is now taken up, and is characteristic in method:

> What is this face, less clear and clearer
> The pulse in the arm, less strong and stronger—
> Given or lent? more distant than stars and nearer than the eye
> Whispers and small laughter between leaves and hurrying feet
> Under sleep, where all the waters meet.

The face, "less clear and clearer," doesn't belong to the ordinary experience of life in time, and the effect of a higher reality is reinforced by the associations of the last two lines—associations that, with their potent suggestion, characteristic of some memories of childhood, of a supremely illuminating significance, recur so much in Eliot's later work:

> We had the experience, but missed the meaning
> And approach to the meaning restores the significance
> In a different form, beyond any meaning
> We can assign to happiness.

The effect depends upon a kind of co-operative co-presence of the different elements of suggestion, the co-operation being, as the spare and nonlogical pointing intimates, essentially implicit, and not a matter for explicit development. What in fact we have is nothing of the order of affirmation or statement, but a kind of tentatively defining exploration.

The rest of the poem adds to the co-present elements the suggestion of a constructive effort, which, though what it constructs is defective and insecure, has a necessary part in the discovery or apprehension:

> I made this . . .
>
> .   .   .   .
>
> Made this unknowing, half-conscious, unknown, my own,
> The garboard strake leaks, the seams need caulking.
> This form, this face, this life
> Living to live in a world of time beyond me; let me
> Resign my life for this life, my speech for that unspoken,
> The awakened, lips parted, the hope, the new ships.

Thus, in the gliding from one image, evocation or suggestion to another, so that all contribute to a total effect, there is created a sense of a supreme significance, elusive, but not, like the message of death, illusory; an opening into a new and more than personal life.

In the *Coriolan* poems it is the unreal actuality that fills the foreground of attention. They deal with the world of public affairs and politics, and it seems natural to call them satires; they are certainly great poetry, and they come as near to great satiric poetry as this age is likely to see. Again we have a search for the real among temporal unrealities. "Triumphal March" gives us the great occasion, the public event, the supremely significant moment. The reduction and deflation of the "significance" is effected by sudden uncommented slides of the focus, or shiftings of the plane. In the opening we share the exaltation and expectancy of the holiday crowd:

> Stone, bronze, stone, steel, stone, oakleaves, horses' heels
> Over the paving.
> And the flags. And the trumpets. And so many eagles.
> How many? Count them. And such a press of people.
> We hardly knew ourselves that day, or knew the City.
> This is the way to the temple, and we so many crowding the way.
> So many waiting, how many waiting? what did it matter, on such a day?
> Are they coming? No, not yet. You can see some eagles. And hear the
>   trumpets.
> Here they come. Is he coming?
> The natural wakeful life of our Ego is a perceiving.
> We can wait with our stools and our sausages.

In the last two lines we have two shifts; first to the level of philosophical observation,

> The natural wakeful life of our Ego is a perceiving

(which has its quasi-musical response towards the end of the poem in

> That is all we could see, etc.),

and then to the mob's natural level of banality (a theme developed in the final paragraph just referred to). Then again we have the tense expectancy; at last the real thing is about to appear:

> What comes first? Can you see? Tell us. It is

> 5,800,000 rifles and carbines,
> 102,000 machine guns,
> 28,000 trench mortars etc.

And it is at any rate one kind of basic "reality" that, with ironical effect, the prolonged inhuman inventory gives us. That is what "comes first," contrasting significantly with the Lord Mayor's Show passage that takes it up at the level of "human interest." Following the Mayor and the Liverymen comes—supreme public moment, climax of the day—the Hero, the Führer, presented in a guise of equivocally godlike self-sufficiency:

> There is no interrogation in his eyes
> Or in the hands, quiet over the horse's neck,
> And the eyes watchful, waiting, perceiving, indifferent.

Comment follows immediately in the sudden shift to the imagery of "consciousness"; imagery that evokes the eternal reality and the escape from time and the flux, and, recurrent as it is in the later poems, indicates the place among them of these satires as something like movements of one work:

> O hidden under the dove's wing, hidden in the turtle's breast,
> Under the palmtree at noon, under the running water
> At the still point of the turning world. O hidden.

"Difficulties of a Statesman" works in the same way as "Triumphal March." Dealing with the unrealities of politics and public affairs, the conventional importances, the loss of ends in the bustle of getting things done, the usurping and frustrating complication of the machinery—

> The first thing to do is to form the committees: 1-5
> The consultative councils, the standing committees, select committees
>   and sub-committees.
> One secretary will do for several committees.

—it places all this by the same kind of abrupt passing invocation of the eternal and ultimate source of significance and peace. It ends with the consummate ironic duplicity of

RESIGN RESIGN RESIGN.

"Burnt Norton," the first poem of the sequence to which "The Dry Salvages" belongs, has the effect of being in a special sense a "fresh start." [3] It is as if the poet were conducting a radical inquiry into the nature and methods of his exploration. The poem is as purely and essentially a poem as anything else of Mr. Eliot's; but it seems to me to be the equivalent in poetry of a philosophical work— to do by strictly poetical means the business of an epistemological and metaphysical inquiry. Of course, in this given case examination of the instruments is necessarily at the same time a use of them in the poet's characteristic kind of exploration. Yet to convey the distinctive character of this poem the stress must fall as I have suggested. Harding, in the illuminating commentary referred to above, registers this character in his own way when he speaks of the poem as being concerned with the "creation of concepts."

The kind of expository generality that distinguishes "Burnt Norton" is well illustrated by the opening:

> Time present and time past
> Are both perhaps present in time future,
> And time future contained in time past.

[3] So here I am, in the middle way, having had twenty years—
Twenty years largely wasted, the years of *l'entre deux guerres*—
Trying to learn to use words, and every attempt
Is a wholly new start . . .

("East Coker," V)

> If all time is eternally present
> All time is unredeemable.
> What might have been is an abstraction
> Remaining a perpetual possibility
> Only in a world of speculation.
> What might have been and what has been
> Point to one end, which is always present.
> Footfalls echo in the memory
> Down the passage which we did not take
> Towards the door we never opened
> Into the rose-garden. My words echo
> Thus, in your mind.

The general propositions of the first ten lines have, by the time we have read the rest of the passage, become clearly part of a *procédé* and a total effect that belong to poetry, and not to the order of abstraction of discursive prose. The particular memory evoked is not an illustration of the general propositions; these, rather, represent a pondering, with results in generalized significance, of the memory, the "illuminative" quality of which, along with the unseizableness—

> the sudden illumination—
> We had the experience, but missed the meaning,
> And approach to the meaning restores the experience
> In a different form

—is marvellously conveyed. The unseizableness—the specific indeterminate status of the experience and the elusiveness of the meaning—we can see being defined, or created, in the paradoxical

> Footfalls echo in the memory
> Down the passage which we did not take
> Towards the door we never opened
> Into the rose-garden.

"Footfalls echo" is a fact, and "memory" becomes the "passage" which, though we did not take it, is thus itself a present fact.

The complex effect of a de-realizing of the routine common-sense world together with the evoking of a reality that lies hidden among the unrealities into which life in time, closely questioned, paradoxes itself is clinched by the sudden shift:

> My words echo
> Thus, in your mind.

The "not" and "never" of the preceding sentence are "thus" (finely placed word) in a way countered. To convey the status of what is apprehended, what stands, in this searching of experience takes both "is" and "is not." The effect is completed by the disjoined next sentence—

> But to what purpose
> Disturbing the dust on a bowl of rose-leaves
> I do not know

—which, in its sudden drop to another plane, to a distancing comment, brings out by contrast the immediacy of what goes before, while at the same time contributing directly to the sensuous presentness of the whole—the words that echo "thus" disturb, in front of us, "the dust on a bowl of rose-leaves" ("dust" and "rose-leaves" together evoke one of those co-presences of opposing associations which seem to replace words by immediate sensation, and the whole sentence, of course, relates back with various subtleties of significance to the "rose-garden" and "time" of the opening paragraph).

The re-creation of, or by, "echoes"—

> other echoes
> Inhabit the garden

(and they are echoes that recur in *Family Reunion* as well as the poems), the restoring "approach to the meaning," continues in a sustained way in the remainder of the section, concluding with, for my "unseizable,"

> Go, go, go, said the bird: human kind
> Cannot bear very much reality.

Regarding this reality we read in the next section:

> Yet the enchainment of past and future
> Woven in the weakness of the changing body,
> Protects mankind from heaven and damnation
> Which flesh cannot endure.

—The reality is sought because, by providing an absolute reference, it is to confront the spirit with the necessity of supreme decisions, ultimate choices, and so give a meaning to life; something not to be found in this "place of disaffection" (which, plainly in this poetry, the spirit cannot endure) where

> Only a flicker
> Over the strained time-ridden faces
> Distracted from distraction by distraction
> Filled with fancies and empty of meaning
> Tumid apathy with no concentration
> Men and bits of paper, whirled by the cold wind
> That blows before and after time,
> Wind in and out of unwholesome lungs
> Time before and time after.
> Eructation of unhealthy souls
> Into the faded air, the torpid
> Driven on the wind that sweeps the gloomy hills of London,
> Hampstead and Clerkenwell, Campden and Putney,
> Highgate, Primrose and Ludgate. Not here
> Not here the darkness, in this twittering world.

"Burnt Norton" develops the specifically religious note no further than the passages quoted above suggest. What is characteristic of the poem is the sustained and marvellously resourceful preoccupation that Harding examines; the preoccupation with re-creating the concept of "eternity."

"East Coker" is at the other extreme from "Burnt Norton": it is personal,[4] running even to autobiography (it is the most directly personal poem of Eliot's we have), and historical. We find ourselves (rightly or wrongly) relating its prevailing mood to Munich and the valedictory editorial of *The Criterion*. It is written, with a passing resurgence of the "echoes," those reminders of the possibility of "consciousness"—

> Whisper of running streams, and winter lightning,
> The wild thyme unseen and the wild strawberry,
> The laughter in the garden, echoed ecstasy
> Not lost, but requiring, pointing to the agony
> Of death and birth,

[4] Mr. Eliot, I think, would object to this way of putting it, but I don't know how to indicate the distinctive quality of the poem without using the adjective.

from "the waste sad time" of the concluding two lines of "Burnt Norton":

> Ridiculous the waste sad time
> Stretching before and after.

It is a discipline of meditation the note of which is:

> I said to my soul, be still, and wait without hope
> For hope would be hope for the wrong thing; wait without love
> For love would be love of the wrong thing; there is yet faith
> But the faith and the love and the hope are all in the waiting.

One section (IV) is a formal and traditional religious poem. The opening section, developing a note of family history, evokes historical time and change and the decay of the old organic culture. The last, starting with a passage of direct autobiography, develops the accompanying reflections and concludes with an inversion, *In my end is my beginning*, of the opening phrase of the whole poem.

"The Dry Salvages" hasn't the personal and historical qualities of "East Coker"; nor has it the abstract generality (for, in spite of the easy way in which we commonly oppose it to "concrete," "abstract" seems the right word) of "Burnt Norton." In its prevailing mode it lies between the other two poems. It is concerned mainly, not with the "creation of concepts," but with dissolving the habit-created "reality" of routine experience and common sense, with their protective (and constructive) anaesthesias. The genius of the poet[5] strikes

---

[5] The extraordinary vitality of language in which the specifically poetic genius is so apparent gets, of course, nothing like representative attention in this review. It is apparent everywhere in the marvellous mastery of rhythm. For a random instance of the metaphorical life take, in the following passage, the characteristic "shuttered"—a good instance of a metaphor that depends obviously on an element of *unlikeness*, of contrasting suggestion (some of the associations of "shuttered room"), for its evocative strength:

> Now the light falls
> Across the open field, leaving the deep lane
> Shuttered with branches, dark in the afternoon . . .
> ("East Coker," I)

Another characteristic manifestation of the genius is this, from the same poem:

> Dawn points, and another day
> Prepares for heat and silence.

us afresh in the opening section as, subtly and inevitably, the symbolic significance of the "river"—

> reminder
> Of what men choose to forget,

and of the sea—

> The river is within us, the sea is all about us,

emerge and are developed. The mind is made to feel how precariously it resists a lapsing away into the flux of the unknown and alien within; our environment of familiarities and certainties dissolves into a daunting indeterminateness of shifting perspectives and recessions. Human experience seems meaningless and vain in its relativity. Our sense and notion of time are unsettled into convicted arbitrariness and vanity by the evocation of times other than human and historical:

> . . . time not our time, rung by the unhurried
> Ground swell, a time
> Older than the time of chronometers, older
> Than time counted by anxious worried women
> Lying awake, calculating the future . . .

The subtlety of resource with which the sapping and unsettling are effected is complementary to the constructive subtlety analysed by Harding in "Burnt Norton."

The "points" clearly comes from the French (*poindre* and *point du jour*). It is a *trouvaille* because of the suggestion, so felicitous in the context, of the regularly punctuating recurrences of time. Another, and equally characteristic, kind of effect is the creative play on "still" in these passages from "Burnt Norton":

> After the kingfisher's wing
> Has answered light to light, and is silent, the light is still
> At the still point of the turning world.

> Only by the form, the pattern,
> Can words or music reach
> The stillness, as a Chinese jar still
> Moves perpetually in its stillness.
> Not the stillness of the violin, while the note lasts,
> Not that only . . .

Here the consummate management of stress and verse-movement is illustrated, too.

The day-to-day actuality of life in time, when we are restored to
it in the second section, the inertia of human continuance, presents
itself in its most desolating aspect as "To-morrow and to-morrow and
to-morrow"—

> There is no end, but addition: the trailing
> Consequence of further days and hours . . .

It is against this background that we have the reminder of the
"moments of happiness . . . the sudden illumination" that promise
a release from the no-meaning of time:

> I have said before
> That the past experience revived in the meaning
> Is not the experience of one life only
> But of many generations . . .

There follow, in the close of the section, new subtleties in the
symbolic use of the "river" and the "sea." The third section develops
the paradoxes of time and change, and the fourth is a formally
Christian invocation. It is in the last section that there comes the
culminating move to which the varied process of constructive exploration, with its accompaniments of negation and rejection, its
indirections and strategic envelopments, has been leading up. The
passage has behind it—is meant to be read with a full sense of its
having behind it—what has gone before in the complex whole that
begins with "Burnt Norton" (to take that as the relevant "fresh
start"). It is introduced immediately by a final preparatory negative,
an admirably and characteristically dry dismissal of the usual traffic in
the "supernormal":

> To explore the womb, or tomb, or dreams; all these are usual
> Pastimes and drugs, and features of the press:
> And always will be, some of them especially
> When there is distress of nations and perplexity
> Whether on the shores of Asia, or in the Edgware Road.
> Men's curiosity searches past and future
> And clings to that dimension. But to apprehend
> The point of intersection of the timeless
> With time, is an occupation for the saint—
> No occupation either, but something given
> And taken, in a lifetime's death in love,

> Ardour and selflessness and self-surrender.
> For most of us, there is only the unattended
> Moment, the moment in and out of time,
> The distraction fit, lost in a shaft of sunlight,
> The wild thyme unseen, or the winter lightning
> Or the waterfall, or music heard so deeply
> That it is not heard at all, but you are the music
> While the music lasts. These are only hints and guesses,
> Hints followed by guesses; and the rest
> Is prayer, observance, discipline, thought and action.
> The hint half guessed, the gift half understood, is Incarnation.
> Here the impossible union
> Of spheres of existence is actual.

For the reader who comes charged with doctrine and acceptance the term "Incarnation" thus introduced will of course have a greater potency than for another. But in that, as I have suggested at the beginning of this review, he will not, for the appreciation of the poetry and of the genius of the poet, be altogether at an advantage. This poetry, in its "re-creation of concepts," is at the same time, and inseparably, preoccupied with the nature of acceptance and belief; one might, in fact, say, adapting Harding, that to take the place of the words "acceptance" and "belief" is its essential aim.

> The hint half guessed, the gift half understood, is Incarnation.
> Here the impossible union
> Of spheres of existence is actual

—these are, no doubt, statements, to be taken as such; but though they imply a theological context, their actual context is the poem. It would be absurd to contend that the passage is not an invitation to a relating of the two contexts, but nothing is gained from the point of view of either poetry or religion by an abandonment of one context for the other, or by any approach that refuses or ignores or relaxes the peculiar discipline that the poetry is. And the critic can hardly insist too much that this affirmation which seems to strain forward out of the poem must, by the reader of the poem, be referred back to what has gone before. And he who doesn't read the poem ignores the poet's genius even while applauding. There is no reason why he shouldn't applaud too Miss Sayers' demonstrations of what the creative mind, on its mettle, can do for orthodoxy.

That the poetry seems to invite a given intellectual and doctrinal frame may be found to recommend it. But the frame is another thing (and the prose is not the poetry—Eliot himself has made some relevant observations). The genius, that of a great poet, manifests itself in a profound and acute apprehension of the difficulties of his age. Those difficulties are such that they certainly cannot be met by any simple reimposition of traditional frames. Eliot is known as professing Anglo-Catholicism and classicism; but his poetry is remarkable for the extraordinary resource, penetration and stamina with which it makes its explorations into the concrete actualities of experience below the conceptual currency; into the life that must be the *raison d'être* of any frame—while there is life at all. With all its positive aspiration and movement, it is at the same time essentially a work of radical analysis and revision, endlessly insistent in its care not to confuse the frame with the living reality, and heroic in its refusal to accept. In any case, to feel an immense indebtedness to Eliot, and to recognize the immense indebtedness of the age, one doesn't need to share his intellectually formulated conclusions, his doctrinal views, or even to be uncritical of the attitudes of his poetry.

To have gone seriously into the poetry is to have had a quickening insight into the nature of thought and language; a discipline of intelligence and sensibility calculated to promote, if any could, real vitality and precision of thought; an education intellectual, emotional and moral. From such a study it would be impossible to come away with a crudely simplifying attitude towards the problems facing the modern world, or without an enhanced consciousness of the need both for continuity and for "fresh starts." As remarked above, Eliot's work is peculiarly relevant to the stresses of our time; and this remains true, in spite of the change of fashions that set in at the beginning of the last decade. His relative distinction and his title to respect and gratitude are certainly not less than they were a dozen years ago. To him, in fact, might be adapted the tribute that he once paid to that very different genius, D. H. Lawrence; he pre-eminently has stood for the spirit in these brutal and discouraging years. And it should by now be impossible to doubt that he is among the greatest poets of the English language.

"Little Gidding"

by D. W. Harding

The opening of the poem speaks of renewed life of un-imaginable splendor, seen in promise amidst the cold decline of age. It offers no revival of life-procession; it is a springtime, "But not in time's covenant." If this "midwinter spring" has such blooms as the snow on hedges,

> Where is the summer, the unimaginable
> Zero summer?

With the sun blazing on the ice, the idea of pentecostal fire, of central importance in the poem, comes in for the first time, an intense, blinding promise of life and (as later passages show) almost unbearable.

The church of Little Gidding introduces another theme of the poem. Anchored in time and space, but for some people serving as the world's end where they can fulfil a purpose outside time and space, it gives contact with spiritual concerns through earthly and human things.

A third theme, important to the whole poem, is also stated in the first section: that the present is able to take up, and even give added meaning to, the values of the past. Here, too, the pentecostal idea comes in:

> And what the dead had no speech for, when living,
> They can tell you, being dead: the communication
> Of the dead is tongued with fire beyond the language of the living.

" 'Little Gidding.' " From *Scrutiny*, XI, No. 3 (Spring, 1943), 216-219. First published in America in *The Importance of Scrutiny* by Eric Bentley (George W. Stewart, Inc., 1948; Grove Press, 1957). Reprinted by permission of the author, F. R. Leavis, and Eric Bentley.

Section II can be regarded as the *logical* starting-point of the whole poem. It deals with the desolation of death and the futility of life for those who have had no conviction of spiritual values in their life's work. First come three sharply organized rhyming stanzas to evoke, by image and idea but without literal statement, our sense of the hopeless death of air, earth, fire, and water, seen not only as the elements of man's existence but as the means of his destruction and dismissal. The tone having been set by these stanzas, there opens a narrative passage describing the dreary bitterness in which a life of literary culture can end if it has brought no sense of spiritual values. The life presented is one, such as Mr. Eliot's own, of effort after clear speech and exact thought, and the passage amounts to a shuddering "There but for the grace of God go I." It reveals more clearly than ever the articles in *The Criterion* did, years ago, what it was in "humanism" that Mr. Eliot recoiled from so violently. What the humanist's ghost sees in his life are futility, isolation, and guilt on account of his self-assertive prowess—"Which once you took for exercise of virtue"—and the measure of aggression against others which that must bring.

The verse in this narrative passage, with its regular measure and insistent alliteration, so effective for combining the macabre with the urbane and dreary, is a way to indicate and a way to control the pressure of urgent misery and self-disgust. The motive power of this passage, as of so much of Mr. Eliot's earlier poetry, is repulsion. But in the poem as a whole the other motive force is dominant: there is a movement of feeling and conviction outwards, reaching towards what attracts. The other parts of the poem can be viewed as working out an alternative to the prospect of life presented in this narrative.

Section III sees the foundation for such an alternative in the contact with spiritual values, especially as they appear in the tradition of the past. Detachment (distinguished from indifference) allows us to use both our own past and the historical past in such a way as to draw on their present spiritual significance for us without entangling us in regressive yearning for a pattern which no longer is:

> History may be servitude,
> History may be freedom. See, now they vanish,
> The faces and places, with the self which, as it could, loved them,
> To become renewed, transfigured, in another pattern.

Once we accept the significance of the spiritual motives and intentions of the past, even the faction connected with the church and community of "Little Gidding" leaves us an inheritance; we can be at one with the whole past, including the sinning and defeated past, for its people were spiritually alive.

> All touched by a common genius,
> United in the strife which divided them.

But the humanist's fate cannot be escaped in so gentle and placid a way; a more formidable ordeal is waiting. In contrast to the leisurely meditation of section III, the fourth section is a forceful passage, close-knit with rhyme, and incisive. Its theme is the terrifying fierceness of the pentecostal experience, the dove bringing fire. This is not the fire of expiation, such as the humanist had to suffer. It is the consuming experience of love, the surrender to a spiritual principle beyond us, and the only alternative to consuming ourselves with the miserable fires of sin and error. This pentecostal ordeal must be met before the blinding promise seen in "midwinter spring" can be accepted.

The final section develops the idea that every experience is integrated with all the others, so that the fullness of exploration means a return, with better understanding, to the point where you started. The theme has already been foreshadowed in Section III, where detachment is seen to give liberation from the future as well as the past, so that neither past nor future has any fascination of a kind that could breed in us a reluctance to accept the present fully.

The tyranny of sequence and duration in life is thus reduced. Time-processes are viewed as aspects of a pattern which can be grasped in its entirety at any one of its moments:

> The moment of the rose and the moment of the yew-tree
> Are of equal duration.

One effect of this view of time and experience is to rob the moment of death of any over-significance we may have given it. For the humanist of Section II life trails off just because it can't manage to endure. For the man convinced of spiritual values life is a coherent pattern in which the ending has its due place and, because it is part of a pattern, itself leads into the beginning. An over-strong terror of death is often one expression of the fear of living, for death is one of the life-processes that seem too terrifying to be borne. In examining one means of becoming reconciled to death, Mr. Eliot can show us life, too, made bearable, unfrightening, positive, inviting:

With the drawing of this Love and the voice of this Calling

> We shall not cease from exploration
> And the end of all our exploring
> Will be to arrive where we started
> And know the place for the first time.

Here is the clearest expression of a motive force other than repression. Its dominance makes this poem—to put it very simply—far happier than most of Mr. Eliot's.

Being reconciled to death and the conditions of life restores the golden age of unfearful natural living and lets you safely, without regression, recapture the wonder and easy rightness of certain moments, especially in early childhood:

> At the source of the longest river
> The voice of the hidden waterfall
> And the children in the apple-tree
> Not know, because not looked for
> But heard, half-heard, in the stillness
> Between two waves of the sea.
> Quick now, here, now, always—
> A condition of complete simplicity
> (Costing not less than everything)

The whole of this last section suggests a serene and revitalized return from meditation to one's part in active living. It includes a reaffirmation of that concern with speech which has made up so much of Mr. Eliot's work and which could have been the bitter futility that it is for the ghostly humanist. The reaffirming passage (introduced as a simile to suggest the integrated patterning of all living experience) is an example of amazing condensation, of most comprehensive thinking given the air of leisured speech—not conversation, but the considered speech of a man talking to a small group who are going to listen for a time without replying. It is one example of the intellectual quality of this poem. In most of Mr. Eliot's poems the intellectual materials which abound are used emotionally. In much of this poem they are used intellectually, in literal statement which is to be understood literally (for instance, the opening of Section III). How such statements become poetry is a question outside the range of this review. To my mind they do, triumphantly, and for me it ranks among the major good fortunes of our time that so superb a poet is writing.

On *Ash-Wednesday*

by *Allen Tate*

Every age, as it sees itself, is peculiarly distracted: its chroniclers notoriously make too much of the variety before their own eyes. We see the variety of the past as mere turbulence within a fixed unity, and our own uniformity of the surface as the sign of a profound disunity of impulse. We have discovered that the ideas that men lived by from about the twelfth to the seventeenth century were absolute and unquestioned. The social turmoil of European history, so this argument runs, was shortsighted disagreement as to the best ways of making these deep assumptions morally good.

Although writers were judged morally, poets purveyed ready-made moralities, and no critic expected the poet to give him a brand-new system. A poem was a piece of enjoyment for minds mature enough— that is, convinced enough of a satisfactory destiny—not to demand of every scribbler a way of life.

It is beyond the scope of this discussion, and of my own competence, to attempt an appraisal of any of the more common guides to salvation, including the uncommon one of the Thirty-nine Articles, lately subscribed to by Mr. T. S. Eliot, whose six poems published under the title *Ash-Wednesday* are the occasion of this review. For it is my belief that, in a discussion of Eliot's poetry, his religious doctrines in themselves have little that commands interest. Yet it appears that his poetry, notwithstanding the amount of space it gets in critical journals, receives less discussion each year. The moral and religious attitude implicit in it has been related to the Thirty-nine Articles, and to a general intellectual position that Eliot has defended in his essays. The poetry and the prose are taken together as evidence that the author has made an inefficient adaptation to the modern environment; or at least he doesn't say anything very helpful to the American critics in their struggles to adapt themselves. It is an astonishing fact that, near as we are to a decade obsessed by "aesthetic standards," there is less discussion of poetry in a typical modern essay on that fine art than there is in Johnson's essay on Denham. Johnson's judgment is frankly moralistic; he is revolted by unsound morals; but he seldom capitulates to a moral sentiment because it flatters his own moral sense. He requires the qualities of generality, copiousness, perspicuity. He hates Milton for a regicide; but his judgment of *Paradise Lost* is as disinterested as any judgment we should find today; certainly no more crippled by historical prejudice than Mr. Eliot's own views of Milton. Yet Eliot's critics are a little less able each year to see the poetry for Westminster Abbey; the wood is all trees.

I do not pretend to know how far our social and philosophical needs justify a prejudice which may be put somewhat summarily as follows: all forms of human action, economics, politics, even poetry, and certainly industry, are legitimate modes of salvation, but the historic religious mode is illegitimate. It is sufficient here to point out that the man who expects to find salvation in the latest lyric or a well-managed factory will not only not find it there; he is not likely to find it anywhere else. If a young mind is incapable of moral philosophy, a mind without moral philosophy is incapable of understanding poetry. For poetry, of all the arts, demands a serenity of view and a settled temper of the mind, and most of all the power to detach one's own needs from the experience set forth in the poem. A moral sense so organized sets limits to human nature, and is content to observe them. But if the reader lack this moral sense, the poem will be only a body of abstractions either useful or irrelevant to that body of abstractions already forming, but of uncertain direction, in the reader's mind. This reader will see the poem chiefly as biography, and he will proceed to deduce from it a history of the poet's case, to which he will attach himself if his own case resembles it; if it doesn't, he will look for a more useful case. Either way, the poem as a specific object is ignored.

The reasoning that is being brought to bear upon Mr. Eliot's recent verse is as follows: Anglo-Catholicism would not at all satisfy me; therefore, his poetry declines under its influence. Moreover, the poetry is not "contemporary"; it doesn't solve any labor problems; it is special, personal; and it can do us no good. Now the poetry *is* special and personal in quality, which is one of its merits, but what the critics are really saying is this—that Eliot's case-history is not special at all, that it is a general scheme of possible conduct that will not do for them. To accept the poetry seems to amount to account to accepting an invitation to join the Anglican Church. For the assumption is that the poetry and the religious position are identical.

If this were so, why should not the excellence of the poetry induce writers to join the Church, in the hope of writing as well as Eliot, since the irrelevance of the Church to their own needs makes them reject the poetry? The answer is, of course, that both parts of this fallacy are common. There is an aesthetic Catholicism, and there is a communist-economic rejection of art because it is involved with the tabooed mode of salvation.

The belief is that Eliot's poetry—all other poetry—is a simple record of the responses of a personality to an environment. The belief witnesses the modern desire to judge an art scientifically, practically, industrially—according to how it works. The poetry is viewed first as a pragmatic instrument, then examined "critically" as a pragmatic result; neither stage of the approach gives us "useful" knowledge.

Now a different heredity-environment combination would give us, of mechanical necessity, a different result, a different quantity of power to do a different and perhaps better social work. Doubtless that is true. But there is something disconcerting in this simple solution to the problem when it is looked at more closely. Two vastly different records or case histories might give us, qualitatively speaking, very similar results: Baudelaire and Eliot have in common many *qualities* but *no history*. Their "results" have at least the common features of irony, humility, introspection, reverence—qualities fit only for contemplation and not for judgment according to their utility in our own conduct.

It is in this, the qualitative sense, that Eliot's recent poetry has been misunderstood. In this sense, the poetry is special, personal, of no use, and highly distinguished. But it is held to be a general formula, not distinct from the general formula that Eliot repeated when he went into the Church.

The form of the poems in *Ash-Wednesday* is lyrical and solitary, and there is almost none of the elaborate natural description and allusion that gave to *The Waste Land* a partly realistic and partly symbolic character. These six poems are a brief moment of religious experience in an age that believes religion to be a kind of defeatism and puts all its hope for man in finding the right secular order. The mixed realism and symbolism of *The Waste Land* issued in irony. The direct and lyrical method of the new poems is based upon the simpler quality of humility. The latter quality comes directly out of the former, and there is an even continuity in Eliot's work.

In *The Waste Land* the prestige of our secular faith gave to the style its special character. This faith was the hard, coherent medium through which the discredited forms of the historic cultures emerged only to be stifled; the poem is at once their vindication and the recognition of their defeat. They are defeated in fact, as a politician may be defeated by the popular vote, but their vindication consists in the critical irony that their subordinate position casts upon the modern world.

The typical scene is the seduction of the stenographer by the clerk, in "The Fire Sermon." Perhaps Mr. J. W. Krutch has not discussed this scene, but a whole generation of critics has, and from a viewpoint that Mr. Krutch has recently made popular: the seduction betrays the disillusion of the poet. The mechanical, brutal scene shows what love really is—that is to say, what it is scientifically, since "science" is truth: it is only an act of practical necessity for procreation. The telling of the story by the Greek seer Tiresias, who is chosen from a past of illusion and ignorance, permits the scene to become *a satire on the unscientific values of the past.* It was all pretense to think that love was anything but a biological necessity. The values of the past were pretty, absurd, and false; the scientific truth is both true and bitter. This is the familiar romantic dilemma, and the critics have read it into the scene from their own romantic despair.

There is no despair in the scene itself. The critics, who being in the state of mind I have described are necessarily blind to an effect of irony, have mistaken the symbols of an ironic contrast for the terms of a philosophic dilemma. It is the kind of metaphorical "logic" typical of romantic criticism since Walter Pater. Mr. Eliot knows too much about classical irony to be overwhelmed by a popular dogma in literary biology. For the seduction scene shows, not what man is, but what *for a moment* he thinks he is. In other words, the clerk stands for the secularization of the religious and qualitative values in the modern world. And the meaning of the contrast between Tiresias and the clerk is not disillusion, but irony. The scene is a masterpiece, perhaps the most profound vision that we have of modern man.

The importance of this scene as a key to the intention of *Ash-Wednesday* lies in the moral identity of humility and irony and in an important difference between them aesthetically. Humility is subjective, a quality of the moral character: it is thus general, invisible, and can only be inferred, not seen. *Irony is the visible, particular,*

and objective instance of humility. Irony is the objective quality of
an event or situation which stimulates our capacity for humility.
It is that arrangement of experience, either premediated by art or
accidentally appearing in the affairs of men, which permits to the
spectator an insight superior to that of the actor; it shows him that
the practical program, the special ambition, of the actor at that
moment is bound to fail. The humility thus derived is the self-respect
proceeding from a sense of the folly of men in their desire to dominate a natural force or a situation. The seduction scene is the picture
of modern and dominating man. The arrogance and the pride of conquest of the "small house agent's clerk" are the badge of science,
bumptious practicality, overweening secular faith. The very success
of his conquest witnesses its aimless character; it succeeds as a wheel
succeeds in turning: he can only conquer again.

His own failure to understand his position is irony, and the poet's
insight into it is humility. But for the grace of God, says the poet in
effect, there go I. This is essentially the poetic attitude, an attitude
that Eliot has been approaching with increasing purity. It is not
that his recent verse is better than that of the period ending with
The Waste Land. Actually it is less spectacular and less complex in
subject matter; for Eliot less frequently objectifies his leading emotion, humility, into irony. His new form is simple, expressive, homo-
geneous, and direct, and without the early elements of violent contrast.

There is a single ironic passage in *Ash-Wednesday,* and significantly
enough it is the first stanza of the first poem. This passage presents
objectively the poet *as he thinks himself for the moment to be.* It
establishes that humility towards his own merit which fixes the tone
of the poems that follow. And the irony has been overlooked by the
critics because they take the stanza as a literal exposition of the latest
phase of the Eliot *case history*—at a time when, in the words of Mr.
Edmund Wilson, "his psychological plight seems most depressing."
Thus, here is the vain pose of a Titan too young to be weary of
strife, but weary of it nevertheless.

> Because I do not hope to turn again
> Because I do not hope
> Because I do not hope to turn
> Desiring this man's gift and that man's scope
> I no longer strive to strive towards such things
> (Why should the aged eagle stretch it wings?)

> Why should I mourn
> The vanished power of the usual reign?

If the six poems are taken together as the focus of a specific religious emotion, the opening stanza, instead of being a naïve personal "confession," appears in the less lurid light of a highly effective technical performance. This stanza has two features that are necessary to the development of the unique imagery which distinguishes the religious emotion of *Ash-Wednesday* from any other religious poetry of our time. It is possibly the only kind of imagery that is valid for religious verse today.

The first feature is the regular yet halting rhythm, the smooth uncertainty of movement which may either proceed to greater regularity or fall away into improvisation. The second feature is the imagery itself. It is trite; it echoes two familiar passages from English poetry. But the quality to be observed is this: it is secular imagery. It sets forth a special ironic situation, but the emotion is not identified with any specific experience. The imagery is thus perfectly suited to the broken rhythm. The stanza is a device for getting the poem under way, starting from a known and general emotion, in a monotonous rhythm, for a direction which, to the reader, is unknown. The ease, the absence of surprise, with which Eliot proceeds to bring out the subject of his meditation is admirable. After some further and ironic deprecation of his worldly powers, he goes on:

> And pray to God to have mercy upon us
> And pray that I may forget
> These matters that with myself I too much discuss,
> Too much explain.

We are being told, of course, that there is to be some kind of discourse on God, or a meditation; yet the emotion is still general. The imagery is even flatter than before; it is "poetical" at all only in that special context; for it is the diction of prose. And yet, subtly and imperceptibly, the rhythm has changed; it is irregular and labored. We are being prepared for a new and sudden effect, and it comes in the first lines of the second poem:

> Lady, three white leopards sat under a juniper-tree
> In the cool of the day, having fed to satiety
> On my legs my heart my liver and that which had been contained

In the hollow round of my skull. And God said
Shall these bones live? shall these
Bones live?

From here on, in all the poems, there is constant and sudden change
of rhythm, and there is a corresponding alternation of two kinds of
imagery—the visual and tactile imagery common to all poetry, without significance in itself for any kind of experience, and the traditional religious symbols. The two orders are inextricably fused.

It is evident that Eliot has hit upon the only method now available
of using the conventional religious image in poetry. He has reduced
it from symbol to image, from abstraction to the plane of sensation.
And corresponding to this process, there are images of his own in-
vention which he almost pushes over the boundary of sensation into
abstractions, where they have the appearance of conventional symbols.[1] The passage I have quoted above is an example of this: for
the "Lady" may be a nun, or even the Virgin, or again she may be
a beautiful woman; but she is presented, through the serious tone
of the invocation, with all the solemnity of a religious figure. The
fifth poem exhibits the reverse of the process; it begins with a series
of plays on the Logos, the most rarefied of all the Christian abstractions; and it succeeds in creating the effect of immediate experience
by means of a broken and distracted rhythm:

> If the lost word is lost, if the spent word is spent
> If the unheard, unspoken
> Word is unspoken, unheard;
> Still is the unspoken word, the word unheard,
> The word without a word, the Word within
> The world and for the world . . .

[1] Mr. Yvor Winters would doubtless call this feature of the poem "pseudo-
reference."

In the Hope of

Straightening Things Out

by R. P. Blackmur

If you think of the body of Eliot's criticism as if it were completed you will see several things more or less clearly, especially if you use your official eye. It has, for example, a vital relation to all the monuments of criticism from Aristotle's *Poetics* to Wordsworth's *Preface* and Coleridge's *Biographia*. It is in vital reaction to Arnold and Pater: the fight with, and use of, Matthew Arnold is lifelong, the fight with Pater is more with his "cause" than with his judgments and is more a foray than a war. Again, Eliot's criticism "owes" a good deal to George Santayana, Rémy de Gourmont, Irving Babbitt, and Ezra Pound. Still again, there is the continuous struggle—the honest wrestling—with the work of I. A. Richards, which it seems to me becomes more intense the more the two men show that their purpose is common. And so on: any one who wished to do so could trace the literary history of Eliot's criticism to the certain conclusion that it is a part of the general literary history. No doubt this work will be done, along with another job about the relations of Eliot's mind to the Christian religion and to the classical world. In short, Eliot as critic is in pretty full and pretty specific relation with all the things a critic ought to be in relation with: the conventional elements of the traditions he supports. With us the type is less common than we believe it used to be.

But there are other accounts of Eliot's criticism which it might be more immediately valuable to take up. There is his indissoluble connection with human behavior; there is his radical allegiance to

"In the Hope of Straightening Things Out." From *The Lion and the Honeycomb* by R. P. Blackmur (New York: Harcourt, Brace & World, Inc., 1955). Copyright 1951 by Richard P. Blackmur. First published in *The Kenyon Review*, Spring, 1951. Reprinted by permission of Harcourt, Brace & World, Inc. and Methuen & Co. Ltd.

language; there is his sense of the constant pressure into the mind—into life—of forces with which neither behavior nor language can cope but to which they must respond.

What I am saying is that Eliot's great concern with order and tradition and hierarchy is in part a result of his direct and constant perception of disorder or of unknowable orders. He knows that human orders are what you do with disorder; he knows that no order remains vital which has lost its intimate contact, at some point, with the disorder or the unknown order which gave it rise. That is why his second thoughts are often better than his first: as in his successive essays on education and the classics, or on the structure of culture or society, or his successive judgments on Milton and Shelley. The *thought* perhaps remains the same but in its second form the thought has renewed and deepened contact with the underlying disorder or unknown order. I could wish, with this in mind, that Eliot might rewrite his paper on Hamlet and his problems, and above all I wish he might write once again on Baudelaire and Pascal. For it is in these three papers, which have been so attractive to so many, that he has too much *rationalized* his attitude towards disorder and the unknown order. In these papers, neither is the fog in the fir trees nor is the salt on the briar rose.

I would suppose such an account of Eliot's criticism could have major interests, but it ought not to be made without some attention to two other matters. After all, we do live and work and have part of our being in our conscious intellectual tradition; and from it we borrow much of our light. In some sense Eliot has lived all his life—in his phrase, all the damage of a lifetime—in intellectual awareness of Coleridge's "three silent revolutions in England." These revolutions were (in Saintsbury's citation from *Table Talk*): "When the professions fell off from the Church; when literature fell off from the professions; and when the press fell off from literature." I think it is the sense of the damage of these revolutions that explains both the tory polemic and the tory rebelliousness of Eliot's mind, what is excessive and what is vital about it. Though of course there are those who believe that the tory lives on, like the Auk, only in the degenerate razor-billed form, yet the truth is that the tory is a permanent nor a devolving type. And this (which is my other pertinent matter) I will illustrate in Eliot's own words from his essay on Dante.

It is when he begins to get really into the *Purgatory* and runs hard on the problem of beliefs in poetry. It is too bad, he says, that the problem has been exaggerated.

But the question of what Dante "believed" is always relevant. It would not matter, if the world were divided between those persons who are capable of taking poetry simply for what it is and those who cannot take it at all; if so, there would be no need to talk about this question to the former and no use in talking about it to the latter. But most of us are somewhat impure and apt to confuse issues: hence the justification of writing books about books, in the hope of straightening things out.

As this last phrase is the least debatable claim for criticism in general I have yet run into, so I trust it will justify the rest of these remarks. It is always the hopeless things, short of futility, that deserve justification most.

There is surely a great deal in Eliot's criticism which can stand straightening out: so many have used it to their own warp. That is why I am so much more interested in putting that criticism together than in taking it apart. This is partly because Eliot—both as poet and critic—has entered into that period of his career when those who will come after him are in reaction against him. It is much more because Eliot's criticism, despite its great influence (he has more than anybody *named* his time, just as in another way he has *undermined* his time, and in another way has *preserved* it), has lacked a general character, and has lacked even the intention of sustained generalization. His essays have been almost entirely topical: what was given him to write about or talk about for money or for a cause; and when they were not, his method has been conversational, for he begs off both the talent and the bent for abstract thought. Even when he undertakes an authoritative air, it is as a short cut, such as a man takes in a argumentative conversation; and there is likely to be a joke or a fresh start or an old memory or an obsessive image in the next sentence. No; the order in Eliot's criticism is that of conversation; and I mean this, as I think he would take it, as a pleasing characterization of a critic so deeply concerned with matters of general order, and I believe it is a characterization that leads to a sense of the unity of his mind.

In support of this characterization, there is a passage in his obituary tribute to Charles Whibley. Whibley, he wrote, had a unity of personality. He goes on:

> In attaining such unity, and indeed in attaining a *living* style, whether in prose or in verse, the practice of conversation is invaluable. Indeed, I believe that to write well it is necessary to converse a great deal. I say "converse" instead of "talk"; because I believe that there are two types of

good writers: those who talk a great deal to others, and those, perhaps less fortunate, who talk a great deal to themselves. It is two thousand and two hundred years since, that the theory was propounded that thought is conversation with oneself; all literary creation certainly springs from the habit of talking to oneself or from the habit of talking to others. Most people are unable to do either, and that is why they lead such active lives. But anyone who would write must let himself go, in one way or the other, for there are only four ways of thinking: to talk to others, or to one other, or to talk to oneself, or to talk to God.

This was written in 1931. At another place he has said that a sound poetic style was the heightened conversation of the time, and in his latest book he has the wonderful remark—for our society—that if you know an author well enough personally you do not need to read him; and indeed that whole book—*Notes Towards the Definition of Culture*—is a warm plea for conversation, and a high sample.

That is why I want to put him together, to add together some of the elements of his unity of personality which have gotten conversationally into his critical writing. It is the order of his personality that gives force to his thought about literature, and it is not a logical, nor a theoretic, nor in any way a systematic order, except as these may enter into the topical and the conversational commitments of the mind. If you do not like the idea of unity of personality, you may try the unity that goes with successive relatively stable states of a deeply held point of view. What he says reflects or illuminates either the personality or the point of view, and you can value a single essay or passage only if you can keep in mind a good many other essays and passages; no one of them, however useful in itself, reflects or illuminates enough by itself. In this he more resembles his image of Montaigne than his image of Pascal: Montaigne is a substance, Pascal a set of orders.

Eliot is a substance besieged by orders. If we want to see this clearly we have only to think of how his criticism runs parallel to his poetry. There is a gap between, but the attraction across the gap is so strong that one train often runs on the other's track. *For Lancelot Andrewes* is only understandable when *Ash-Wednesday* and "Little Gidding" have been well read, and I rather suspect that all three need, at some point but not at all points, the backward illumination of "The Hippopotamus":

> Although he seems so firm to us
> He is merely flesh and blood.

Better than that, it is the shocking characteristic of Eliot's mind that he brings his inner divergences, the division of his startling allegiances, rather nearer the surface than most minds, and sometimes they explode through. W. H. Auden put it very well when he said in *The New Yorker* that Eliot is a household with

> at least three permanent residents. First there is the archdeacon, who believes in and practices order, discipline, and good manners, social and intellectual, with a thoroughly Anglican distaste for evangelical excess. . . . And no wonder, for the poor gentleman is condemned to be domiciled with a figure of a very different stamp, a violent and passionate old peasant grandmother, who has witnessed murder, rape, pogroms, famine, flood, fire, everything; who has looked into the abyss and, unless restrained, would scream the house down. . . . Last, as if this state of affairs were not difficult enough, there is a young boy who likes to play slightly malicious jokes. The too earnest guest, who has come to interview the Reverend, is startled and bewildered by finding an apple-pie bed or being handed an explosive cigar.

Auden was right; but he should have said at once that these people live very close together, and are in either a conversational or poetic order of things one and the same: that is, in the unity of personality. There is an inner violence of this sort connected with every formidable assertion of order. It is even a type, with special emphasis on the small boy, in this country. Eliot differs from the type in the *quantity* of all three denizens of his jungle that get into his work: the quantity of behavior that gets into his language. Most get only a trace; Eliot gets the sense of the whole force. It seems to me that both the essays and the poems get their compositional strength through the succession of violent and tragic and formal gestures that inhabit them; they cry to each other, and are *together* a voice.

Let what has been said be taken as a particular preface to thinking about Eliot's criticism; here is a general preface, which has more to do with the nature of literary people (more smugly, the state of culture) than it has with Eliot. He wrote essays on the Metaphysicals and the Elizabethans with a serious running effort in mind to correct the estimation of the main course of literature, in short to correct Arnold. What happened was that the reputation of Marvell, the Herberts, Donne, Tourneur, and Webster went up. What he wrote about Jonson seems to have been less effective, for it put Jonson into the Empyrean. And it is clear that what he wrote about Milton and Shelley and Swinburne had more effect than he intended, for certain classes of people quit reading these poets at all. People went out and read or refused to read what Eliot wrote about. They also took their Eliot neat, undiluted with other reading: as with Dryden, Samuel Johnson, and the seventeenth century preachers. After the *Wasteland,* Jessie Laidlaw Weston went out of print. After *Ash-Wednesday* the Book of Common Prayer had a *literary circulation,* as if like the Bible it too had become a monument of English prose; and indeed it may be said that there sprung up a whole literary generation whose only knowledge of Christianity was what they got by reading Eliot—I mean those who did not read the prayer book. Again, Eliot rebuilt Baudelaire on the rock of original sin, which is at least firmer ground than the perfumed swoon in which Arthur Symons had left him. Again, partly because of Eliot's quotations in his own poems from Dante and partly from the effects of his long essay on him, a "cult" for Dante spread through Bloomsbury and Cape Cod. No modern critic has had anything like the effect of Eliot on the literary people. How he got it I think lies partly in the force of the unity of his personality, some of it in the small-boy part: since he has persuaded so many people who had nothing but personality that the poet had only an impersonal relation to poetry. But his effect came partly, and more properly, from the pressure of the fact that he talked about literature as such, relating it only to life, to that old peasant grandmother of his, and because he has never failed in an extraordinary skill at quotation. In any case he became a literary dictator unexampled in our times: nobody but a dictator could make Ezra Pound *il miglior fabbro* by a simple dedication.

It is worth noticing about literary dictatorships that they only partly work. There is no police power in this dictatorship, only the power communicated through fashion, and fashion is impervious to what lies in the realm of tedious or too laborious change. Eliot as dictator failed in at least three of his Orders in Council: that the poetry of our time should resemble that of Ben Jonson when it got done resembling Webster and Marvell: that it should take up the power of statement found in Dryden: that it should take stock of Dryden's poetic successor, Samuel Johnson. It is notable that Eliot has not himself been in the least able to follow his own Orders in these respects. Not only the fashion but also the possibilities were evidently against it. But with these exceptions, Eliot has created and imposed a taste—a set of habits in reading and writing—of very high standards; has set going a serious criticism with respect to these standards; and has set abroad a current of ideas which has vitalized the profession of literature by reducing the claims made for it and then eloquently affirming the claim that was left. He did a great deal on

a task which everybody wanted done but which most people concerned had doctrinal difficulties of Art for Art or of the New Knowledges to prevent them. This was the task of bringing literature back
into the common enterprise. It was the archdeacon perhaps who
thought he was up to that job; but it was a lonely job and he got the
company, if not the help, of the violent grandmother and the mali-
cious boy. Let us say that they both let him know what he had to deal
with—themselves—and also, for their own part, kept things lively.

On this sort of statement no conclusion is possible except to stop;
as a statement, it is too general. Luckily there is plenty left to tackle.
No man not a fool or a saint is out of his time—or the ideas of his
time. Eliot has been centrally concerned (we had an example above)
in what Richards has called the great plague of contemporary poets,
the relation between thought and feeling, the relation between belief
and poetry; and Richards compelled the form in which Eliot under-
took to deal with that plague. Richards took instinctively to the
twinning of science and poetry; Eliot twinned poetry and religion.
Poetry for both of them lay so to speak in the middle: the relation
between the twins raised the question of belief. Richards wanted to
get rid of belief in favor of pseudo-statement; Eliot did not want to
get rid of belief at all, certainly not for pseudo-statement, yet he knew
that poetry did not require the allegiance of belief; both the grandmother and the small boy told him that. Poetry was more like behavior than belief, and required only the kind of belief that behavior
requires. What he did was simple; he excluded thought *as such* from
poetry and said that poetry dealt with the experience or feeling of
thought which might or might not—probably *not*—have been the
poet's thought; and similarly he said that poetry dealt with belief as
the experience or feeling of belief which probably had to be, from the
nature of belief, the poet's own belief. This is not at all the same
thing as the willing suspension of disbelief; it is a positive and poetic
attitude towards belief and thought where both of them show the
aspect of behavior.

I simplify and summarize from various places in the essays. The
clearest single statements of Eliot's position may be found in the
long essays on Shakespeare and Dante, and all that he says there
strikes me as sensible so far as either poetry or criticism can be
sensible. Eliot does not need the kind of sense that is needed by
Richards' much wider and more philosophical enterprise. Eliot can
afford, what Richards cannot, to bring his divided allegiances into
the open precisely because his belief is a kind of behavior, and what

a poet and critic can afford he must certainly do: it is his one possible extravagance.

One of the reasons he can afford it, I think, is because he has tradition, a slogan word and a slogan thing, but a real word and a real thing, too. Tradition for Eliot is the weapon and resource of individual talent. Tradition is the positive cumulus, good and bad, aside from ourselves, and we have to find out for ourselves all that grandmother will not tell us of what it is. It is the hardest work to find out what is already there. It is also, when we have it, our means of protection against what we are not. It is what is impersonal in the personality, and it is the materials of which we make the form—the mask—of personality: the public shape which stands between the world and the denizens of our jungle. If we are really thinking of Eliot, and not of a doctrine which we dislike, the word tradition should always be associated with the idea of the individual and with the idea of personality. Otherwise we shall not understand Eliot's rich personal insistence on impersonality as the means of escaping the abuses of personality which pass for creation and authority and originality. As order is what we do with disorder, impersonality is what we do with personality. Eliot knows too well that what is called "personality" is the private creation out of the damage of a lifetime, just as he knows that "romanticism"—like a good meal or good whiskey—often alone avails to make private life tolerable. Personality and romanticism cross loneliness and obscure isolation. But Eliot also knows—as the result of these things too much discussed—that it is the disorder within no less than the disorder without that requires the assertion of order and tradition and impersonality.

Thus Eliot has never repudiated the three doctrines found in the early essay, "Tradition and the Individual Talent." First that, by tradition, all literature forms one order and that each new work alters the whole order. Second, the different and later remark that orthodoxy exists whether we know it or not. The first is manifesto thinking which he needed to get work done; the second is deep observation about the structure of the mind. To these let us add a third from the book on the definition of culture to the effect that orthodoxy—right thinking or belief—requires the constant prodding of fresh heresy; which seems to me to put the first two together in the form of insight as to how tradition changes.

The second doctrine in the early essay was the doctrine of the poet as the filament of platinum, as the catalyst in whose presence, unaltered, combinations of emotions and feelings take place. I believe that what this says in essence is that the poet only uses language well by getting himself out of the way; that language uses him; that language is real, the result of a tremendous historical collaboration, and that its reality is somehow objective and ought so far as is possible to be submitted to: so that oneself—let alone the reader— might "know" what has been written. It has always seemed to me that Eliot must have heard read the same words I heard in Professor Wood's course in Indian Philosophy, for the notes were very old when I heard them used: "The reality in words, gentlemen, is both superior to and anterior to any use to which you can put them." These words were accompanied by a strenuous forward rubbing of the hands on the desk, as if somehow the reality of words was being rubbed both into the grain of the wood and the grain of our minds. Eliot's filament of platinum may well have an ancestor in words spoken in Emerson Hall.

The third doctrine from the early essay was the doctrine that, so far as the writing of poetry *itself* goes, but without regard to the kind of poetry or the extra-literary value of the poetry, one age, one stage of development of mind or spirit, is as good as any other. Feeling and emotion are absolute and final, and the poet of any age has enough to go on—even more in youth than later; he has only to improve his technical processes. This is rather like Croce's rule that it is the quantity not the quality of poetic gift that differs. For Eliot then, it was only technically that the poet could improve himself —in the theoretic form of feelings—in the means of communication. I see no reason to believe that Eliot would repudiate this notion if asked, but I suspect he might for once quote Shaw approvingly, that this situation is a grand example of how youth is wasted on the young.

It is in relation to these three notions that I want to consider the idea of the objective correlative as found in the paper on *Hamlet*. These are Eliot's words: "The only way of expressing emotion in the form of art is by finding 'an objective correlative'; in other words, a set of objects, a situation, a chain of events which shall be the formula for that *particular* emotion; such that when the external facts, which terminate in sensory experience, are given, the emotion is immediately evoked." This has been called a doctrine, and as a doctrine it has flooded the language of criticism. I would rather call it an observation put into the form of a notion: that is, an observation which was the result of numberless observations about the way the individual talent acts as a catalyst between the feelings and emotions, not necessarily his own, that he wants to write about and the language, the words, in which he must write. It is a metaphorical account of how feelings and emotions get into the words with the least interference by the "mere" personality. This metaphor does not in any way presuppose success: the observation was made in the course of an examination of *Hamlet* where the material of feelings and emotions was intractable and no satisfactory "objective correlative" was found. Eliot was making a metaphor about Shakespeare's failure, as he saw it, to give the right words and actions in the right relation or sequence to express the emotions and feelings that were already there in Prince Hamlet, in his mind and the impulses of his behavior. It was not, as I see it, a metaphor about the poet's own relation to *his* feelings and emotions and to *his* language. The inconsistency with his other notions about tradition and order and behavior and belief would make the acceptance of the objective correlative as a doctrine for poetry impossible even in a mind with such deeply divided allegiances as Eliot's. If I am right, most of the arguments about this notion as doctrine or principle take place only in the critics' own minds and concern Eliot only as a mistaken development of what he wrote in his book review of Robertson on *Hamlet*. The whole situation lacks clarity.

Eliot's own doctrine of poetry, as he has united it in his personality, seems to me to turn up in what he says about the triad of feeling, emotion, and sensibility. While everybody and his dog seem able to play with the objective correlative, many people seem unable to understand the distinctions and the relations of this triad. They appear to me simple to understand by good will, though, since that commodity is short, awkward to state simply.

Feeling is the fundamental term: concrete, sensory, nuclear, somehow in experience, whether actual or imagined, always particular: the hand rubbing into the grain of the desk.

Emotion is feelings organized by a force whether within or without the psyche. Emotion is feelings, organized, generalized, abstracted, built into a form, theoretic or not. You can hurt a man's feelings, you cannot hurt a man's rage; but you can rouse his rage by hurting his feelings. And so on. A congeries of feelings may mount, may organize, may crystallize into the emotion of sexual love, or, by a twitch of phase, into the emotion of another kind of love. Art is full of particular emotions in the sense that the abstract or theoretic form, the emotion, is good only in that instance. Further, emotion in art, like life, is made sometimes out of feelings alone, sometimes out of feelings and emotions modifying each other, and sometimes out of one emotion working on another form of emotion.

> And so each venture
> Is a new beginning, a raid on the inarticulate
> With shabby equipment always deteriorating
> In the general mess of imprecision of feeling,
> Undisciplined squads of emotion.
>
> (East Coker, V)

Sensibility is the discipline of the squads, the precision of the feeling. Sensibility for the poet is his stock, his reservoir, his cumulus, of feelings and perceptions in various stages of organization; and thus represents his residual skill to respond sensibly. Sensibility is what you draw on to make fresh responses. Live language and particularly live poetry make the great objective reservoir of sensibility: the traditional and impersonal source of what power you have over your own sensibility.

It is as simple as that, and I hope it will not seem that I have twisted Eliot to my own purposes; I think I depend only on the language as it is in the dictionary and in usage and *thereby* in Eliot's own use; and I would say that that use depended on Eliot's own observation as an individual struggling with his talent—which of course differs from those of people of different education and temperament. It is the observation of the man who could write: The spirit killeth, the letter giveth life. That is the small boy's way of insisting on the genuine, but with a violence belonging to the grandmother, and in the vocabulary of the archdeacon.

But let us have some samples of other observations: all, so to speak, expert beyond experience. I think they will add up to an order dealing with disorder and with unknown order. But they will add differently for different people.

No verse is "free" for the man who does a good job. That is, there is real work in poetry like the work in carpentry.

Poetry is a mug's game. That is, no matter how hard you work, you are likely to find you have been taken in.

Crabs and sea-anemones. Imagination is full of memory. "Six ruffians seen through an open window playing cards at night at a small French railway junction where there was a water-mill, such memories may have symbolic value, but of what we cannot tell, for they come to represent depths of feeling into which we cannot peer." That is, there is the unknown order struggling towards incarnation.

Poetry may have three meanings: what is immediate, what comes by study, and what only gradually reveals itself. The incarnation in poetry is slow.

Poetry sees beneath beauty and ugliness: it sees the boredom, the horror, and the glory. The incarnation of poetry is deep.

Poetry, by its music, by its discovered rhythm—which may come from the internal combustion engine in airplane or ship or car, as well as from river and sea and garden and wind—by its music poetry may persist, its meaning may persist, after the words have stopped. Though the incarnations in poetry may last, all incarnations are only partial.

Poetry may be legitimately concerned with the actual whereas one's prose reflexions are concerned with the ideal. That is, poetry incarnates—manifests—only what of the ideal, of the ultimate real, can be found in the actual feelings and emotions.

I have been using, unexplained, the word *incarnation* in my appendages to Eliot's remarks; and I have done so deliberately as a means of getting at the important fact of Eliot's religion. Incarnation is a religious word: I am the more justified in using it here because Eliot in his book on culture has himself used it. Culture, he says, is essentially the incarnation of the religion of a people. Poetry is a part of culture when it exists and is certainly a part of what we mean by culture. The adventure of incarnating religion in poetry is what Eliot has been up to all along, and not only religion but the conditions of religion: as it is in the actual world, all that is under and aside and apart from it. It is this point of view which infects Eliot's criticism with its special problem and its final ideal. This is how he puts it in the book on culture:

> Aesthetic sensibility must be extended into spiritual perception, and spiritual perception must be extended into aesthetic sensibility and disciplined taste before we are qualified to pass judgment upon decadence or diabolism or nihilism in art. To judge a work of art by artistic or by religious standards, to judge a religion by religious or artistic standards should come in the end to the same thing: though it is an end at which no individual can arrive.

It seems to me that here is the feeling, the emotion, the justified impulse; it is how Eliot's mind works; it is how he finds it necessary to dine with the Opposition. Poetry is an act of incarnation; but the incarnation is slow, deep, partial, and only of what has been made actual. The real and the ideal are far off.

But what a relief it is not to have too many claims made for poetry. What a relief to read a man who never cheats on poetry, who insists on the gift and the genuine, but who is to this extent not fooled: He knows that poetry is only a part of the enterprise. He knows that poetry saves nobody, but shows rather the actual world from which to be saved or not, and shows also what has been made actual, what has been actually felt, of aspiration. A living language, for Eliot, has to do with a living religion. All this is in a remark which ought still to have the widest circulation: "Poetry is a superior form of amusement."

Mr. Eliot's Solid Merit

by *Ezra Pound*

[. . .] If Mr. Eliot weren't head and shoulders above the rank of the organized pifflers, and if he didn't amply deserve his position as recognized head of English literary criticism I would not be wasting time, typing ribbon, and postage, to discuss his limitations at all. [. . .]

The great division in all—I mean ALL, contemporary writing—is between that little that has been written by men who had "clarified their intentions"; who were writing with the *sole aim* of registering and communicating truth or their desire, and the overwhelming bulk composed of the consciously dishonest *and* of those whose writing has been affected at second or tenth remove by economic pressure, economic temptation, economic flattery, by "if you can only put it in the right form," and so on.

If I, who have always been a banned writer, have discovered this, what is to be said of the "victors"?

There are all degrees and nuances, from the poor damn'd cringing hacks who fluff up and say they only write what they think, and that "of course they will answer questions" and then slink off beaten and silent when you ask them anything vital, or who boast that their expression is not limited, merely that they never WANT to run further than the end of the chain, up through the men who aren't for sale but get a little, just a little, good-natured or perhaps only humorous.

Eliot has paid the penalty of success. Given the amount of that success, the low degree of penalty paid is proof of his solid capacity. [. . .]

"Mr. Eliot's Solid Merit" (abridged). From *Polite Essays* by Ezra Pound (London: Faber & Faber Ltd., 1937; New York: New Directions, 1940). Copyright 1937, 1940 by Ezra Pound. First published in the *New English Weekly*, July 12, 1934. Reprinted by permission of Dorothy Pound ("Committee for Ezra Pound") and New Directions, publishers. All rights reserved.

The merit of an author who can pass through the dolorous gates and write *in* the "citta dolente" among the unstill gibberings of "fellow reviewers," "fellow employees," doddering geezers doing notes on sixty volumes a week, etc. AND still enrich formal discussion of heterogeneous writers with paragraphs as clear, and deep, as incisive and as subtle as the delicate incision of a great surgeon, IS A POSITIVE MERIT, and it is a merit whereto Eliot almost ALONE in our time could lay any valid or sustainable claim.

After recovering from one's irritation that an intelligent man CAN, or could a decade ago, still write about Ben Jonson in language that could get into the *Times Literary Supplement;* after recovering from the quite foolish and misguided attempt to read through the *Selected Essays,* one can by using it properly, i.e., as grazing ground in unhurried (if any) hours, find critical estimates so just that one must believe them a permanent part of literary valuation. They may not be of commanding immediacy, but that is all that could possibly be urged against them with any justice, and IMMEDIACY itself is of small use unless it be built up on a mass of EXACT knowledge, *almost* any detail of which might be stigmatized as "minor." [. . .]

> Even if we except also Jonson and Chapman, those two were notably erudite, and were notably men who *incorporated their erudition into their sensibility*: their mode of feeling was directly and freshly altered by their reading and thought. In Chapman especially there is a direct sensuous apprehension of thought, or a recreation of thought into feeling. . . .
>
> Two most powerful poets of the century. . . . Each of these men performed certain poetic functions so magnificently well that the magnitude of the effect concealed the absence of others.
>
> A philosophical theory which has entered into poetry is established, for its truth or *falsity in one* sense ceases to matter, and its truth in *another* sense is proved.
>
> Interesting to speculate whether it is not a misfortune that two of the greatest masters of diction in our language, Milton and Dryden, triumph with a dazzling disregard of the soul.
>
> Sometimes tell us to "look into our hearts and write." But that is not looking deep enough; Racine or Donne looked into a good deal more than the heart. One must look into the cerebral cortex, the nervous system, and the digestive tracts.

The first and second of these quotations (italics mine) are certainly NOT dead academicism, pedantry or mere university lecturing. They are criticism definitely shot at NEW creation; at a reinvigoration of writing.

If the third, fourth, and fifth excite discussion it is fundamental discussion; it is not aimed at producing a quiet reposing place for anonymities (as, for example, the editor X. R.), who slouch crumbling and cringing on the margin of the literature that provides them with beef and board; who have never signed a statement or answered a question in their twenty or forty years of trading, maggots living in or on the mental activity of their time but contributing nothing to its life, parasites in the strict sense, with the mind one would suppose inherent in parasitic condition.

That any man should have been able to get past such obstacle and to print paragraphs of literary criticism that will last as long as there are any students of English poetry concerned with just opinion and assessment of its value, is not only reason for tribute and compliment, but is an inalienable certificate of the native and persistent vigor and acuteness of an author's perceptions. [. . .]

The Style of the Master

by William Empson

I do not propose here to try to judge or define the achievement of Eliot; indeed I feel, like most other verse writers of my generation, that I do not know for certain how much of my own mind
he invented, let alone how much of it is a reaction against him or
indeed a consequence of misreading him. He has a very penetrating
influence, perhaps not unlike an east wind. All I can do here is to
put down a few reminiscences of him, from meetings much rarer
than I should have wished; stories greatly in his favor, I should have
thought, but you never know how people will take things. And when
I have tried out my Eliot anecdotes on an anti-Eliot man he has
generally taken them as confirming his worst impressions. So they
are not designed to flatter (and, by the way, I could not have invented them) but they are a sort of witness to the Eliot legend, and
it deserves to be recorded.

My most impressive memory is of walking up Kingsway with him
after some lunch, probably about 1930, when finding myself alone
with the great man I felt it opportune to raise a practical question
which had been giving me a little anxiety. "Do you really think it
necessary, Mr. Eliot," I broke out, "as you said in the preface to the
Pound anthology, for a poet to write verse at least every week?" He
was preparing to cross into Russell Square, eyeing the traffic both
ways, and we were dodging it as his slow reply proceeded. "I had in
mind Pound when I wrote that passage" began the deep sad voice,
and there was a considerable pause. "Taking the question in general,
I should say, in the case of many poets, that the most important
thing for them to do . . . is to write as little as possible." The grav-

"The Style of the Master." From *T. S. Eliot,* edited by March and Tambimuttu
(London: Editions Poetry, 1948; Chicago: Henry Regnery Co., 1949). Reprinted by
permission of Henry Regnery Co.

ity of the last phrase was so pure as to give it an almost lyrical quality. A reader may be tempted to suppose that this was a snub or at least a joke, but I still do not believe it was; and at the time it seemed to me not only very wise but a very satisfactory answer. He had taken quite a weight off my mind.

In this kind of case, indeed, the Johnsonian pessimism was quite practical and helpful; one felt more doubtful about it in generalizations. There was a party (I forget everybody else in the room) where Eliot broke into some chatter about a letter being misunderstood. "Ah, letters," he said, rather as if they were some rare kind of bird, "I had to look into the question of letters at one time. I found that the mistake . . . that most people make . . . about letters, is that after writing their letters, carefully, they go out, and look for a pillar-box. I found that it is very much better, after giving one's attention to composing the letter, to . . . pop it into the fire." This kind of thing was a little unnerving, because one did not know how tragically it ought to be taken; it was clearly not to be regarded as a flippancy. There was some dinner including a very charming diplomat's wife, who remarked to Eliot that she too was very fond of reading. She didn't get much time, but she was always reading in bed, biographies and things. "With pen in hand?" inquired Mr. Eliot, in a voice which contrived to form a question without leaving its lowest note of gloom. There was a rather fluttered disclaimer, and he went on "It is the chief penalty of becoming a professional literary man that one can no longer read anything with pleasure." This went down very well, but it struck me that the Johnsonian manner requires more gusto as a contrast to the pessimism; perhaps after all, looking back, a mistaken complaint, because if untruth is all that is required to justify this sort of quip it was surely quite untrue that he no longer read anything with pleasure.

My earliest memory of Eliot, speaking of untruth, was when he came to Cambridge to give the Clark lectures and was prepared to receive undergraduates after breakfast on Thursdays; this was in the middle 1920's. At the first of these very awed gatherings someone asked him what he thought of Proust. "I have not read Proust" was the deliberate reply. How the conversation was picked up again is beyond conjecture, but no one cared to plumb into the motives of his abstinence. It was felt to be a rather impressive trait in this powerful character. Next week a new member of the group asked what he thought of the translation of Proust by Scott Moncrieff, and Eliot delivered a very weighty, and rather long, tribute to that work. It was not enough, he said, to say that it was better than the original in many single passages; it was his impression that the translation was at no point inferior to the original (which, to be sure, was often careless French), either in accuracy of detail or in the general impression of the whole. We were startled by so much loquacity from the silent master rather than by any disagreement with what he had said before; in fact it seemed quite clear to me what Eliot meant—he did not consider he had "read" a book unless he had written copious notes about it and so on. I no longer feel sure that this was what he meant, but I am still quite sure that he was not merely lying to impress the children; maybe at the earlier meeting he hadn't bothered to listen to what they were saying.

Perhaps the most charming case of his peculiar note, which however wilful in its sadness is always at the opposite pole to malice, occurred when a younger poet (long ago now) published a diary. I should explain that Eliot takes cheese rather seriously; as witness the pronouncement, "I find I can no longer travel except where there is a native cheese. I am therefore bounded, northwards by Yorkshire . . ." and the rest of the points of the compass were all tidy (I think he had a fair run to the south) but I no longer know what they were. The younger poet had recorded a lunch with "Tom," at which he had told Tom that simplicity and deep feeling were what made good poetry, and Tom had agreed. This was what gave his own poetry its lasting qualities ("Yes" Tom had said) and on the other hand gave good reason to prophesy that the poetry of Tom would only prove a passing fashion. Tom had seemed much struck by this. Meeting Eliot not long after I made bold to mention the diary, and he said "Very interesting. He did me the kindness . . . to send me the proofs . . . of the parts . . . concerning myself." I said I hoped he had found them all right. His manner became a trifle severe, though not noticeably sadder. "I found it necessary," he said, "in the interests of truth, to correct the name of the cheese."

Murder in the Cathedral

by John Peter

At a time when *The Cocktail Party* is being hailed on all sides as a masterpiece and when *The Family Reunion* (now seen as a predecessor to that masterpiece) is likely to receive from critics rather more than its due, it should be salutary to pause for a while, to cast our attention back to Eliot's first play. Already there are those who will contend that Eliot's dramatic productions to date reveal a steady growth in power and capacity, that *The Cocktail Party* is as much an improvement on *The Family Reunion* as was that play on *Murder in the Cathedral*. It would be pleasant to accept this view of the plays; is it, however, possible? I have elsewhere given some of my reasons for finding the two later plays unsatisfactory.[1] Here I should like, by way of filling out an incomplete statement and balancing it, to consider what claims *Murder in the Cathedral* may have on our attention. Broadly speaking it is mainly to the verse and to the inner coherence of the two later plays that I think a critic is obliged to object, though it seems to me that a more "philosophical" critic might also find grounds for objection in Eliot's handling of his psychological and his religious content. I take it that to such a critic the manner in which the two subjects, Religion and Psychology, tend to replace and proscribe one another would be clear enough. He would recall Freud's stigmatizing of religion as "the universal obsessional neurosis," he would appreciate the difficulties involved in trying to reconcile the Christian idea of "free will" with the psychologist's notion of "conditioning," and he might well question whether in Eliot's later plays any reconciliation of the

[1] *Scrutiny* XVI, 3 and XVII, 1.

two had really been effected. To juxtapose is, after all, not necessarily
to reconcile. *Murder in the Cathedral* is a play which, from its nature, does not exclude the possibility of faults of this kind: the verse
might be poor, the general dramatic conception might be contra-
dictory, Thomas' motivation might be inconsistent with his religious
significance. It seems to me worthwhile considering the play in some
detail to see whether any of these criticisms can be levelled against
it. Initially, however, I wish briefly to compare *Murder in the Cathedral* not with Eliot's later plays but with an earlier play that offers
itself very readily for the purpose: I mean Tennyson's *Becket*. Almost
all the differences between these two poetic dramas could be called
fundamental and significant: the principal difference is not even
merely one of merit, or only consequentially so. It is the difference
between, on the one hand, a derivative, circumscribing tradition, a
tradition that has been revived without being invested with any
new validity, and on the other a tradition which, for all its modesty,
is altogether the opposite of this. The tradition from which Tennyson derives is of course the Elizabethan—the *point de départ* also
for the poetic dramas of Blake, Keats, Shelley, Wordsworth and,
frequently, Byron. To anyone who has studied even the best plays
by these poets this is at once a cause for some misgivings. Recollect-
ing the constricting bonds of precedent which crippled his predecessors, the stiffness and awkwardness of their plots and their all but
shameless verbal reminiscences from Shakespeare, it is somewhat
warily and without undue expectation that we approach Tennyson's
play. It isn't long before these misgivings are confirmed.

Becket (and we can say this quite categorically) tries to be Shakespearian and fails in the attempt even more conspicuously than did
its predecessors. At first it is merely the resemblances to an Elizabethan drama that one notices. The convention of five acts is used;
there is a developed "story"; and there is a subplot worked up between Henry and Rosamund. Following his model Tennyson introduces approximations to the *Romeo and Juliet* nurse type (Margery)
and to the type of Macduff's small son (Geoffrey). His imitation ex-
tends even to the more wearisome characteristics of the original:

> Fitzurse: Why—why, my lord, I follow'd—follow'd one—
> Becket: And then what follows? Let me follow thee.

These are no doubt peripheral considerations: *mala prohibita* rather
mala in se: prohibited, we might add, rather because of what they
indicate than because of what they are. Coming closer to the sub-

stantial differences between Tennyson's and Eliot's plays we come closer, too, to the reason why (despite praise of it in 1910 as "the greatest literary drama of recent years") *Becket* cannot be held to make any very serious claim to our attention.

In Eliot's play, as we shall presently be observing, the idea of Thomas suffering a "tragic" death (in the sense that, say, the death of Othello is tragic) is nowhere entertained. The "murder" in the cathedral is not primarily a murder at all, but an act of redemption. Tennyson, by contrast, has the gross outlines of Shakespearian tragedy so deeply imprinted upon his mind that he tends continually to reproduce them. Now if this were all there might be little to which one could reasonably object; but we can see that Tennyson is never comfortable in his emulation and that indeed the Shakespearian pattern is, for his purposes, unsuitable and irksome—especially in the defective sense in which he understands it. As he sees it tragedy clearly implies no more than the fall from eminence, and usually the death, of some prominent figure, this fall being directly attributable to the hero's own imperfections. This admissible but transparently over-simplified interpretation of plays like *Macbeth, Lear,* and *Othello* was of course generally accepted in the Laureate's time and no doubt, as is the way with Laureates, he saw no reason for trying to transcend it. Applied to his own *Becket,* however, the conception gives rise to a persistent anomaly which he has nowhere contrived to solve: I mean the anomaly that arises when, having taken as his chief character a saint, he is thereafter obliged to endow the saint with a variety of gratuitous imperfections to account for his "fall." The result of this is to invest the whole play with an uncertainty that can hardly be condoned. If on the one hand Becket is proud and wilful then he is no martyr, and his death is merely a personal downfall with no significantly religious implications. If on the other hand he is a saint, it is fatal, or at least absurd, to represent him as impetuous and headstrong, constantly requiring the restraining admonitions of John of Salisbury, plainly his superior in most respects. The poet can't eat his cake and have it too. I suppose one may charitably suppose that, without the fatal magnetism attracting him towards the Elizabethans, his Victorian piety might, for all its stiffness, here and there have struck out a genuine spark. But as things are this doesn't happen. We are left with an impression of central inadequacy around which the several lesser weaknesses— diction, characterization and so on—cumulatively group themselves. The play, especially when set beside *Murder in the Cathedral,* needs a lax criterion even to be called unimpressive.

Eliot, who read it before setting to work on his own play, admits that he found it bad.[2] One can assume that he also found it something of an object lesson, helping him to a clearer idea of what he himself wished to do. Tennyson for instance, by beginning with Becket still in his office of Chancellor and friendly to the King, is forced to effect the change to a refractory and estranged Archbishop during the playing; and he does it far too abruptly. Eliot on the other hand— inclining as always towards the dramatic unities—rings up the curtain on a Thomas who is already mature, already on the eve of his martyrdom. Skilful references block in the background of his past (the Tempters of course are very useful here) and the play takes on that tautness and pregnancy that comes with condensation. But this is not all. There is no John of Salisbury in Eliot's play and no call for Becket to refer to him in Tennyson's terms: "My other self, Who like my conscience never lets me be." For Eliot places Becket's conscience within himself, treating the Tempters merely as objectified facets of his own consciousness; and it is through this modification that he avoids all Tennyson's uncertainty. All thought of a fall-through-arrogance, all idea of a struggle at the character level, is accordingly bypassed and the dramatic effect is placed beyond all this, in a context of religious redemption. King Henry himself does not appear, being present only indirectly. The whole technique aims at such simplification and intensification as will give appropriate weight to the issues which are discussed: that is, the persistent conflict between the values of the world and those of the spirit,[3] and the idea of the redemption of sin through the death of a martyr. There are no superfluities; and at the same time there is a texture which will bear examination in some detail.

Like a Greek tragedy (it is of course the classical rather than the Elizabethan tradition we are conscious of here) *Murder in the Cathedral* opens with a Chorus, that of the Women of Canterbury, and like its Attic counterpart this Chorus gives us a good deal of information (often simply atmospheric) about the time, place and potentiality of the scene. The immediate emphasis is obvious:

[2] So far as I know he has not had occasion to say so publicly.

[3] Even the title seems to have been chosen so as to summarize this. Just so, in "Sweeney among the Nightingales," a detective-story atmosphere ("The silent man in mocha brown," "the lady in the cape") is used to contrast with the picture of Agamemnon's "stiff dishonoured shroud," the mere contrast being enough to suggest a criticism of our modern attitude to murder: that it is no more than an entertainment, with none of the spiritual significance given to it in the *Oresteia*.

> Are we drawn by danger? Is it knowledge of safety, that draws our feet
> Towards the cathedral?

Eliot uses a seeming contradiction, characteristically, to stress the point. We are aware at once that there is both danger and safety and that, though hyperconscious of it, the Chorus know that the danger only indirectly threatens them:

> There is no danger
> For us.

Twice that "For us" is emphasized at the beginning of a line. The Chorus are, as they realize, initially present merely as lookers-on, and they put an accent on their own impotence by speaking of their limbs and organs as if these were out of their direct control:

> Some presage of an act
> Which our eyes are compelled to witness, has forced our feet
> Towards the cathedral.

Quickly the atmosphere of strain and expectancy is evoked, a simple visual image being loaded from line to line with more and more significance:

> While the labourer kicks off a muddy boot and stretches his hand to
>   the fire,
> The New Year waits, destiny waits for the coming.
> Who has stretched out his hand to the fire and remembered the Saints
>   at All Hallows,
> Remembered the martyrs and saints who wait? and who shall
> Stretch out his hand to the fire, and deny his master?

The interest shifts from Peter (and Christ) to Thomas. We are told that he "was always kind to his people" but that "it would not be well if he should return." It becomes clear that it is he whom the danger threatens, and with this knowledge the position of the Chorus also clarifies.

This is ambivalent. At one level they are simply the poor women of Canterbury, immersed in the routine of existence and fearful lest anything should occur to upset that routine. Like the laborer, with his orthopterous color adaptation—he who

> bends to his piece of earth, earth-colour, his own colour,
> Preferring to pass unobserved—

their dominant effort is to efface themselves, to avoid being implicated in any of the dangerous actions that are afoot. To appreciate this fully is crucial, for it is in terms of the modification of this attitude that much of the significance of the "murder" is embodied and expressed. Salvation is presented, not by talking about it (as Tennyson would have been tempted to do), but by showing it operating in the consciousness of the Chorus. Again, at another level the Chorus are transparently more than their natural selves. Like their equivalents in Greek tragedy they present a commentary on the action, anticipating and preparing us for developments, rousing us, with their passionate dithyrambs, to participate wholeheartedly in the emotional crises that arise, supplying the action with a background that is, like music, all-pervasive. It is in this their second rôle, that they now speak of moments of vision "in a shaft of sunlight," and it is as a flash of clairvoyance that their concluding apostrophe to December is made:

> Shall the Son of Man be born again in the litter of scorn?

For all its specificity this is wide enough to suggest Thomas' own case and the redemption which is in turn to be made possible through his martyrdom. Meantime the Chorus fall silent—and the priests enter upon the stage.

> For us, the poor, there is no action,
> But only to wait and to witness—

Almost at once the tone of the verse alters. This is emphasized by the First Priest's use of two of the Chorus' lines. Significantly the next line ("He who was always kind to his people") is not given and the Priests fall to discussing the temporal effects of Thomas' return with the Messenger, speaking of his pride and isolation, gladly affirming that he will tell them what to do. Although there is nothing in the treatment of these characters that can be called positively unsympathetic I think this section is designed (apart from its content of sheer information) to show that it is not primarily for such at these that Thomas will die. The Priests are presented almost as sanguine and certainly as being capable of taking care of themselves. Their piety is tinged with worldliness and they have just enough cynicism to quote loosely from Ecclesiastes, abandoning themselves to a flux of external events:

> For good or ill, let the wheel turn.
> The wheel has been still, these seven years, and no good.
> For ill or good, let the wheel turn.
> For who knows the end of good or evil?
> Until the grinders cease
> And the door shall be shut in the street,
> And all the daughters of music shall be brought low.

This fidgety acceptance of mere change is what the Chorus criticize as they burst out again. They know that the present is perilous and a change for the better hardly possible:

> Ill the wind, ill the time, uncertain the profit, certain the danger.

They appeal to Thomas to return to France:

> You come with applause, you come with rejoicing, but you come bringing death into Canterbury:
> A doom on the house, a doom on yourself, a doom on the world.

To them, who "do not wish anything to happen," who go on "living and partly living," Thomas' return seems only to presage catastrophe. From the first touch of sharpness ("our brains unskinned like the layers of an onion") the intensity of their foreboding increases. When they have done the Second Priest reproves them for croaking (isn't the image rather a comment on him than on them?) "like frogs in the treetops." Thomas, entering, reproves him in turn.

> Peace. And let them be, in their exaltation.
> They speak better than they know, and beyond your understanding.
> They know and do not know, what it is to act or suffer.
> They know and do not know, that action is suffering
> And suffering is action. Neither does the agent suffer
> Nor the patient act. But both are fixed
> In an eternal action, an eternal patience
> To which all must consent that it may be willed
> And which all must suffer that they may will it,

That the pattern may subsist, for the pattern is the action
And the suffering, that the wheel may turn and still
Be forever still.

This is likely to be dismissed as Eliotese, and perhaps with some reason; but its extreme inexplicitness is not arbitrary, the passage being kept deliberately ambiguous so as to allow it to be spoken again a little later on, in a completely different context, without seeming irrelevant there. Some "small matters" are discussed, and Thomas speaks of his crossing and its political significance. And at this stage the drama enters upon a new development.

The material facts of the situation being now adequately suggested, Eliot's next endeavor is equally to present the repercussions that they occasion in Thomas' mind. The remainder of Part One anatomizes these. It does so, not by the Elizabethan technique of soliloquy, but through a technique of allegory or "objectification" that is close to that of the *autos* of Calderón.[4] It is typical of Eliot's early meticulousness (it has worn thin since, I fear) that he should mark the transition from one reality to another unambiguously: here he does it by modulating into those terse, Anglo-Saxon-like locutions which are so often in other modern poets merely idiosyncratic. Hearing the articles begin to disappear from Thomas' speech ("End will be simple, sudden, God-given") and the abruptness with which he concludes ("All things prepare the event. Watch.") we are prepared for the First Tempter, who enters at once. He is the first of three whom, since their temptations offer only temporal and material benefits, Thomas finds it fairly easy to resist. They are introduced, these three, partly to show the truth of Thomas' saying,

The impossible is still temptation,

partly to give added point to what succeeds. Apart perhaps from

4 Compare A. A. Parker, *The Allegorical Drama of Calderón* (1942), pp. 82-3: "They [the *autos*] deal with another plane of experience; they are conceptual and not realistic. . . . This is what Calderón in his later *autos* so often does: he allows his audience to follow each step in the train of thought as it emerges from the mind of a character on the stage actually conceiving the action before their eyes. The importance of this strikingly original device lies in the remarkable clarity it can give to an abstract theme. . . ." I suppose we may recall what Harry says in *The Family Reunion:*

> Perhaps my life has only been a dream
> Dreamt through me by the minds of others.

noting the poet's bizarre use of a piece of the "Musgrave Ritual" [5] we need not pause here, and can proceed straight on to the Fourth Tempter.

This figure, entering with congratulations, is at once endowed with a more sinister import. "Who are you?" Thomas asks. "I expected Three visitors, not four." Meeting with no answer more definite than "I always precede expectation" he is forced to ask the question again, and again it is evaded. The two figures hold the stage, fencing cautiously with their speeches. Thomas is suspicious, we can see, and especially since the Tempter seems to be stating a case with which he can only agree. Counselled to

> Think of pilgrims, standing in line
> Before the glittering jewelled shrine

he replies (the line is something of an actor's crux):

> I have thought of these things.

The Tempter confuses him with obliquities; then his advice becomes more explicit:

> Seek the way of martyrdom, make yourself the lowest
> On earth, to be high in heaven.
> And see far off below you, where the gulf is fixed,
> Your persecutors, in timeless torment,
> Parched passion, beyond expiation.

With this Thomas begins to see what the temptation involves—an ultimate vitiation of his martyrdom through hypocrisy—and he bursts out:

> No!
> Who are you, tempting with my own desires?
> . . . Others offered real goods, worthless
> But real. You only offer
> Dreams to damnation.

With the Tempter's retort ("You have often dreamt them") and Thomas' appeals to be freed from the damning weight of his pride,

[5] From Conan Doyle's story. I see this has been noted before, in 1948, by Grover Smith, in *Notes and Queries*, CXCIII, 431-2.

we reach the point—and it should in its way be almost blood-curdling—where the Tempter quotes to Thomas his own words, noticed earlier, concerning action and suffering. This is a device, classic in its neatness, to show how inextricably mixed Thomas' motives still remain. We see that the whole dialogue with the Tempters has symbolized an introspective process and that hitherto it has been a comparatively simple matter for the Archbishop to isolate and discard the temptations. Now, however, tempter and tempted begin to merge: Thomas is no longer the vigilant custodian over his own mind but is involved in a tangle of motives which he himself can only partially analyze. Some external prompting is needed to help him to his final decision.

This comes, as it must, from the Chorus, his spiritual dependents. After an orchestral *crescendo* of doubt and confusion Thomas is shown listening to their clamorous hopelessness, image after image in their speech suggesting a single sense of horror and panic—

> The forms take shape in the dark air:
> Puss-purr of leopard, footfall of padding bear,
> Palm-pat of nodding ape, square hyaena waiting,
> For laughter, laughter, laughter. The Lords of Hell are here.

It is with their last cry, identifying their own balance between hope and despair with his decision, that resolution breaks across his hesitancy.

> O Thomas Archbishop, save us, save us, save yourself that we may be saved;
> Destroy yourself and we are destroyed.

> THOMAS
> Now is my way clear, now is the meaning plain. . . .

The archbishop, to sum up the matter tersely, here realizes that his decision is no longer personal or autonomous. Involved in the integrity with which he must resolve the struggle in his own conscience is the spiritual integrity and well-being of the whole Church, and particularly of these members of it, the women of Canterbury. But a terse comment like this does scant justice to the dramatic effectiveness at this point. That the poet should have been able to make his point so clearly, while at the same time, through the dexterous orchestration of the voices, preserving all the dramatic suspense latent in the situation, is surely very much to his credit. Such a marriage of poetry and excitement is a far cry from the verbose inertia of the poetic dramas of the nineteenth century.

Thomas, his decision achieved, is allowed to address the audience briefly—a gesture which is useful, technically, to suggest that the act is now nearly over, and also to anticipate the direct address of the Interlude. Then the curtain falls on a scene of resignation in which we see him finally and irrevocably dedicated to what he now recognizes as his necessary purpose:

> Now my good Angel, whom God appoints
> To be my guardian, hover over the swords' points.

It is a good curtain and indeed, to my mind, a good act. Few verse dramatists of the past three hundred years have been able to see so clearly what is to be done; fewer still have been able, having perceived it, so precisely and effectively to get it done. There is a touch here that English drama has not felt since the Jacobeans—something which, when one remembers the precedents Eliot had in 1935, is all the more remarkable.

Perhaps what follows can be treated rather more summarily. It will be appreciated that by the end of Part I the play is (at least in one, not unimportant respect) virtually over. The fundamental implications of the action are now clearly before us and it only remains for the dramatist to show the factual outcome of the inward struggle, Thomas' visible death and its effects. I do not think Eliot had any illusions about the danger of a drop in emotional temperature at this point, for it seems to be deliberately that he introduces several technical developments in the central and later sections of the play. One feels that these are diversionary, designed to hold an interest which might otherwise begin to flag. It is only at the end, when a richer and less explicit significance returns to the action, that the *ars* is once more *celare artem*.

In the Interlude that separates Parts I and II the approach is at once bold and appropriate. What could be more natural than to find an Archbishop preaching a sermon, and what better form could there be in which to cast Thomas' generalized animadversions on his own fate? The short scene is enriched by a sort of duality, Thomas' remarks being addressed both to a hypothetical congregation (the Chorus) and to the audience. He speaks very pregnantly, and the sermon is something of a model for its kind. It insists briefly upon

two appropriate fundamentals—the Christian conceptions of rejoic-
ing" and "peace"—and then as briefly analyzes the idea of martyrdom. The relevance of the Crucifixion to any other martyrdom (a
relevance implicit throughout the play) here becomes specific:

> Just as we rejoice and mourn at once, in the Birth and in the Passion of
> Our Lord; so also, in a smaller figure, we both rejoice and mourn in the
> death of martyrs,

and the whole meaning of Thomas' self-abnegation, and of the fourth
temptation, is explained:

> A Christian martyrdom is never an accident, for Saints are not made by
> accident. Still less is a Christian martyrdom the effect of a man's will to
> become a Saint, as a man by willing and contriving may become a ruler
> of men. A martyrdom is always the design of God, for His love of men, to
> warn them and to lead them, to bring them back to His ways. . . .

After this a personal note is allowed to sound and the scene comes
naturally to its conclusion.

Part II again opens with a Chorus. It is a comparatively intricate
and sensuous one and may in fact owe something (if only rhyth-
mically) to the very different Chorus which opens Act II of *Becket*.[6]
First there is the sea-bird "driven inland," convenient symbol for the
Chorus themselves, driven from their wonted security. Then the mention of a Spring which is more like death than birth—an image for
the context generally. There is insistence on the unnaturalness of
the season:

> Longer and [a faint shock] darker the day,

and on the sense of potentiality:

> But a wind is stored up in the East.

The crow and the owl supply two quick contributory effects and

---

[6] Is it the wind of the dawn that I hear in the pine overhead?
No; but the voice of the deep as it hollows the cliffs of the land.
Is there a voice coming up with the voice of the deep from the strand,
One coming up with a song in the flush of the glimmering red?
Love that is born of the deep coming up with the sun from the sea. . . .
The dialectic development here is superficially rather like Eliot's choruses.

then the imagery modulates into religious writing proper, reaching something of a climax of appositeness in

And war among men defiles the world, but death in the Lord renews it.

We hear again the note of anxiety and mistrust—

Between Christmas and Easter what work shall be done? [7]

—and this is reinforced through a passage where the flashing, colorful glimpses of Spring are seen as if against a backdrop of shadow and apprehension. The Chorus hover in anticipation:

We wait, and the time is short
But waiting is long.

There follows a stylized passage, alternative to the Chorus (though not necessarily, one may suppose), to denote the passage of time, the Priests chanting phrases from the Epistles for the feast days of St. Stephen, St. John the Apostle and the Holy Innocents: perhaps it is enough to mention that these are appropriate to the situation at this point, even the "very babes" of the last being relevant, a glance at the Chorus. Then, with the interest fixed upon the fourth day after Christmas, as yet unsanctified, the Knights enter for the first time and Thomas' arraignment takes place.

What follows now is dramatic enough in itself not to need any tricks of presentation to set it off, and the dramatist has wisely allowed the murder to take place quite simply. Two Choruses crammed with horrifying imagery from the animal world punctuate the action, the diction ultimately shading off into what is almost inarticulate, sheer atmospheric music. So we proceed to the *fortissimo* of the penultimate chorus, which accompanies the actual killing. This is, in the vulgar sense, the climax of events and it is accordingly right that the chorus should be simplified and hyperbolical. When it is over the Knights advance to the front of the stage and address the audience directly.

Their address is again a form of diversion to hold our interest, and there has been a tendency to dismiss it as irrelevant, or as irritating, like the last act of *Saint Joan*. I should agree that the rationaliza-

---

[7] A good example of the ambiguity through which the dramatist achieves many of his effects. The period may mean no more than "winter"; or it may refer to the life-span of Christ; or, more obviously, it may simply anticipate Thomas' death.

tions of the Knights are usually neither effective nor convincing in the Theatre (though I think a good director could make them so), but the dramatist's purpose in inserting them at this point should not be overlooked. There are at least three useful ends that they serve. First, simply, the previous relationship between the audience and these actors is disturbed, and this helps to disguise the faint touch of anticlimax which, just here, might otherwise be felt. Secondly, and more substantially, the Knights' speeches are useful for stressing the irreconcilable divergence between the values of the world, their values, and the values to which Thomas appeals. Nothing could underline Thomas' sincerity more effectively than the First Knight's speech, with its recurrent clichés—"fair play," "under dog," "sense of honour" and so on. By such dexterous touches as the Second Knight's "I am going to appeal not to your emotions but to your reason" our mistrust is subtly evoked: the more so since the whole force of what has gone before has been to show us how shallow these material arguments are. The whole clash has been between two orders, one spiritual, one temporal, and we are invited to see how impossible it has been to find a compromise between them. Consequently when the Second Knight sneers at Thomas for saying that the two were incompatible ("God knows why") our sympathies are all, where they should be, with Thomas. The silent advocate pleads best. Obviously on the plane of personal conviction the Knights are, and should be represented as, sincere; obviously too there are degrees of sincerity which are beyond them. The subtlest plea, that of the Fourth Knight, is perhaps too ingenious even to be called sincere on the personal level; yet it, too, is already negatived by what we have seen taking place in the episode of the Fourth Tempter.[8] The whole force of this apparently unnecessary *divertissement* is to show us a broad clash of values and an inherent, conquering strength in those which (as to the Knights) usually seem most nebulous, the values of religion. Thirdly, and more simply

---

[8] It may be unfortunate that the parallel between the four Knights and the four Tempters should be so clear in the play, and that in the theatre the doubling of these parts should make it so much clearer. For if we press the correspondence between the fourth Tempter and the fourth Knight too far we may even be tempted to infer that Thomas' death *is* a form of suicide, that it is partly his own consciousness (as represented by this Tempter-Knight) that wills his death. Perverse or not, I have heard this argued. It is true in a sense of course, as we can see from his behavior when he commands the priests to fling open the cathedral doors; but his "will" to die is a matter of dedication and not a form of self-destruction, from whatever motives, as the Knight suggests. The part of the Knight and the part of the Tempter in fact, though often assigned to one actor, are antithetic, not parallel.

again, these speeches allow a pause to intervene between the initial re-
vulsion heard in the penultimate chorus and the tone of reconciliation
that we find in the last.

When the Knights have finished speaking we feel sincerity in a
deeper dimension return with a perceptible jar. I feel the treatment
here, in the conclusion of the play, is again reminiscent of a technique in music. The "theme" is stated quite fully in the speeches
given to the Priests and there is, in what we might call a ratiocinative
or factual sense, little to add to these. They explain how the Church
has been strengthened by Thomas' death, how the Knights are now
reduced to spiritual suicide, how the Archbishop is already translated.
But there is, as yet, no emotional resolution. As in a musical recapitu-
lation this material is immediately restated, this time with all the
emphasis the poet can command. For the first time the Chorus become resonantly affirmative, sounding their praises of God in terms
of a creation that has lost all its frightfulness. The purring leopard,
the patting ape, the waiting hyaena—these are all recognized as necessary units in an intelligible whole, implying, even by negation, the
glory of God:

> The darkness declares the glory of light.

Once again a martyr has redeemed the crumbling faith, and now the
Chorus are free to sing triumphantly of what before they had so
dreaded, the act of death and the benison proceeding from it. Gradually, in strong, liturgical rhythms, they build a firm statement of this
recaptured peace, their voices falling silent upon an epitome which
cannot but be impressive to whoever has attended the full meaning of
the play:

> Blessed Thomas, pray for us.

Only by virtue of his martyrdom is Thomas "Blessed"; only by virtue
of what they had flinched from do the women of Canterbury now
have an intermediary and advocate with God. There is true Aristote-
lian *peripeteia* here; and there is also, it seems to me, an economy
and vitality of statement that no modern reader or theatre-goer should
be encouraged to neglect.

We return, then, to the questions posed at the outset. If we agree
(and I think there may be a number of people reading this prepared

to agree) that in *The Family Reunion* and *The Cocktail Party* the verse is often disappointing, the basic conception of the drama not always coherent and the treatment of the material sometimes inept, should we be inclined to level similar criticisms at *Murder in the Cathedral*?

For myself I do not see how we can do this in any way that is likely to be convincing. The motivation of Thomas and the reactions of the Chorus, two things which between them make up the real kernel of the play, are effectively coherent throughout, and such "psychology" as is implied in the scene with the Tempters, far from militating against the religious implications of the theme, serves only to confirm them. That is, the play is lucid and integral in a way in which, to me, the later plays are not. At the same time, as I have tried to suggest, it would be unfair to think of it as possessing merely the lucidity of shallowness. Let us by all means acknowledge that it is not *King Lear*, not by a long chalk, and that in comparison with an achievement of that order it must appear rather premeditatedly lucid, almost scant; we have still to concede that such lucidity is in any case preferable to the arch mystifications of *The Cocktail Party*, like the toasts to Lavinia's aunt and Reilly's song. Reilly's behavior throughout the first scene of that play has apparently been widely objected to, and it is well-known that his creator has countered by referring to the *Alcestis* of Euripides. I am not sure that I understand this rebuttal but to the extent that I do it seems to me a very odd one, and rather frivolous. For to take up an attitude like that, as if anything implausible or unintelligible can be justified merely by producing a remote or unsuspected (and unilluminating) "source" for it—to claim that sort of license—is surely to reduce literature to the level of acrostic, and criticism to code-breaking. It is true that, like so much of Eliot's work, *Murder in the Cathedral*, with its snatch from the Musgrave Ritual, is not absolutely free of affectation of this kind. Is it, however, in any sense as cryptic a performance as the later play? Again, though the part of Becket is often badly acted, with a swallowed sob at the end of his sermon, and though the mimed slaying always seems to occasion some embarrassment, the play does as a rule come across in the theatre as a balanced and dramatic experience. This *The Family Reunion* certainly *doesn't* do. Nor, to my mind, even with adroit actors and actresses, is *The Cocktail Party* much more successful in the theatre, where (to offer only two of the possible objections) the meagreness of the verse is quite as evident as it is on the page, and the Noel Cowardish slickness of a good deal of the dialogue even more disturbing. As to the verse in *Murder in the Cathedral,* the Chorus have only to be properly rehearsed, and allowed to speak in unison instead of singly, for its virtues to become apparent. I have only seen—I should say heard—this done once, but I think there can be no question that it is the right procedure. When it *is* done the play becomes positively gripping.

It might of course be argued that these particular comparisons are not to be pressed too vehemently. In writing of *The Cocktail Party* I had occasion to observe that the problems confronting the dramatist when he wrote that play were much more knotty than those involved in writing *Murder in the Cathedral,* and in a recent article Eliot has made his own admissions to this effect.[9] Essentially, I suppose, a comparison between the early play and its successors resolves itself into a comparison between what is in many ways a limited work of art, one which proposes to itself a few specific objectives and succeeds admirably with them, and two more ambitious if less successful undertakings. In these circumstances it is easy enough to accuse the critic of comparing chalk with cheese, or to throw Browning at him:

> Ah, but a man's reach should exceed his grasp,
> Or what's a Heaven for?

But this is also to demand from him an incontinence which it should be beyond his willingness to grant: he should know that his concern is not with approximations and potentialities, but only with what has been positively and demonstrably achieved. Eliot himself, in his early essay on *Hamlet,* was disposed to place that play well below both *Coriolanus* and *Antony and Cleopatra* on the grounds that there was more actual achievement in the two later plays. I cannot agree with this judgment but I am in sympathy with the attitude underlying it, and with the critic's deliberate reservation of his attention to those qualities in the plays which he felt he could really demonstrate to be there. Without some such admission, tacit or not, of his fallibility in dealing with the more nebulous issues that a work of art may raise it seems to me a commentator is simply abdicating his responsibilities, turning from poised and substantiated judgments to mere conjectures and assertions. And soon he finds himself discussing, not a particular piece of writing, but a ghost—the play as it may possibly have existed in the dramatist's mind or the novel as it might have appeared had it not

[9] See *The Atlantic Monthly* for February, 1951.

been written as it is. That in terms of actual achievement *The Cocktail Party* is a better play than *Murder in the Cathedral* does not seem to me a defensible proposition. Certainly I believe that until it *is* defended, and cogently and convincingly, we should suspect that it is only our wish to accept it that allows us to find it acceptable.

The Cocktail Party

by Denis Donoghue

In *The Cocktail Party,* as in *The Family Reunion* and *The Waste Land,* Eliot proceeds by indirection; he ensnares his audience. To speak of his work in these terms is to point again to the conditions which govern communication between the contemporary artist and society. The characteristic situation of the modern artist, which—despite boredom and natural misgivings—we continue to describe as "alienation," is particularly relevant to an important problem in modern drama. Professor Fergusson has observed that as theatre poetry was freed from the limitations of modern realism it lost its public status as a mirror of human nature. Obey's *Noah* and Eliot's *Murder in the Cathedral* throw light upon contemporary experience, but only obliquely or at best "experimentally": the literal moorings are cut and the resulting drama is arbitrary in its own way. Each poetic dramatist discerns his own beautiful, consistent, and intelligible dramatic idea while the formless public, looking the other way, is engrossed in the commercially profitable shadows on the cave-wall.[1] In his more recent plays Eliot moves his drama into a position between the audience and the cave-wall, hoping to entice them into drama, into consciousness, and perhaps even into spirituality by offering them something which from a distance looks familiar. The trap is prepared with great subtlety.

The surface of the play exhibits all the features of a comedy of manners; the silly party, the urban setting, the trivial chatter:

"The Cocktail Party" (abridged). From *The Third Voice* by Denis Donoghue (Princeton: Princeton University Press, 1959; Oxford University Press, 1959). Copyright 1959 by Princeton University Press. Reprinted by permission of the author, Princeton University Press, and Oxford University Press.

[1] Francis Fergusson, *The Idea of a Theater* (Princeton University Press, 1949), p. 224.

JULIA: I've always wanted to go to California. Do tell us what you were
    doing in California.
CELIA: Making a film.
PETER: Trying to make a film.
JULIA: Oh, what film was it? I wonder if I've seen it.[2]

The opening scene is packed with ironic stichomythia of this kind,
brought over from *A Game of Chess* and comically flattened for the
occasion. The inner rhetoric[3] of the play operates on a "high" comic
surface: Lady Klootz, the tigers, monkeys, and decayed mansions help
to pacify and control an audience temperamentally suspicious of Holi-
ness. [. . .]

In 1939 Eliot expressed the view that "we have today a culture
which is mainly negative, but which, so far as it is positive, is still
Christian." [4] Accordingly, the surface appearance of *The Cocktail
Party* is designed to offer no obstacle to the "negative" aspects of our
culture; on the other hand, the texture of the play is such that its
images, to the extent to which they are "positive," are Christian. A
typical passage reads:

> JULIA: Celia! I see you've had the same inspiration
>   That I had. Edward must be fed.
>   He's under such a strain. We must keep his strength up.
>   Edward! Don't you realise how lucky you are
>   To have *two* Good Samaritans? I never heard of that before.
> EDWARD: The man who fell among thieves was luckier than I:
>   He was left at an inn.
> JULIA: Edward, how ungrateful.
>   What's in that saucepan?
> CELIA: Nobody knows.
> EDWARD: It's something that Alex came and prepared for me.
>   He *would* do it. Three Good Samaritans.
>   I forgot all about it.

The images in this passage are either domestic or Christian. The
Christian images arise naturally from the situation; the domestic de-

---

[2] *The Cocktail Party* (London: Faber & Faber, Ltd., 1950), pp. 13-14.

[3] "By rhetoric is meant: the art of persuasion, properly in the service of dialectic or poetic; improperly, in the service of argument on the pleading of a
'cause'; in *extremis* or in abstraction, the art of persuasion uprooted, flourished
for its own sake, with its eye on itself." R. P. Blackmur, "The Lion and the
Honeycomb," *Hudson Review*, III, No. 4 (Winter, 1951), 487.

[4] *The Idea of a Christian Society* (London: Faber & Faber, Ltd., 1939), p. 13.

tails are so authentic that they support the Christian references without strain. It is easy to understand, therefore, why a secular or neutral audience would accept such a passage, complete with its Christian terms. The same audience would react strongly to the dogmatic and "exclusive" fervor of *The Man Born to be King*.

The Cocktail Party is a realistic play, up to a point. Shortly after it was completed, Eliot said that he had intended to create characters whose drawing-room behavior was generally correct. The most important thing was that people should speak in character.[5] These remarks were designed primarily to enable the playwright to evade the invitation to "explain" his play, and they are accurate only to a limited extent. The truth is that while *The Cocktail Party* contains no Chorus, no Eumenides, and no lyrical duets, the anti-realistic forces which it utilizes are deployed with much greater success than in *The Family Reunion*. These forces are necessary because *The Cocktail Party* invokes the "real" world only to the extent required to engage the attenton of its audience. [. . .] The play invites us, not to observe an interesting slice of life or to suspend our disbelief, but to *envisage* a society in which the vague humanistic motion of our lives would be changed into something more dynamic, more "real" and simultaneously more Christian. "Motion" becomes "action." Eliot's basic procedure is one by which neutral images are exposed to the danger of picking up a specifically Christian infection. The mood is optative.

Perhaps the most convenient way to illustrate this procedure is by examining those images which seem to dominate the text. Fortunately, part of the work has been well done for us by William Arrowsmith, who points out that the main images in the play are those involving sight and blindness, light and dark. He quotes Julia's "I must have left my glasses here, / And I simply can't see a thing without them"; Reilly's "And me bein' the One Eyed Riley"; Celia's "I can see you at last as a human being," followed by Edward's "I'm completely in the dark"; Julia's "You must have learned to look at people, Peter / . . . That is, when you're not concerned with yourself / But just being an eye." There are several other instances including the following little sequence:

JULIA: Well, my dears, I shall see you very soon.
EDWARD: When shall we see you?
JULIA: Did I say you'd see me?[6]

[5] *World Review* (November, 1949), pp. 20-21.
[6] "English Verse Drama II: *The Cocktail Party*," *Hudson Review*, Autumn, 1950, p. 413.

The imagery of vision is undoubtedly of great importance in *The Cocktail Party* and it bears an obvious relation to the theme of spiritual progress. But these images operate still more positively, and to an end of great moment.

Eliot introduces the visual reference quite casually, by cliché:

EDWARD: And what is the use of all your analysis
    If I am to remain always lost in the dark?
UNIDENTIFIED GUEST: There is certainly no purpose in remaining in the dark
    Except long enough to clear from the mind
    The illusion of having ever been in the light.

Clearly, the second reference is sharper than the first. The Unidentified Guest, catching the cliché, holds it, literally, to the light. The pattern is similar to that in which Harry's consciousness, in *The Family Reunion,* reveals that the illusions of Wishwood are no longer tenable. In *The Cocktail Party* we have begun to be aware of the pattern by the middle of the second act. Gradually, while we are wondering how to interpret it, Eliot unobtrusively leads it in a positively religious direction. A late stage in the process is reached when Julia speaks of Celia to Sir Henry Harcourt-Reilly:

    Oh yes, she will go far. And we know where she is going.
    But what do we know of the terrors of the journey?
    You and I don't know the process by which the human is
    Transhumanised: what do we know
    Of the kind of suffering they must undergo
    On the way of illumination?

The formality of the last phrase is enough to differentiate it even from the imagery of vision which has gone before; we feel that the phrase marks a definite stage in the action. It is at this point that Eliot brings into play the Christian potentialities of the imagery. The source may well be St. John of the Cross, whose writings have influenced Eliot's thought since before *Sweeney Agonistes.* We cite the following passage from *The Illuminative Way*: "This tranquillity and repose in God is not all darkness to the soul, as the dark night is, but rather tranquillity and repose in the divine light and in a new knowledge of God, whereby the mind, most sweetly tranquil, is raised to a divine light." [7] It is characteristic of *The Cocktail Party* that its main images

[7] *The Mystical Doctrine of St. John of the Cross,* Introduction by R. H. J. Steuart, S. J. (London: Sheed & Ward, Ltd., 1948), p. 159.

are (a) common and domestic, (b) employed in the *Alcestis* of Euripides, from which Eliot's play is remotely derived, and (c) capable of
supporting a heavy spiritual burden, when required, without shelving
mundane reference. We note that Eliot uses such words as "atone,"
"salvation," and "crucifixion" only in the later stages of the play. Their
relatively unobtrusive use has been made possible by the continuous
activity of the imagery of vision, sometimes employed as simple denota-
tion, at other times it harnesses latent implications of spiritual
vision. [. . .]

Let us revert to Mr. Arrowsmith's conclusions. He asks: if, by metaphor, Edward and Lavinia and, at first, Peter and Celia, are said to
be "completely in the dark," what are we to make of Harcourt-Reilly
and Julia and Alex? Julia is said to be "very observant," but she cannot, she says, see without her glasses, and one lens is missing: she is,
in effect, blind in one eye. In response to her query Harcourt-Reilly
sings, "And me bein' the One Eyed Riley." We have, then, three metaphorical conditions: blindness, half-sight, and full vision, exhibited,
respectively, by Edward, Julia, and Celia. The meaning of Julia's half
sight is to be found in a proverb: In the kingdom of the blind the one-
eyed man is king. The intent of the imagery, then, is: the parable of a
moral miracle, the recovery of sight. [. . .][8]

In "Poetry and Drama" Eliot declared that while he was inclined to
go to a Greek dramatist for the theme of *The Cocktail Party* he determined to do so merely as a point of departure, and to conceal the
source as much as possible. The source, he revealed, was the *Alcestis*
of Euripides. As an instance of his debt to Euripides he cited the Un-
invited Guest in *The Cocktail Party*; the eccentric behavior of this
character, his apparently intemperate habits, and his tendency to
burst into song, are modeled on the behavior of Heracles in the
Alcestis.[9]

The relationship between Heracles and Sir Henry Harcourt-Reilly
is the only point of contact which Eliot has specified between the
two plays. Professor Heilman has elucidated several other affinities.[10]
Few of these are amenable to paraphrase, but we may bear in mind
that Eliot's treatment of his source is characterized by the assign-
ment of a spiritual dimension to physical facts. On some occasions
the relation between the two plays is quite straightforward: compare,
for example, the Servant's

[8] Arrowsmith, *supra*, footnote 6, pp. 413-14.
[9] T. S. Eliot, *Selected Prose* (Baltimore: Penguin Books, 1953), p. 83.
[10] Robert B. Heilman, "*Alcestis* and *The Cocktail Party*," *Comparative Literature*, V, No. 2 (Spring, 1953), 106.

> Noble she is, indeed; but Admetus is blind to that.
> He will see the truth when he has lost her . . .[11]

with Edward's

> And yet I want her back.
> And I *must* get her back, to find out what happened
> During the five years that we've been married.
> I must find out who she is, to find out who I am.

More significantly, the physical death of Alcestis has, as its counterpart in *The Cocktail Party*, the spiritual death of broken marriage.
Alcestis simply affirms:

> I have chosen that you should live rather than I,
> because I honour you as my husband . . .

The corresponding passage in *The Cocktail Party* presents, in Lavinia,
a much more complex motive:

> I thought that there might be some way out for you
> If I went away. I thought if I died
> To you, I who had been only a ghost to you,
> You might be able to find the road back
> To a time when you were real—for you must have been real
> At some time or other, before you ever knew me:
> Perhaps only when you were a child.

Even the presentation of Sir Henry Harcourt-Reilly is similarly
complicated. In the *Alcestis* Heracles's roistering has ancient sanction.
David Paul has pointed out that as a traditional Satyric figure in
Greek drama Heracles always appears in a state of Bacchic jollity; in
the *Alcestis* this helps to reduce him from a status which would otherwise be too big for the play.[12] Some students of *The Cocktail Party*,
recalling the role of Heracles, have presented Sir Henry Harcourt-
Reilly as a "whole Christian man," [13] but this seems a mistake. Indeed,

[11] *Alcestis and Other Plays*, trans. Philip Vellacott (Baltimore: Penguin Books,
1953), p. 126.
[12] David Paul, "Euripides and Mr. Eliot," *Twentieth Century*, CLII, No. 906
(August, 1952), 175.
[13] Arrowsmith, *supra*, p. 421.

Eliot appears to have planned that this character would overflow every realistic vessel, however large, however "whole." He never allows us to forget the symbolic function of Reilly, Julia, and Alex as Guardians; to keep this in our minds he makes it impossible for us to accept them on realistic terms. Professor Heilman, sensing this point, argues that in the presentation of Reilly Eliot has successfully created an air, if not of the inexplicable, at least of the unexplained, of the quizzically irregular, of the elusive. From the time when Reilly tells Edward that he has started "a train of events / Beyond your control," and Lavinia confesses, "Yet something, or somebody, compelled me to come," we are given continual impressions of mysterious forces in action. Psychiatry takes on a spiritual dimension.[14] Indeed, while the *dramatis personae* do not include the Eumenides, one feels that they are hovering in the wings, driving Celia as they have already driven Harry.

This sense of the elusive, the unexplained, applies not only to Reilly but also to Julia and Alex. Alex serves as the conventional bore but the emphasis on his "guardianship" is so strong that we soon ignore the slight extent to which, on realistic terms, he is credible.[15] Similarly with Julia: Edward calls her "a dreadful old woman," and yet we are often warned that she has a degree of perception far beyond our expectations. For example, Alex's "She never misses anything unless she wants to"; Celia's "There isn't much that Julia doesn't know"; Edward's "Julia is certainly observant"; Peter's "You never miss anything"; Alex's "Julia is really a mine of information"; and Lavinia's "Nothing less than the truth could deceive Julia."

Does it not seem, then, that Eliot *wants* his audience to be confused by these three, Reilly, Julia, and Alex?[16] He wants us to feel that in some rather intangible way they stand apart from the realistically credible Edward, Lavinia, Celia, and Peter. This prepares us for their emergence as the spiritual Guardians which they have been from the very beginning. The form is that of "qualitative progression," the "confusion" leading eventually and joyously to clarity.[17]

Julia is, of course, the leader, the power to which Reilly is witness and servant. Her emergence in this role at a late stage in the play,

[14] Heilman, *supra*, footnote 11, p. 115.

[15] Heidi Heimann ["A God in Three Disguises," *World Review* (June, 1950), 66-69] suggests a perceptive comparison between Eliot's Alex, Cocteau's Heurtebise in *Orphée*, and the stranger who advises Joseph in Thomas Mann's *The Young Joseph*.

[16] *World Review* (November, 1949), 66-69.

[17] Kenneth Burke, *Counterstatement* (2d ed.; Los Altos, California: Hermes Publications, 1953), pp. 124-25.

after her early exhibition as the silly old woman of Mayfair, is a
comic *tour de force.* Near the end of the play we realize that as director
of the plot she is the latest, and not the least interesting, of those
stage managers who have directed dramatic affairs at intervals since
Aristophanes. Her place in this rich tradition is secure: she stands
beside the hero of *The Acharnians* with Prospero of *The Tempest* and
the Duke of *Measure for Measure.*

No simple correlation between *Alcestis* and *The Cocktail Party,* in
respect of character or incident, is possible without severe distortion
of both plays. Even in the case of Reilly there is strong evidence in
favor of Professor Heilman's view that he represents not just Heracles
but Heracles-plus-Pheres. Certainly, Pheres's function as truth-teller
has been taken over by Reilly: the interview between Reilly and
Edward in the first act is the counterpart of Pheres's denunciation of
his son over the coffin of Alcestis.

One of the most interesting and disturbing relations between the
two plays arises in the treatment of Alcestis herself. Eliot, while
combining Heracles and Pheres into the single role of Reilly, takes
precisely the opposite course in the case of Alcestis, whom he divides
into two characters. As the wife who died and was eventually restored
to her husband she becomes Lavinia, the life of whose marriage is
saved. As the woman who sacrificed herself she becomes Celia, who is
finally martyred in Kinkanja. We would speculate somewhat on this
division.

In the course of *The Cocktail Party* Reilly says that those who choose
the lift of common routine

> Learn to avoid excessive expectation,
> Become tolerant of themselves and others,
> Giving and taking in the usual actions
> What there is to give and take. They do not repine
> And are contented with the morning that separates
> And with the evening that brings together
> For casual talk before the fire
> Two people who know that they do not understand each other,
> Breeding children whom they do not understand
> And who will never understand them.

Lionel Trilling has rebuked Eliot for this passage. There is, he argues,
no reference to the pain which is an essential and not an accidental

part of the life of the common routine. There is no reference to the principles, the ethical discipline, by which the ordinary life is governed: all is habit. There is no reference to the possibility of either joy or glory. This failure to conceive the actuality of the life of common routine is typical, he maintains, of modern literature since ᴛolstoi. Eliot's representation of the two "ways" of life, that of the ommon routine and that of the "terrifying journey" to beatitude, xemplifies how we are drawn to the violence of extremity. We imgine, with nothing in between, the dull not-being of life and the ntense not-being of death; but we do not imagine Being, we do not imagine that it can be a joy.[18]

Many students of *The Cocktail Party* have had a similar feeling that the play does scant justice to the virtues which make the routine life possible. But to remain too long with this idea is to run the risk of missing a related but much more crucial point. The real defect of *The Cocktail Party*, a defect of drama and rhetoric, is that it presents the life of the common routine and the way of beatitude as totally discrete.

Professor Fergusson would detect a similar representation in Eliot's plays as early as *Murder in the Cathedral*. In an Introduction to Pascal's *Pensées* Eliot observed: "Capital, for instance, is (Pascal's) analysis of the *three orders:* the order of nature, the order of mind, and the order of charity. These three are *discontinuous;* the higher is not implicit in the lower as in an evolutionary doctrine it would be." This notion, Professor Fergusson remarks, throws light upon *Murder in the Cathedral*. In that play the Chorus is in the order of nature; the Tempters, Priests, and Knights are in the order of the mind; and Thomas is in the order of charity. Only the first two orders are visible to us, unless by Grace; but it is only in the order of charity that Thomas and the form and meaning of the play are finally intelligible. In the play this order is represented by the doctrine which Thomas expounds in the sermon, and also by the abstract scheme of the play: the three orders and the three parts of society. Hence the mechanical feel of the play as a whole. The dramatis personae are as discontinuous from each other and from any common world as the parts of a machine, but they move according to the will of God as that is presented by the theological doctrine. It is an idea of the divine plan, and of human experience as subject to it, which comes from modern idealism:

[18] Lionel Trilling, *The Opposing Self* (London: Secker and Warburg, 1955), pp. 145-47. Similarly, D. W. Harding [*Kenyon Review*, xviii, No. 3 (Summer, 1956)] refuses to accept Edward and Lavinia as properly representing "the human condition."

one is reminded of Leibniz's preestablished harmony. In *Murder in the Cathedral*, therefore, the whole realm of experience represented by the *Purgatorio*, the direct sense of moral change and of analogies which make the three orders not completely discontinuous—in short, the appeal to a real world which all may in some sense perceive—is lacking.[19]

The lack is concealed to some extent in *Murder in the Cathedral* by the fact that the play, almost by definition, transcends the everyday world of experience or presents it only in circumscribed conditions. But *The Cocktail Party*, confronting such a world, shows that here Eliot has been unable to make the analogical act, or at least to render it dramatically convincing.

In this context it is important to establish the precise meaning of "analogy." Father William Lynch has proposed a description of its intent and in doing so has taken *The Cocktail Party* as his text. He describes the analogical as that habit of perception which sees that different levels of being are also somehow one and can therefore be associated in the same image, in a single act of perception. And, by contrast, we describe as "manichean" all those habits of perception which dispose levels of being in a relationship of hostility or complete separation. For example, every attitude is manichean which—like Forgael in *The Shadowy Waters*—despises the finite, the limited, the human levels of reality, which does not believe in the limited image as a path to the infinite. *The Cocktail Party* is a case in point; it presents two solutions to two human desires. One woman is sent back to "the monotony and dross of her human love"; the other takes up a divine and contemplative vocation. But, says Father Lynch, the psychiatrist speaks truer than he knows in saying that each is but another form of loneliness. One is tempted to wish that it had been the same woman who had taken up the two vocations in the one act and the one situation. Eliot's breakdown of the matter into two situations and two salvations represents a failure and an evasion.[20]

"Monotony and dross of her human love" is too strong as a description of the relationship between Edward and Lavinia at the end of the play; it is not as bad at that; but the larger point remains.[21]

[19] Fergusson, *supra*, footnote 1, p. 217.

[20] William Lynch, S. J., "Theology and the Imagination," *Thought*, Spring, 1954, pp. 66, 67, and 84.

[21] Compare an earlier statement by Walter Stein ["After the Cocktails," *Essays in Criticism*, III, No. 1 (January, 1953), 90, 94]: "The disturbing conclusion emerges that *The Cocktail Party* is (unwittingly) a Manichean play. Its vision is not that of a humane . . . Christianity, but approximates to a radical division of existence

When Eliot divided Alcestis into two separate characters and presented each as representative of a certain way of life, he could hardly avoid writing a manichean play.

It may be argued, of course, that whether the rhetorical tendency of *The Cocktail Party* is manichean or not is critically irrelevant, that the only valid criteria are formal and dramatic. We would argue, however, that the reasons which have been advanced to prove the play manichean are precisely those which cause the play to be, as drama, defective.

Father Lynch in another context has complained that *The Cocktail Party* is "filled with a contempt for reality," [22] by which he means, we infer, that we are made to feel that the activities of Edward and Lavinia, the life of the common routine, are negligible. There is no doubt, of course, as to the supreme importance of Celia's progress, the "way of illumination," but we feel that the two fables are unrelated, that they are not encompassed by an analogical act which guarantees the value of each. This is true. But if, having considered the Christian objections to this separation, we now concentrate on its purely dramatic issues, we find that the separation results in a gross discontinuity of tone. We feel a serious incongruity between the tone of the Edward-Lavinia story and that of Celia's martyrdom. The contrast between *The Cocktail Party* and *Alcestis* is instructive at this point; Professor Heilman has noted that *Alcestis* is, in our terms, romantic comedy, but its distinction lies in its daring flirtation with tragedy.[23] *Alcestis* encompasses this range of tone because its characters are sufficiently large, which means sufficiently complex; the frequent changes of tone are sanctioned by the manysidedness of Admetus, Alcestis, and Heracles. Furthermore, the changes of tone in *Alcestis* do not result in the isolation of any of the characters; none of them is restricted by association with a single tone. In *The Cocktail Party*, on the other hand. Eliot, in addition to dissolving Alcestis into two separate characters, isolates these characters still further by a crude disparity of tone. Lavinia and Celia, and all they represent, are from the beginning of

into spheres of Nature and Transcendence sharply separated from each other: where the transcendent is not merely approached by way of the disclosure of Nature's essential imperfections, but finally embraced as a—literally—*desperate* alternative to the latter's graceless essence."

See also Malcolm Mackenzie Ross, "Fixed Stars and Living Motion in Poetry." *Thought* (Autumn, 1952), 384-85.

[22] William Lynch, S. J., "Confusion in our Theater," *Thought* (Autumn, 1951), 351.

[23] Heilman, *supra*, footnote 11, p. 106.

the play separate. Their worlds are thrust apart even farther by the
fact that Eliot's treatment of Lavinia's activities is for the most part
comic while his presentation of Celia's history is in a tone of high
seriousness.

On the whole, the characteristic tone of the episodes involving
Lavinia seems just right. Given that the play is a comedy of manners,
the tone of these parts is finely adjusted. Professor Wimsatt has observed that the homely, patched-up felicity of Edward and Lavinia,
glimpsed as they prepare for the second cocktail party, is beyond
cavil convincing and just dramatic enough to be interesting.[24] The
real fault occurs, he maintains, in the treatment of Celia's martyrdom.
At the pinnacle, in the third act, one part of the double outcome,
that of martyrdom, aims at something the opposite of tame and shoots
too far wide of the comic into the sensationally gruesome:

> It would seem that she must have been crucified
> Very near an ant-hill.

Something more muted, unheroic, was surely required; perhaps a
phalanx of abstractions might have served the purpose best, lines such
as the later

> . . . hunger, damp, exposure,
> Bowel trouble, and the fear of lions.

The occasion seemed to demand that the specific, the detailed exhibition of death be avoided. In retrospect the gruesomeness is to some
extent sidetracked when Lavinia explains to Sir Henry Harcourt-
Reilly:

> It came to me, when Alex told about Celia
> And I looked at your face. It seemed to convey to me
> That the way in which she died was not important
> Or the fact that she died because she would not leave
> A few dying natives.

At this point one recalls Harry's "insensitivity" to his brother's accident
in *The Family Reunion;* again, in the wider context of values which
Harry was engaged in imposing, a mere matter of concussion was, indeed, unimportant. To seize these details as evidence, on realistic

---

[24] W. K. Wimsatt, Jr., "Eliot's Comedy," *Sewanee Review*, Autumn, 1950, p. 667.

terms, of Harry's cruelty or Reilly's insensitivity would be absurd. But while one can explain the incidents in terms of the intellectual and rhetorical patterns of the plays, the quality of the tone which they involve imposes itself, regardless of our rationalization. Similarly, the degree of explicitness in Alex's report remains an artistic flaw because the details, however easy to "explain," impress their own quality on the "feel" of the play. The disparity, in qualitative terms, between the presentation of the two plots is excessive. The proper antidote to the Mayfair plot would surely have involved the emergence in Mayfair of serious moral concerns. No rhetorical law demanded the crucifixion near an ant-hill. [. . .]

The norm of the play's language is fine virile speech, clean and "easy," from which the smoke and shadow of *The Family Reunion* have been very largely eliminated. The verse is so pliant that, as Professor Wimsatt has observed, it makes possible the little joke tied in at the end of the phrase as if without effort:

> Finding your life becoming cosier and cosier,
> Without the consistent critic, the patient misunderstander.

or the sinister incompleteness of:

> Mr. Peter Quilpe
> Was a frequent guest . . .

or the flattened summation, far echo of *Prufrock* or *Gerontion*:

> Each way means loneliness—and communion.
> Both ways avoid the final desolation
> Of solitude in the phantasmal world
> Of imagination, shuffling memories and desires.

We are reminded that the presiding virtues of the play are chasteness, restraint, terseness, and precision.

Very occasionally in *The Cocktail Party* Eliot loses control of his "poetry." In this passage, for instance, in which Edward cries out to Lavinia:

> O God, O God, if I could return to yesterday
> Before I thought that I had made a decision.
> What devil left the door on the latch

> For these doubts to enter? And then you came back, you
> The angel of destruction—just as I felt sure.
> In a moment, at your touch, there is nothing but ruin.
> O God, what have I done? The python. The octopus.
> Must I become after all what you would make me?

This exhibits again, as we have seen in *The Family Reunion*, the tendency of Eliot the poet to break loose from the restraints of the dramatic context. The description of Lavinia as "angel of destruction" is brilliantly ironical, but it is the poet's irony, not Edward's. Such double talk occurs much less frequently in *The Cocktail Party* than in *The Family Reunion* and, as a result, the rhetoric of the later play is much firmer. Where it persists, however, it accounts for a certain feeling of insecurity which merges into that larger unsteadiness of tone which we have already observed. *The Cocktail Party*, in its entirety, does not quite hold fast.

In *Murder in the Cathedral* the question of a viable alternative to sanctity did not seriously arise to confront either Thomas or the audience: the order of Grace determined the conditions of the drama. In turn, *The Family Reunion* recognized a mundane alternative, sneering at it, however, assigning it to the stupid brother John. *The Cocktail Party* is a more ample play because it at least gives serious representation (in the comic mode, admittedly) to a way of life other than that which issues in beatitude or martyrdom. The implications of the play's "argument" have pleased no one, but it is important in Eliot's development as the first play to make some appeal to "a real world which all may in some sense perceive." [25] It points to a more successful play, *The Confidential Clerk*.

[25] Fergusson, *supra*, footnote 1, p. 217.

For Other Voices

by Hugh Kenner

Mr. Eliot admits no actor to his intimacy. That is one meaning of the marked change that pervades his verse when he writes for
the stage. His poems, he has nearly told us, he conceives in some
psychic center where the obscure phatic sensations of his own voice
take their origin. When you are writing such poetry, "The way it
sounds when you read it to yourself is the test," and the sensation of
reading to yourself what you have written is permeated by the way
it feels to be speaking: larynx, lips, and nameless intimate zones of
feeling, all affirming, urging, intertexturing their modulations of a
fluid of sound, in a prolonged ritual courtship of the silence which
at last closes round the utterance.

> Revive for a moment a broken Coriolanus . . .

Not the least of the pleasures such a line implies is the pleasure of
uttering it.

Shakespeare wrote plays in the same way; that is why he never
lacks willing actors to singe their wings in his flame. He makes
thrilling speaking; and often, difficult hearing. But Eliot's plays reverse the premise not only of Shakespeare's plays but of Eliot's poetry:
they exist not to be spoken but to be heard. Though it is true that
others besides the author will experiment with the sensations of
enunciating "Gerontion" or *The Waste Land,* that is *per accidens.*
But that stage verse shall be spoken by other people is the essential
condition of its existence. And Mr. Eliot's way of distinguishing and
identifying his characters seems inseparable from a reluctance to allow
any of them access to the central pleasure of enunciating Eliotic

"For Other Voices." From *Poetry,* XCIV (October, 1959), 36-40. Copyright 1959
by Hugh Kenner. Reprinted by permission of the author.

verse. "In a play," he has said, "you write for other voices, and you
do not know whose voices they will be": a truth, but one which did
not intimidate Shakespeare, whose central act of sympathy was always
with the actor. Eliot is careful to keep his sympathies on this side
of the footlights; he writes (at least after *Murder in the Cathedral*)
on behalf of the audience, whose experience of the play is likely to
be not merely more comprehensive than that of anyone on stage, but
profounder.

There are small indications that the actor is even fended off a little
by the poet, when the poet has anything to do with the matter, as
though the actor whose vocal apparatus will caress these words con-
stitutes in some obscure way a threat, to be countered by mobilizing
Old Possum's whole repertory of courteous evasions. Miss Alison
Leggat, whose responsibility it was to develop for the first time the
part of Mrs. Guzzard in *The Confidential Clerk,* has recalled the pro-
ducer's concern to admonish the cast, before a rehearsal at which the
author was to be present, that they were on no account to ask the
author about the meaning of anything; and one or two perplexed
spirits who could not forbear to disregard this warning heard only
his claim not to have the least idea. Miss Leggat was told only that
in playing Mrs. Guzzard she was to combine Pallas Athene with a
suburban housewife, and later received a copy of the play inscribed
"To the Perfection of Guzzards." Only Mr. Alec Guinness, who brings
to a part his own ritual of furtive detachment, seems ever to have
been conspicuously intimate with an Eliot character, less by empathy
than conaturality. It is said that Rex Harrison played the same part
in the London production of *The Cocktail Party* as though baffled
by it, which may help explain *The Cocktail Party*'s relative unsuccess
in London.

At the heart of each of the postwar plays lies a problem analogous
with this disquieting freedom enjoyed by the actors. Some mystery to
which no one possesses the whole key condemns everyone on stage
to state with explicit candor very little at a time. No obfuscation can
be blamed on the language they employ. It is the clearest verse ever
written, and every discernible poetic means assists to make it clearer.
Parallelisms explicate the structure of long speeches, diamond-like
precisions of diction clinch shorter ones. A metric, not of recurrences
but of groupings, adjusts salient words to one another. Novelty of
metaphor is eschewed; symbols are absent; epithets do not astonish
but inform. The language of these plays is upper-middle-class English colloquial speech, raised from badinage to system. We have only
to listen for five minutes to the admirable English cast speaking *The*

Cocktail Party in the Decca recording to see how intimate is the phrasing of the verse with that of English talk: its run has nothing in common with the deliberate unemphatic phrasing of any spoken American. It is not "prosaic"; its system of communicating is unlike that of prose, which appeals to shared meanings and agreed areas of understanding. The verse of *The Elder Statesman,* like the language of Euclid, is coolly adequate to anything that requires saying. Spoken prose is never quite adequate to what it is saying: hence its ritual of unfinished sentences, gesturing hands, meeting eyes.

The Elder Statesman begins with badinage modulating into a love scene:

MONICA: How did this come, Charles? It crept so softly
   On silent feet, and stood behind my back
   Quietly, a long time, a long long time
   Before I felt its presence. . . .

Before long the world of the lovers offsets the loveless world of Monica's father, the Elder Statesman, whose speech (we are to listen, not doze between rhetorical thrills) has a kind of bloodless adequacy because he is a ghost:

   Perhaps I've never really enjoyed living
   As much as most people. At least, as they seem to do,
   Without knowing that they enjoy it. Whereas I've often known
   That I didn't enjoy it.

That is the way Lord Claverton talks. It is "poetry" by no definition but this one, that it embodies the exact meaning that requires embodying, at this point in this fable. The same is true of this ghost's conversation with one of the ghosts who return from his past:

LORD CLAVERTON: Why should I feel embarrassment? My conscience was
   clear.
   A brief infatuation, ended in the only way possible
   To our mutual satisfaction.
MRS. CARGHILL: Your conscience was clear.
   I've very seldom heard people mention their consciences
   Except to observe that their consciences were clear.
   You got out of a tangle for a large cash payment
   And no publicity. So your conscience was clear.
   At bottom, I believe you're the same silly Richard

> You always were. You wanted to pose
> As a man of the world. And now you're posing
> As what? I presume, as an elder statesman;
> And the difference between being an elder statesman
> And posing successfully as an elder statesman
> Is practically negligible. And you look the part.
> Whatever part you've played, I must say you've always looked it.

This extraordinary explicitness isn't making a point of throwing cards on the table, or dramatizing its own candor; it is simply a function of the language Eliot gives characters to speak in the most matter-of-fact way. Mrs. Carghill neither *wields* this talk nor is subsumed by it; she utters it and is detached from it. A Lear, a Cassius, an Antony, by being preternaturally articulate becomes a function of the capacity of the English language for expressiveness: an upwelling: an overflow: anything, in fact, but an embodiment of human privacy articulating what it chooses to articulate. One cannot conceive of a silent Othello, and Cordelia's silences are a mode of speech; but Lord Claverton and Mrs. Carghill have their reticences and their blighted areas.

The tension of *The Elder Statesman,* in fact, is located in the very idea of human privacy. It is a tension between privacies of two sorts: the sort which withholds itself behind a role and one day withers into a ghost—

> If I've been looking at this engagement book, to-day,
> Not over breakfast, but before tea,
> It's the empty pages that I've been fingering—
> The first empty pages since I entered Parliament.

—and the blessed sort which can give itself into communion with another person precisely because it *is* a privacy, a self, a serene personal entity, this and not an interfering determination to make its existence felt. "I've been freed," Lord Claverton sums up a few minutes before the end of the play,

> . . . from the self that pretends to be someone;
> And in becoming no one, I begin to live.
> It is worth while dying, to find out what life is.

Then the lovers, Charles and Monica, close the play as they opened it:

MONICA: We will go to him together. He is close at hand,
  Though he has gone too far to return to us.
  He is under the beech tree. It is quiet and cold there.
  In becoming no one, he has become himself.
  He is only my father now, and Michael's.
  And I am happy. Isn't it strange, Charles,
  To be happy at this moment?

The play's form is as simple as mediaeval music: a precarious compromise between something as sparely intimate as *At the Hawk's Well* and the innocent pretensions of a formal theatre. The actors who can combine the authority and self-effacement it demands are to be found, one supposes, in some ideal world not very different from ours but less avid of brilliance. The work will never attract Mr. Elia Kazan. Mr. Eliot can be forgiven if he doesn't much care. He has written, perhaps under the illusion that he was serving a theatre that exists, the most intimate of his works, so much so that the lyric dedication of the book to his wife is perfectly in keeping. That drama is the most personal of forms is one way of stating this play's theme. As Lord Claverton was able to enter into reality only through others, through a daughter he had hitherto tried to keep to himself, a son he had constrained, and a former lover he had allowed to be bought off, so his poet is set free from the lyric flame by writing for other voices, not knowing whose voices they will be.

T. S. Eliot: The End of an Era

by Donald Davie

I

I find it very surprising that all readers seem to either accept or reject the *Four Quartets* as a whole—and yet not really surprising, since the cleavage comes plainly not along any line of literary fact, but is flagrantly ideological: the religiously inclined applaud the Quartets, the more or less militantly secular and "humanist" decry them. As simple as that.

At any rate, I find it still surprising (and depressing) that no one should yet have remarked to my knowledge how the third Quartet, "The Dry Salvages," sticks out among the rest like a sore thumb. At first sight it is not only incongruous with the others, strikingly different in conception and procedure, but different unaccountably and disastrously. One could take it by itself and prove convincingly that it is quite simply *rather a bad poem*. It amazes me that, so far as I know, no one has yet done this; and until very lately I thought I was the person to do it. In fact, I aim to do it here and now—but now with the proviso that all I can say against it is true only so far as it goes, that from another point of view all the vices become virtues and fall into place. It is possible, of course, that all other readers have been clever enough to see the thing aright from the start. But it goes without saying that I don't think so. Here at any rate, to begin with, is my case against "The Dry Salvages."

II

Leavis and Rajan have both applauded the opening lines of the poem, and Helen Gardner was so misguided as to choose them for

"T. S. Eliot: The End of an Era." From *The Twentieth Century*, CLIX, No. 950 (April, 1956), 350-362. Copyright 1956 by the *Twentieth Century*. Reprinted by permission of the author and *The Twentieth Century*.

the basis of her claims for Eliot specifically as a manipulator of
language:

> I do not know much about gods; but I think that the river
> Is a strong brown god—sullen, untamed and intractable,
> Patient to some degree, at first recognized as a frontier;

Miss Gardner says that the "strong brown god" is "a personification
which the poet's tone makes no more than a suggestion, a piece of
only half-serious myth-making." But the first line has not sufficiently
defined the tone (a single line hardly could) for this to be true; and
indeed it is to my ear still too uncertain, eight lines later, to carry
the journalistic cliché, "worshippers of the machine," by giving it the
invisible quote marks which, as Miss Gardner allows, such an inert
and faded locution requires. What in any case, we may well ask, is
the tone in which we could hear without embarrassment the first
line spoken? "I do not know much about gods"—who could conceivably start a conversation like that without condemning himself from
the start as an uncomfortable poseur? Is it not rather like

> Poems are made by fools like me
> But only God can make a tree?

What is it but a gaucherie? And yet there *is* a tone in which we
have been addressed, which hovers here in the offing, a tone familiar
enough but still far from acceptable, a tone which has indeed become
a byword as a type of strident uncertainty in the speaker and of cor-
respondingly acute embarrassment in the hearer—it is the tone of
Whitman.

But what is Eliot thinking of, that he should talk like Whitman?
And our bewilderment deepens:

> Unhonoured, unpropitiated
> By worshippers of the machine, but waiting, watching and waiting,
> His rhythm was present in the nursery bedroom,
> In the rank ailanthus of the April dooryard,
> In the smell of grapes on the autumn table,
> And the evening circle in the winter gaslight.

"Worshippers of the machine"; then the incredibly limp "watching
and waiting"; and finally, limpest of all, "his rhythm was present."

"His rhythm was present in the nursery bedroom"—could anything
be more vague and woolly? After this statement has been issued, we
know not a tittle more about the relation between river and bedroom
than we did before. And the poetry is not just bad, but unaccountably so. For "His rhythm was present in" represents just that bridge-
work, that filling in and faking of transitions, which Eliot as a post-
symbolist poet has always contrived to do without. From first to last
his procedure has been the symbolist procedure of "juxtaposition
without copula," the setting down of images side by side with a space
between them, a space that does not need to be bridged. There is an
example just over the page in "The Dry Salvages":

> The salt is on the briar rose,
> The fog is in the fir trees.

For now, from "The river is within us" through to the end of the
first section, the poetry picks up, the diction becomes distinctively
Eliotic and fine; and only an unwonted straightforwardness, the vul-
nerable stance face to face with the subject, the overtness of the evocation, are there to trouble us with something pre-symbolist and old-
fashioned.

But, then, what shall be said of the famous Sestina of the second
section, which Rajan calls "as intricately organized as anything Eliot
has written"? Shall I be thought laughably naïve for calling attention
to the rhymes? In the first sestine comes an extremely beautiful perception:

> The silent withering of autumn flowers
> Dropping their petals and remaining motionless;

The rhymes found to correspond to these in the later sestines are as
follows, in order:

> . . . the trailing
> Consequence of further days and hours,
> While emotion takes to itself the emotionless
> Years of living among the breakage . . .
> . . . the failing
> Pride or resentment at failing powers,
> The unattached devotion which might pass for devotionless . . .
> Where is the end of them, the fishermen sailing
> Into the wind's tail, where the fog cowers?

We cannot think of a time that is oceanless . . .
Setting and hauling, while the North East lowers
Over shallow banks unchanging and erosionless . . .
No end to the withering of withered flowers,
To the movement of pain that is painless and motionless . . .

Should we not be justified in seeing here a case of sheer incompetence? Is it not plain that the trouvaille at the head of the page, 'Dropping their petals and remaining motionless', gets the poet into more and more patent difficulties (and dishonesties) once the rhyme on it has been taken up as a determining feature of his stanza-form? "Emotionless"—how? "Oceanless"—grotesque! "Erosionless"—does he mean "uneroded"? And "movement . . . pain . . . painless . . . motionless"—our confidence in the poet has by this time been so undermined that we cannot, in justice to ourselves, take this as anything but incantatory gibberish. Faced with this, we have to feel a momentary sympathy with the rancor even of a Robert Graves—who, whatever his limitations, would never allow such slapdash inefficiency into his own verses.

The next passage reads:

It seems, as one becomes older,
That the past has another pattern, and ceases to be a mere sequence
Or even development: the latter a partial fallacy
Encouraged by superficial notions of evolution
Which becomes, in the popular mind, a means of disowning the past

Is this the poet who wove to and fro the close and lively syntax at the beginning of *East Coker*, or the passage from *Burnt Norton* beginning "The inner freedom from the practical desire"? How can we explain that the same poet should now proffer, in such stumbling trundling rhythms, these inarticulate ejaculations of reach-me-down phrases, the debased currency of the study circle? And worse is to come— Possum's little joke:

The moments of happiness—not the sense of well-being,
Fruition, fulfilment, security or affection,
Or even a very good dinner . . .

At the dismal jocularity of that "very good dinner," we throw in our hands. The tone that Miss Gardner thought established in the

very first line can now, we realize, never be established at all. Or
else, if we prefer to put it this way—it has been very thoroughly
established, as excruciatingly unsettled, off-key. To be sure, the diction now picks up again for a while, though still liable to such upsets
as the lame gabble, "not forgetting/Something that is probably quite
ineffable: . . ." But Section III begins with *Krishna,* which sticks
in the throat even of Dr. Rajan (who for the most part seems to be
reading a different poem): "Mr. Eliot is never happy in 'the maze of
Oriental metaphysics' and his wanderings this time are uncomfort-
ably sinuous." And there is, as Rajan further notes, a self-advertising
virtuosity, almost Euphuistic, about "the future is a faded song, a
Royal Rose or a lavender spray . . ."

At this point re-enter Whitman, conspicuously. S. Musgrove, author
of *T. S. Eliot and Walt Whitman,* compares with this passage turning
on "Fare forward, travellers," Whitman's "Song of the Open Road";
and he comments (p. 55):

> Once again, Eliot has employed Whitman's material and manner in
> order to reject his philosophy. For Whitman, time stretches away in one
> infinite linear direction, towards a positive and perfect future, in which
> the possession of something actual, something better than the present,
> awaits the growing spirit of man. For Eliot, the sense of a direction is
> illusory; time is an eternal present which can never yield more than is
> now known, in which the only kind of possession conceivable is one
> alike in kind to dispossession from the demands of the self. . . .

This is a good deal less than fair to Whitman, who is at pains in
"Song of the Open Road" to make it clear that there is no destination
to the voyaging, no end to it, no perfection to be aimed at or achieved
except in the process of still and still going on. Thus Eliot, with his
"Fare neither well nor ill, so it be forward" (my words, of course, but
a fair summary of Eliot's drift), has dropped from Whitman only his
optimism, substituting for it the Chekhovian compassion which strips
its objects of all dignity:

> Fare forward, you who think that you are voyaging; . . .

And to be sure, Musgrove talks as if the one unforgivable thing
about Whitman, what proves his vulgarity, is precisely his optimism
—a good example of that rigid neo-Augustinian temper among Eliot's
adherents which very properly enrages a secular liberal like Kathleen
Nott. For Whitman's optimism is not by any means the worst thing

about him. There is beneath and beside it what Lawrence pointed to
—"Always wanting to merge himself into the womb of something or
other"; that is, the drive to "transcend" the self by losing it in identification with some inhuman process, of which, as Wyndham Lewis
pointed out long ago, the process of time is perhaps the most obvious
and popular. Moreover, as Lawrence and, following him, Yvor Winters have shown, this drive is especially marked in the American
literary tradition, from Emerson and Melville to Hart Crane[1]—its
obsessive symbol very frequently, as here in "The Dry Salvages," the
sea. And, sure enough, Rajan comes aptly in once more with the
suggestion that Section IV, "Lady, whose shrine stands on the pro-
montory," "perhaps owes something to the sermon in *Moby Dick.*"
Even the Hinduism fits in, if one recalls Yeats's remark about "those
translations of the Upanishads, which it is so much harder to study
by the sinking flame of Indian tradition than by the serviceable lamp
of Emerson and Walt Whitman." And yet, when one recalls also
Yeats's verdict on Emerson and Whitman, "writers who have come to
seem superficial precisely because they lack the Vision of Evil," one
finds it unaccountable that Eliot, the author of the essay on Baudelaire, however American, should have fallen into this trap of ecstatic
merging with the process.

The last section begins with an admirable new departure, in the
vigor of

> To communicate with Mars, converse with spirits . . . ;

but then it modulates, through a very beautiful yet again strangely
uncritical treatment of the Bergsonian *durée* in music ("but you are
the music/While the music lasts"), into the inhuman conclusion that
human life for all but the saints is mere purposeless *movement,*
scurrying activity, only at fleeting uncontrollable moments elevated
into the meaning and dignity of true *action.* We realize that the poet
indeed meant the shocking "emotionless" of the sestina; and if that
helps to validate the poetry of that passage, it only makes the poet
seem even less humane.

III

If we are to turn the force of these numerous objections we have
to go a long way round—and yet in a way we need to go no further

---

[1] One traces it as far afield as Berenson, in his remarks on Umbrian space-
composition and "the religious emotion."

than Hugh Kenner's essay on "Eliot's Moral Dialectic" (*Hudson Review,* 1949). Kenner there distinguishes the predominant structural principle of this poetry as a diagram in which two terms (life and death, beginning and end) are first opposed, then falsely reconciled in a third term, and then truly reconciled in a fourth term, a metaphysical conception. His examples are Section III of "Burnt Norton," where the opposed terms light and darkness are combined in the parody-reconciliation of the "flicker" in the twilit murk of London, only to be truly reconciled paradoxically in the metaphysical Dark Night of the Soul; and Section III of "Little Gidding," where the opposing terms attachment and detachment are reconciled in parody in "indifference," only to be truly reconciled in Love.

Section III of "East Coker" yields up the same pattern:

> . . . So the darkness shall be the light, and the stillness the dancing.
> Whisper of running streams, and winter lightning,
> The wild thyme unseen and the wild strawberry.
> The laughter in the garden, echoed ecstasy
> Not lost, but requiring, pointing to the agony
> Of death and birth.
>   You say I am repeating
> Something I have said before. I shall say it again.
> Shall I say it again? In order to arrive there,
> To arrive where you are, to get from where you are not,
>   You must go by a way wherein there is no ecstasy.
> In order to arrive at what you do not know
>   You must go by a way which is the way of ignorance . . .

Darkness and light, stillness and dancing, are two pairs of opposed terms. They are reconciled in "the agony/Of death and birth." Birth, coming from the dark to the light, is a sort of death, for as soon as we are born we begin to die; and death, going from the light to the dark, is a sort of birth—into eternal life. And the stillness of a seizure, the dance of pain, are reconciled in agony. But this is a false reconciliation which is at once abandoned for the true one carried in the borrowings from St. John of the Cross. Thus, "I shall say it again/Shall I say it again?" is an ironical trap. Musgrove suggests an allusion to Whitman's "Do I contradict myself? Very well, I contradict myself." This points it up even more; for the point is that Eliot *is* contradicting himself even as he *seems* to repeat himself—inevitably, because it is characteristic of the terms he is thinking in that the false reconciliation, being a parody of the true one, is very hard—all but impossible—to distinguish from it in words, even in words charged to the utmost, as in poetry.

Since the third sections of "Burnt Norton," "East Coker," and "Little Gidding" are thus broadly parallel in structure, one would expect to discern the same structure in Section III of "The Dry Salvages," which is the Whitmanesque passage I have just discussed. But "The Dry Salvages," as we noted at the start, is the odd one out in all sorts of ways; and though the pattern is there, it is there only with a difference, and is hard to discern.

> And the way up is the way down, the way forward is the way back

—here are the terms opposed, right enough. But we look in vain for the false reconciliation, though the image of the traveller is obviously apt for it—since travelling is the same state whether one travels from here to there, or there to here. But this parody-reconciliation is ruled out of court when the poet jumps at once to his insight (a restatement, as Kenner has noted, of the insight of "Tradition and the Individual Talent"):

> You cannot face it steadily, but this thing is sure,
> That time is no healer: the patient is no longer here.

Yet the parody-reconciliation *is* present in the lines that follow, though never overtly offered—it is there precisely in the shade of Whitman that haunts the passage, the Whitmanesque tone that hovers here as an overtone.

But we can, and must, go further. This diagram that Kenner has brilliantly extricated he does not offer to us merely as the structural principle informing these passages and others like them. He hints that the same diagram informs the *Four Quartets* as a whole. If this is so, then *The Dry Salvages,* the third of them, should appear as the false reconciliation, the parody. And here it seems we may at last be coming near to understanding, and forgiving, its peculiarities.

It is generally recognized that parody is to be found in the *Four Quartets,* that in "East Coker," for instance, when the poet says, of the lyric at the start of Section II, "That was a way of putting it—not very satisfactory:/A periphrastic study in a worn-out poetical fashion," we are meant to take this at its face value and to agree that the passage referred to is, therefore, a parody. But when Kenner asks us to compare "Down the passage which we did not take" at the start of "Burnt Norton" with the "cunning passages, contrived corridors" of Gerontion (himself, as Kenner argues, a living parody of the true self-surrender that we find in Simeon), we are advised that we must look for parody elsewhere in the *Four Quartets,* where it is not explicitly pointed out to us by the poet. For instance, the false reconciliation which I have pointed out in "East Coker," "the agony/Of death and birth," while it looks back to the significantly theatrical image, "with a hollow rumble of wings, with a movement of darkness on darkness," looks forward surely to "The wounded surgeon plies the steel" and the much elaborated skull-and-crossbones conceit which occupies the whole of Section IV of the poem. Several readers have objected to this as strained and labored; and since the necrophily which informs it has already been shown as a parody of the true reconciliation between dark and light, should we not take it that the strain and the laboring are deliberate, a conscious forcing of the tone, a *conscious* movement towards self-parody? What is it in fact but what we were warned of in the typically opalescent lines from "Burnt Norton"—

> The crying shadow in the funeral dance,
> The loud lament of the disconsolate chimera?

It is my argument, then, that in the sense and to the degree in which Section IV of "East Coker" is a parody the whole of "The Dry Salvages" is a parody. It is hardly too much to say that the whole of this third quartet is spoken by a nameless persona; certainly it is spoken through a mask, spoken *in character,* spoken in character as the American. This, and nothing else, can explain the approximations to Whitmanesque and other pre-symbolist American verse-procedures; and the insistent Americanism, of course, as all the commentators have noted, is a quality also of the locale persistently evoked by the images—of the Mississippi and the New England coast for instance. It is thus that the incompetence turns out to be dazzling virtuosity; and the inhumanity of the conclusion reached turns out to be only a parody of the true conclusion reached in *Little Gidding,* which is thoroughly humane in its insistence that all varieties of human folly and imperfection are the conditions for apprehending perfection, that the world is therefore necessary and to that extent— even the worst of it—good.

IV

There remains only one question. Admitting, as we have had to admit, that the *Four Quartets*—and "The Dry Salvages" no less than every other part—represent a superbly controlled achievement of its kind, what are we to say of that kind? What kind of poetry is this, in which loose and woolly incoherent language can be seen to be—in its place and for special purposes—better than clear and closely articulated language? This is a question raised not just by the *Quartets* but by Eliot's work as a whole. The opening paragraph of the fifth section of *Ash-Wednesday* is what Leavis says it is—a magnificent acting out in verse movement and word play of "both the agonized effort to seize the unseizable, and the elusive equivocations of the thing grasped." But it is also, from another point of view, what Max Eastman says it is—an "oily puddle of emotional noises." It is easy to say that Leavis's point of view is right, and Eastman's wrong—that any poetic effect can be seen and judged only as it plays its part in the economy of a whole poem, and that any amount of violence done to language, any amount of sheer ugliness, can be justified as means to a justifiable poetic end. But this is to assert that Eastman's pang of angry discomfort, which I suppose is shared by every sensitive reader at least at a first reading, is not a protest against ugliness on behalf of beauty, but only a protest against the functional in favor of the pretty. Are we in fact prepared to waive the claim "beautiful" which we make for those lines of poetry which move us to applause as surely as the lines from *Ash-Wednesday* move us to rebellion? And are we, moreover (for this, too, is implied), prepared to waive the claim "poetry" for those lines we applaud—unless, that is, their engagingness can be seen as functional?

Well, we—you and I, dear reader—may be prepared to waive these claims. What is quite certain is that not only that legendary figure, the common reader, but the enthusiast and the specialist—a person like Dr. Rajan—is not prepared to do so; not prepared because he has not realized it is what is required. More, the poet himself—a poet like Robert Graves—is not prepared to do so. And (what perhaps should make us pause) younger poets than either Graves or Eliot *have* realized what is required of them by poetry like Eliot's and have refused—at least where their own writing is concerned—to waive their claims to poetry and to beauty in the old-fashioned pre-symbolist sense.

"Pre-symbolist," yes. For it is pre-eminently symbolist and post-symbolist poetry that waives these claims and insists that the reader waive them also. Eliot waives them when he says, in "East Coker," "The poetry does not matter." The exegetes cushion the shock of this by taking it to mean "*That sort* of poetry doesn't . . . ," the sort which we have just heard called "A periphrastic study in a worn-out poetical fashion," which we have agreed to consider as parody. Well, that interpretation can be allowed to stand for classroom consumption. But it isn't what Eliot means, or it isn't all that he means. He means what he says: the poetry doesn't matter, and beauty doesn't matter—for no verse can be judged either poetic or beautiful except in so far as it is seen to be expressive; and what it has to express may demand, as it does in "The Dry Salvages," rather the false note than the true one, the faded and shop-soiled locution rather than the phrase new-minted, the trundling rhythm rather than the cut, woolliness rather than clarity—

> See now they vanish,
> The faces and places, with the self which, as it could, loved them.

Woolliness becomes the only sort of clarity, the wrong note is the right note, and nothing is so beautiful as what is hideous—in certain (not uncommon) poetic circumstances.

If it is true that Kenner's essay has made everything else on the *Quartets* (and not on them only but on Eliot's work in general) seem like literary curiosities, none of these curios is so appealing to me as Anthony Thorlby's essay, "The Poetry of *Four Quartets*," which was published after Kenner's (in the *Cambridge Journal*, 1952) but was obviously not written in the light of that. Thorlby is seriously wrong about the *Quartets*; nothing could be further from the truth than his assertion, "What is remarkable in Mr. Eliot's use of imagery is not that it is symbolic or capable of interpretation, but that the interpretation is essential to its poetic coherence." Or rather, if this is true in one sense, if we take "interpretation" to mean "seeing the place of any part in relation to the whole," it is certainly untrue if we take it to mean, as Thorlby does, that each image as we come to it must be construed, like the images of allegory. What is appealing and important about Thorlby's essay is that it represents a man recognizing that the symbolist revolution in poetry has happened, and trying to come to grips with it. To be sure, Thorlby does not acknowledge that the revolution he perceives is the symbolist revolution; indeed, he writes as if it were inaugurated specifically by the *Four*

Quartets, seemingly unaware that the revolution was over, and successfully over, long before Eliot began to write, and that all Eliot's poems, the earliest as well as the latest, are constructed on that assumption—that the symbolist procedures have arrived and supplanted all others. Then, again, Thorlby's objections to the procedure as he detects it could be easily countered by anyone versed even a little in symbolist theory; for his argument rests upon a hard and fast distinction between "having an experience" and "seeing the significance of that experience"—a distinction made untenable by Bergson. Nevertheless, Thorlby at least perceives the essentially post-symbolist nature of the poetry of the *Quartets*—which is more than can be said for most of the commentators—even if he hasn't the label to tie on to it. And he grasps quite a lot of the implications of the symbolist revolution in terms of the revised expectations that the reader must now entertain—a matter of crucial importance which is hardly ever touched upon.

Thus it is very nearly correct—it is entirely correct from most points of view—to say with Thorlby:

> Mr. Eliot's poetry is *about* the many forms in which the life of poetry has flourished; which is a very different thing from simply accepting one form and creating within it a poetry of life.

And it is entirely correct to say, as he does:

> Mr. Eliot, then, is not standing outside his material looking in upon the experience he is writing about, composing it into one form; he is himself at the centre . . . looking around him upon so many of the problems of to-day which he hopes to illumine by its light.

This last point is the vital one. If no one has made it before Thorlby, that was (I suspect) for fear of falling foul of the master's own propaganda for impersonality in poetry, on the gap between the man who suffers and the poet who creates. Eliot was playing perfectly fair in this, and one can hardly resent his insistence when one finds critics, deaf to all his warnings, reading "Gerontion" as a *cri du coeur* rather than what it is—the rendering of the state of mind of an imagined persona, from which the poet is wholly detached. From this point of view Eliot is indeed impersonal, standing quite aside and apart from his creation—my diagnosis of "The Dry Salvages" as parody makes the point all over again. And yet Thorlby is right, too: in another sense Eliot is never outside and apart from his poems. No post-symbolist poet can be outside his poem as Milton was outside *Lycidas*; and no post-symbolist poem can ever be as impersonal as *Lycidas* was for John Crowe Ransom when he called it "a poem nearly anonymous." If Eliot enters his own poems only disguised as a persona, wearing a mask, at least he enters them. Reading a parody, we are inevitably aware (though as it were at one remove) of the parodist. Perhaps no other kind of poet is so much in evidence in his own poems as the parodist is, the histrionic virtuoso, always tipping the wink. And if Eliot thus enters into his own poems, his reader must do likewise, changing his focus as the poem changes focus, knowing when to give almost full credence to what the poetry says, when to make reservations according as he detects the voice of now one persona, now another parodying the first.

I share Thorlby's preference for a kind of poetry which stands on its own feet, without my help, as an independent creation, a thing to be walked round, and as satisfying from one standpoint as from another. And so I hope I shall not be thought lacking in gratitude to Eliot for the *Four Quartets,* nor lacking in respect for the prodigious achievement of that poem, if I say that I hope for quite a different sort of poem in the future, a sort of poem more in harmony with what was written in Europe before symbolism was thought of, even (since symbolist procedures are only the logical development of Romantic procedures) before Romanticism was thought of. I am not forgetting the lesson of "Tradition and the Individual Talent." I knew that history cannot be unwritten, that there can be no question of putting the clock back; the post-post-symbolist poetry I look for may be more in harmony with pre-Romantic poetry, it can never be the same. There cannot be a conspiracy to pretend that the symbolist revolution never happened. (The annoying thing of course is that, because Eliot has been seen by the influential critics most often in the perspective of the specifically English tradition rather than in the perspective of Europe as a whole, it is commonly held that he has done just what I seem to ask for, has re-established continuity with the poetry of the seventeenth and eighteenth centuries. And he has really done so—but only in relatively superficial ways.)

If I hope for a different sort of poetry, that hope is reasonably confident—not because I give much weight to the younger poets of today who, when they think in these terms at all (they seldom do), declare that the post-symbolist tradition is "worked out"; not even because the respectable poetry written in England and America by poets younger than Eliot is plainly not written according to his prescription; but simply because the *Four Quartets* represent a stage of such subtlety and intricacy in the post-symbolist tradition that it is impossible to think of its ever being taken a stage further. Surely no poet, unless it be Eliot himself, can elaborate further this procedure in which the true key is never sounded, but exists in the poem only as the norm by which all the voices that speak are heard as delicately off-key, as the voices of parody. It is, at any rate, in this hope and this confidence of something quite different in the offing, that I have written the second half of my title: "T. S. Eliot: *The End of an Era*."

Chronology of Important Dates

1888   T. S. Eliot born in St. Louis, Missouri.

1906-9   Undergraduate at Harvard. Discovery of the symbolists and Laforgue.

1909-10   Graduate student at Harvard. Early poems, including "Portrait of a Lady" and beginnings of "Prufrock."

1910-11   Studies in France and Germany. "Prufrock" completed.

1911-14   Graduate student at Harvard. Commenced work on the philosophy of Francis Herbert Bradley.

1914-15   Study in Germany cut off by war. Residence at Oxford. Short satiric poems. "Prufrock" published in Chicago, June 1915. Marriage to Vivien Haigh-Wood, July 1915.

1915-16   Teaching and book reviewing in London. Bradley thesis completed.

1917-20   Employee of Lloyd's Bank. Numerous editorial and reviewing assignments. Writing of French poems, quatrain poems, "Gerontion." *Prufrock and Other Observations* published June, 1917. *Poems* published 1920. *The Sacred Wood*, 1920.

1921-25   London correspondent for *The Dial* (1921-2) and *La Nouvelle Revue Française* (1922-3). Editorship of *The Criterion* commenced October, 1922. Dial Award for *The Waste Land*, 1922. *Poems 1909-1925*, including *The Hollow Men*. Joined Faber & Gwyer, later Faber & Faber, publishers.

1926-27   "Fragment of a Prologue," "Fragment of an Agon," essays on Seneca.

1927-31   Confirmation in the Church of England and assumption of British citizenship, 1927. *Ariel Poems*, 1927-30; *Ash-Wednesday*, 1930; essay on Dante, 1929; *Coriolan*, 1931.

1932   *Selected Essays*, including most of *The Sacred Wood*.

1932-34   *The Use of Poetry and the Use of Criticism* (1933) and *After Strange Gods* (1934). *The Rock*, 1934.

1935   *Murder in the Cathedral. Poems, 1909-1935,* including "Burnt Norton."

1939   *The Family Reunion.*

1940-42   Appearance of "East Coker," "The Dry Salvages," and "Little Gidding," published with "Burnt Norton" as *Four Quartets,* 1943.

1947   Death of T. S. Eliot's first wife, after long illness.

1948   Nobel Prize for Literature. *Notes Towards the Definition of Culture.*

1950   *The Cocktail Party.*

1955   *The Confidential Clerk.*

1957   Marriage to Valerie Fletcher. *On Poetry and Poets.*

1959   *The Elder Statesman.*

Notes on the Editor and Contributors

HUGH KENNER, editor of the anthology, teaches at the University of California (Santa Barbara). His books include *The Invisible Poet: T. S. Eliot, The Poetry of Ezra Pound,* and *Wyndham Lewis.*

R. P. BLACKMUR, poet and critic, teaches at Princeton University. His principal essays are contained in *Language as Gesture* (1953).

DONALD DAVIE, author of *Purity of Diction in English Verse* and *Articulate Energy,* is Lecturer in English at the University of Cambridge.

DENIS DONOGHUE teaches English at University College, Dublin. *The Third Voice,* a study of modern British and American verse drama, was published in 1959.

WILLIAM EMPSON, one of the inventors of twentieth century textual criticism (*Seven Types of Ambiguity, Some Versions of Pastoral, The Structure of Complex Words*) is Professor of English at Sheffield University.

D. W. HARDING was one of the founders of *Scrutiny,* and a member of its editorial board throughout its existence of nearly twenty years.

F. R. LEAVIS, the principal editor of *Scrutiny,* is Fellow of Downing College, Cambridge. He was Eliot's pioneer supporter in the British academic world.

WYNDHAM LEWIS (1884-1957), painter, novelist, and controversialist, was associated with Pound and Eliot from 1914 until his death. His *Blasting and Bombardiering* (1937) contains other reminiscences.

ARTHUR MIZENER, who teaches English at Cornell University, has published widely on twentieth century literature. He is best known for his biography of Scott Fitzgerald.

GEORGE L. K. MORRIS, abstract artist, painter and sculptor, lives in New York City, where he was born in 1905. His work has frequently been exhibited. From 1937 to 1943 he was Art Editor of *Partisan Review.*

S. MUSGROVE, author of *T. S. Eliot and Walt Whitman,* teaches at the University of Auckland, New Zealand.

JOHN PETER, a *Scrutiny* alumnus, teaches at the University of Manitoba. His essays on *The Family Reunion* and *The Cocktail Party* appeared in *Scrutiny* (XVI, No. 3, 1949, and XVII, No. 1, 1950).

EZRA POUND, poet and instigator, first met Eliot in the autumn of 1914, engineered the first publication of "Prufrock," and edited the author's draft of *The Waste Land* into its present form. He now lives in Italy.

ELIZABETH SEWELL, British philosopher and critic, is the author of *Paul Valéry, The Structure of Poetry, The Field of Nonsense,* and *The Orphic Voice.* She has taught at Ohio State, Vassar, Fordham, Princeton, and Bennett College.

ALLEN TATE, poet and man of letters, teaches at the University of Minnesota. His *Collected Essays* were published in 1959.

Selected Bibliography

General discussion of Eliot and his work may be found in F. O. Matthiessen, *The Achievement of T. S. Eliot* (1935) (3d ed.; New York: Oxford University Press, 1959); Helen L. Gardner, *The Art of T. S. Eliot* (1949) (New York: E. P. Dutton & Co., 1959); D. E. S. Maxwell, *The Poetry of T. S. Eliot* (1952) (New York: Hillary House, Inc., 1959); and Hugh Kenner, *The Invisible Poet: T. S. Eliot* (New York: Ivan Obolensky, Inc., 1959).

Books with a special point of view include Elizabeth Drew's *T. S. Eliot, The Design of his Poetry* (New York: Charles Scribner's Sons, 1949), a Jungian interpretation; George Williamson's *Reader's Guide to T. S. Eliot* (1953) (New York: Noonday Press, 1957), a poem-by-poem paraphrase; Grover C. Smith's *T. S. Eliot's Poetry and Plays* (Chicago: University of Chicago Press, 1956), which concentrates heavily on sources; and R. H. Robbins' *The T. S. Eliot Myth* (New York: Henry Schumann, Inc., 1951), an expression of wholesale irritation.

The periodical literature is endless. *T. S. Eliot, a Selected Critique*, edited by Leonard Unger (New York: Holt, Rinehart & Winston, Inc., 1948) is a generous selection of pieces from the 1930's and 1940's. *T. S. Eliot, a Study of his Writings by Several Hands*, edited by B. Rajan (New York: Funk & Wagnalls Co., 1948), is brief and systematic. *T. S. Eliot, a Symposium* edited by Richard March and M. J. Tambimuttu (Chicago: Henry Regnery Co., 1949) and *T. S. Eliot, a Symposium for His Seventieth Birthday*, edited by Neville Braybrooke (New York: Farrar, Straus & Cudahy, Inc., 1958) were compiled as birthday tributes. Yvor Winters, *In Defense of Reason* (Denver: Alan Swallow, 1947); A. Alvarez, *Stewards of Excellence* (New York: Charles Scribner's Sons, 1958); and Cleanth Brooks, *Modern Poetry and the Tradition* (Chapel Hill: University of North Carolina Press, 1939) contain valuable sections on Eliot.

The serious student will need Donald Gallup, *T. S. Eliot, A Bibliography* (New York: Harcourt, Brace and Co., Inc., 1953), which lists Eliot's entire output up to 1950.

TWENTIETH CENTURY VIEWS

British Authors

TWENTIETH CENTURY VIEWS

American Authors

TWENTIETH CENTURY VIEWS

European Authors